D1126380

This brilliant and extensive tour of the Russian mind supplies startlingly fresh insights. Using sharp anecdotes, Ronald Hingley portrays the national brand of leg-pull *(vranyo),* analyzes the Russian's tendency to keep his official and personal psyche in separate compartments, and deals with that splendid traditional institution, the *skandal.*

As well as discussing the conflicting claims that the Russian mentality is, in spectacular excess, either kind or cruel, generous or mean, energetic or torpid, Hingley describes the phenomena in Russia of campus revolutions, women's lib, female political assassins, alcoholism, the cult of youth, and much more. *The Russian Mind* is a provocative book that will have great appeal to the American mind.

**RONALD HINGLEY** is University Lecturer in Russian at Oxford University and the author of over twenty books on Russian literature, language, history, and politics, including a recently published major biography of Chekhov.

# THE RUSSIAN MIND

OTHER BOOKS BY RONALD HINGLEY

*Chekhov: a Biographical and Critical Study*
*Up Jenkins!*
*Soviet Prose: a Reader*
*Under Soviet Skins: an Untourist's Report*
*Russian: a Beginners' Course*
*The Undiscovered Dostoyevsky*
*Russian Writers and Society*
*Nihilists*
*The Tsars: Russian Autocrats, 1533–1917*
*Russian Revolution*
*The Russian Secret Police*
*A Concise History of Russia*
*Joseph Stalin: A Personal and Political Biography*
*A New Life of Anton Chekhov*

# THE
# RUSSIAN
# MIND

❧ Ronald Hingley ❧

CHARLES SCRIBNER'S SONS / New York

Copyright © 1977 Ronald Hingley

Library of Congress Cataloging in Publication Data

Hingley, Ronald.
  The Russian mind.

  Bibliography: p. 282
  Includes index.
  1. National characteristics, Russian.  2. Russia—
Social life and customs.  3. Russia—Intellectual life.
I. Title.
DK32.H56      947        77-7286
ISBN 0-684-14923-0

THIS BOOK PUBLISHED SIMULTANEOUSLY IN
THE UNITED STATES OF AMERICA AND IN CANADA-
COPYRIGHT UNDER THE BERNE CONVENTION

ALL RIGHTS RESERVED. NO PART OF THIS BOOK
MAY BE REPRODUCED IN ANY FORM WITHOUT
THE PERMISSION OF CHARLES SCRIBNER'S SONS.

1 3 5 7 9 11 13 15 17 19 v/c 20 18 16 14 12 10 8 6 4 2

PRINTED IN THE UNITED STATES OF AMERICA

181168

# CONTENTS

CONTENTS

# THE RUSSIAN MIND

# *I*

# FOREGROUND AND
# BACKGROUND

## *LIFE-ENHANCERS OR LIFE-DENIERS?*

How has Russia most impressed, provoked and fascinated Western Europeans throughout the ages? Partly as a tantalizing combination of the familiar and the unfamiliar. Some form of this mixture has been bemusing visitors since they began to discover the country in the sixteenth century.

Early travelers did not know what to make of this mysterious people: Muscovites, as they were then commonly known. On the one hand they were European in their complexions, in their general physical type. They were also found to be devout Christians. For such reasons visitors from the West could not easily regard them as orientals or Asiatics. But were they indeed fellow-occidentals? Hardly, for their notables wore flowing Eastern robes; inferiors prostrated themselves before superiors in the kowtow; upper-class women were kept in a form of purdah. Then again, there was the vast power—absolute and yet, impossibly, seeming to be constantly on the increase—wielded by the Russian supreme ruler, the autocratic Tsar of Muscovy. That remote, revered, unpredictable potentate treated all his subjects, high and low, as his slaves, disposing of their persons and property as his own. Surrounded by self-abasing minions, he generated an 'off-with-their-heads' atmosphere at once frightening, comic, inscrutable and devious; and could thus easily be confused in the alien mind with a caliph, sultan or Grand Cham. Greeks of the classical period had once looked eastward at the Persian Great King in much the same way: awe spiked, as may be seen in Aristophanes, with somewhat contemptuous amusement at the barbarian's expense.

To leap from Muscovy across half a millennium to the present-day USSR is to find Russia's authoritarian politics a continued object of fascination to the West. Now organized on principles termed Marxist-Leninist, and constituting the largest ethnic element in an amalgam termed Soviet, the Russians have—according to their official spokesmen—spent the last sixty years pioneering a new, freer, more democratic way of life than any previously adopted by any other society: one allegedly bound, by a happy dispensation, sooner or later to spread itself over the entire globe in accordance with certain inexorable and scientific laws of historical development. This thesis has found many devoted disciples in the West, though by no means all Western Marxists have been prepared to accept it in its ultra-russocentric form. Moreover, a sharply opposed view has also found favor outside the Kremlin's orbit: that Russian totalitarian controls represent a form of slavery more sophisticated and far-reaching than any previously known in history. The obligation placed on USSR-domiciled Russians, together with other Kremlinized and Kremlin-dominated citizens, to affirm enthusiastically from time to time that they are free, happy and fulfilled, is (in this view) merely a supreme insult added to so many injuries—an indignity which even the slaves of Periclean Athens were spared.

Despite the admitted importance of Russian politics, medieval as well as modern, the country's fascination for many of its Western addicts has derived less from its system of government than from the lure of the quaint, the bizarre, the incongruous. It is in Russian literature that many foreigners have first encountered such features. A policeman is thrown into a river tied to a bear. A civil servant looks in his mirror one morning and discovers that his nose has mysteriously disappeared from his face in the course of the night. A dog solemnly lectures his owner on citizens' rights. A young man takes a general's ear between his teeth, and then hangs on to it for several paragraphs while the author of the tale discourses at leisure on the possible causes and implications of this event.

For drawing these first tentative samples of the Russian ethos from literature rather than life no apology is offered, since the activities of the imagination as expressed in belles-lettres can be the most potent illustration possible of a collective national mind. The above samples happen to come from the works of Leo Tolstoy, Gogol, Michael Bulgakov and Dostoyevsky respectively. And if one seeks to reinforce them by seeking further instances of such casual incongruity in life, history and legend, there will be no need to look far. A sixteenth-century Tsar, Ivan the Terrible, is presented with an elephant and orders the slaughter of the beast for failing to bow to him; yet the same dread monarch is too frightened, too superstitious to quell the lunatic naked monk who wanders around publicly denouncing his sovereign as a limb of Satan.[1] Two centuries later the ebullient giant Potemkin, favorite of Catherine the Great, takes as his concubine the wife of Prince Dolgoruky, his subordinate general in the Turkish campaign of 1791, and responds to the titled cuckold's protests by hoisting him aloft in the presence of his brother officers, holding him in the air by the sashes of his decorations and giving tongue. 'You bastard!' yells the gargantuan fornicator. 'It was I who gave you and the others these honors. You don't deserve them. You're all a load of crap and I have every right to do what I like with you and yours.'[2] More recently, to take a less rumbustious absurdity, the Tsar-Emperor Nicholas I amiably settles the route of Russia's first major railway, that linking St. Petersburg and Moscow, by seizing a ruler and drawing a line between the two cities on a map: a line which the engineers faithfully follow, down to minor detours accidentally caused at points where the emperor's fingers chance to have protruded.[3]

Nor has the twentieth century been immune from similar absurdities, in which obscenity and cruelty have all too often found their part. The monstrous drunken Rasputin—a major architect of the Empire's downfall, the absurdly rumored lover of the last reigning empress—indecently exposes himself in a Moscow restaurant while introducing the company to the only true and legitimate ruler of Russia: his erect penis.[4] A post-revolutionary tyrant, Stalin, rocks with helpless laughter as one of his police chiefs, K. V. Pauker, enlivens a social occasion by imitating the last minutes on earth of Zinovyev, the political rival recently sentenced to death, and thus to judicial assassination, by the dictator himself through the first big Moscow show trial. The doomed Zinovyev is mimicked as calling in vain—even while he is dragged off to be shot—on the name of Jehovah, and as thereby cravenly apostatizing with his final breath from his atheist Marxist creed. After nearly choking with laughter, Stalin soon ensures that the very author of this sally, the malign Pauker, shall be liquidated in turn.[5] Now, Pauker and Zinovyev were both Jewish, while Stalin was a Georgian; still, where else but on Russian soil would this grotesque pantomime have seemed so much in place?

It must be hastily added that not one of these stories is fully authenticated, while those first invoked come from avowed works of fiction. But of all of them it may be suggested that, even if they are not true, it would have been necessary to invent them. All convey an atmosphere which may be provisionally called, in however superficial a sense, Russian; and which, however much the conception of things Russian may be modified and expanded on later pages, may at least serve as the starting point for an investigation. For good or ill, it was the special atmosphere conjured up by such episodes, true or imaginary, which seized so violently on my youthful imagination as to divert me many years ago from the study of the Greek and Latin classics to that of Russia, her language, literature and history. What, compared with these intriguing monstrosities, was a mere Gorgon's head or robe of Nessus? And where, to my adolescent brain, was the attraction of a long-vanished people dedicated at least in theory to a policy of μηδὲν ἄγαν ('nothing in excess'), compared to the fascination exercised by those live heirs of the Scythians who seemed so gloriously to proclaim and act out the slogan EVERYTHING IN EXCESS?

Having provisionally identified, however superficially, certain incidents as characteristically Russian, one may now ask what specific features they present to the eye of sober analysis. Violence at once stands out as a characteristic element. Still, many other peoples have been no less violent than the Russians, surely, and one may proceed to seek other typical ingredients. Suddenness and unpredictability are among them, as may be further illustrated from the methods of nineteenth-century criminals in the Siberian city of Irkutsk. A rich merchant, capped and swaddled in furs, is staggering drunkenly out of some hostelry into the sub-zero temperature of the main thoroughfare, when he is suddenly lassoed from a careering troika manned by whooping highwaymen, and towed helplessly over the ice at high speed to a remote alley where he is plundered and stripped, and has his throat cut.[6] The victim could no doubt have been 'mugged' in some more static, less theatrical style. But that would have spoiled the fun. The dynamism, the excess of zeal—as typical a feature of the Russian as a total absence of zeal—are characteristic. How dull and conventional the procedures of a mere Dick Turpin or Procrustes seem by comparison.

Then again, there is that pervasive episode in Russian history: the mock execution as meted out, for example, to the high-placed embezzler Baron Shafirov by Peter the Great. Condemned to beheading, the baron is solemnly led out to die and dutifully lays his head on the block, after which he hears the headsman's axe whistle through the air: to strike the block, not the suddenly pardoned victim.[7] Similarly, in 1742, under Peter's daughter Elizabeth, the gouty elder statesman Ostermann is first sentenced to be broken on the wheel, then has his penalty commuted to beheading; he too places his head on the block as one executioner clutches him by the hair and another takes a grip on the axe—whereupon the presiding official suddenly flourishes a piece of paper and proclaims that 'God and the Empress have spared your life.'[8] Need one, then, be surprised to find the youthful novelist Dostoyevsky sentenced, a century later, to execution by firing squad at the behest of the Emperor Nicholas I? Here is another carefully stage-managed scene culminating in a preordained last-minute commutation whereby the young man learns, within minutes of expected death by shooting, that he is to suffer Siberian imprisonment and exile in its place: all (another characteristic feature) for the crime of participating in what was little more than a private political discussion group.[9]

Though these are all examples of mock executions which ended well for the victims, the contrary switch has by no means been excluded. One thinks of those minor NKVD officials who were ordered to confess to invented crimes, thus implicating Zinovyev, Kamenev and their co-defendants in the first great Moscow political show trial. The understanding was that the lives of these false witnesses would be spared. But once sentence of death had been pronounced they had no way of compelling Stalin to keep his side of the bargain, and they were of course duly shot along with all the others.[10] This too represents a long-standing national tradition: witness, for example, the fate of the seventeenth-century General Shein, as recounted by the German scholar and traveler Olearius. Defeated at Smolensk by the Poles and accused of treachery by his own troops, the general was solemnly requested—by the very Patriarch of Moscow among others—to take part in a form of pageant whereby he would first be led out to the chopping block *pour encourager les autres,* but then pardoned at the last moment. In the event, though, everything went according to a second, yet more secret, plan into which poor Shein had not been initiated; and before the wretched man could raise his head to protest it was already rolling on the ground.[11]

A similar style has sometimes been cultivated on a collective level, and by no one more than the arch-russifier Stalin. His defeat of Finland in the Winter War of 1939–40 having led to the release from Finnish custody of numerous Red Army prisoners-of-war, the dictator paraded these returning warriors in a victory march through Leningrad under banners ('The Fatherland Greets Its Heroes')—straight through the city to railway sidings. Here cattle trucks were ready to transport one and all to the concentration camps which were the common fate of those Soviet troops who, for whatever reason, had allowed themselves to be captured by the enemy.[12] Similarly, in 1944, an entire small Soviet Caucasian nation—that of the Chechens—was invited to join local troops in celebrating Red Army Day on 23 February: whereupon, at a given signal, these carousing hillsmen—men, women, children, Party members and all—were rounded up at gunpoint and conveyed in Lend-Lease Studebaker trucks to the nearest railhead: a prelude to concentration camp or exile.[13]

Such examples of the sudden switch, the volte-face, figure frequently in Russian myths and folklore, as when the seventeenth-century rebel chief Stenka Razin suddenly decides, in the popular folk song, to hurl his favorite concubine—a captured Persian princess—to drown in the turbulent waves of the Volga. Nor are these folklore examples of the volte-face inevitably in the direction from benevolence to cruelty. In

another, less well-known, Russian folk song, the ataman Ku-
deyar, robber baron and terror of peaceful villagers, is transformed with even greater dramatic abruptness into Brother
Pyaterim, a saintly monk. How like the KGB 'hit man' Captain
Nicholas Khokhlov, who was sent to Germany in 1954 to
murder a prominent *émigré* Russian politician but laid aside
his weapon, resembling a cigarette case and specially designed
to fire poisoned bullets, and confronted his prospective victim
with something only a shade less daunting, a confession, *à la*
Dostoyevsky, of his mission and of his decision not to go
through with it.[14] Russian life, lore, art and myth abound in
these dramatic conversions of plus into minus and vice versa.
They are not of course an exclusive Russian monopoly, as the
biblical transformation of Saul into Paul illustrates; but they
seem more prominent and typical in a Russian context than
anywhere else.

To seek further clues to the essential 'Russianness' of such
episodes is to be struck by the frequency with which the concept of authority is invoked. Where sudden humiliation, cruelty or death are concerned, authority's most natural role is
that of dispenser rather than recipient. The Tsars, Potemkin,
Stalin—these figures are not easily seen as victims. But less
adroit, less fortunate Russian potentates have found themselves on the receiving end. They have included several
crowned victims of assassination: Peter III in 1762, Paul I in
1801, Alexander II in 1881 and the ex-Emperor Nicholas II
in 1918. Another unfortunate, Tsar Ivan VI, spent over
twenty years in solitary confinement from infancy before
being stabbed to death on the Empress Catherine's instructions when an abortive attempt was made to free him. And
though the supreme dictators of the Soviet period have remained immune from such turns of fortune's wheel, despite
an unsuccessful attempt on Lenin's life, their nearest henchmen have not escaped unscathed. Judicially murdered
(Zinovyev, Kamenev and so many others), assassinated in

emigration (Trotsky), or peacefully—but how suddenly!—deposed (Khrushchev), they have often figured in the kind of dramatic volte-face which seems so characteristic of Russian life and fiction.

The religious world, too, seems to provoke certain characteristic responses directed toward deflating or overthrowing divine or clerical authority. Long before the post-1917 revolutionary government began to attack religion more systematically, the Russian landowner had been apt to duck his local priest in the pond to amuse his guests, or even to coop the poor man in a barrel and roll him downhill. Nor were the very symbols of religion immune. There is Dostoyevsky's story, in his *Diary of a Writer* of 1873, of the peasant who privily removed from church his edible pellet, symbolizing the Host and issued to him during Communion, stuck it on a post and then proceeded to aim a rifle at the Body and Blood of Christ. There are also the same writer's sacrilegious scenes, especially notable in his novel *Devils*. Here a live mouse is surreptitiously introduced into the case containing a holy icon; an aged Bible-seller has pornographic literature inserted in her stock of trade; and a holy man pelts pilgrims with boiled potatoes.

In seeking to understand such phenomena rather than to add further examples such as could be supplied indefinitely, one seems to find their essence less and less in factors discussed above: the obsession with authority, the element of volte-face, the suddenness, the violence, the cruelty. None of these, especially the last, can fairly be claimed as a Russian monopoly. No, for the secret surely lies more in the motivation underlying such manifestations. There seems to be, to put it mildly, a lack of proper or seemly proportion between cause and effect in these sudden acts of violence or absurdity. A rational stimulus may be detected when one scans a given episode; but it seems nothing beside the element of maniac self-assertion expressed in the reaction, whether one thinks of the lassoers of Irkutsk, the princess-drowning Razin, the elephant-slaughtering Tsar or Stalin's acts against the Chechens and his own soldiers. In all these cases there seems to be an intelligible initial impulse: personal gain, bolstering of prestige, maintenance of military discipline and so on. And yet the motive, no sooner discerned, at once seems to disappear from sight owing to the spectacular and disproportionately exuberant nature of the action to which it gives rise.

In other cases the link between stimulus and reaction is even more remote. Why should a young man, piqued to learn that his mother has become the mistress of an abbot, react by taking a tame canary, tying it to a tree and discharging a double-barreled shotgun at it, as in Dostoyevsky's novel *A Raw Youth*? There is perhaps no point in asking, and in another, parallel, episode from Dostoyevsky the history of the text shows that its author explicitly desired to mystify the reader, and that the search for a rational explanation is therefore doomed from the start. This is the episode in *Devils* describing Stavrogin's astonishing treatment, in a county town's respectable local club, of a harmless, middle-aged member who is in the habit of remarking from time to time in the course of conversation, 'No, sir, you cannot lead *me* by the nose.' Stavrogin suddenly, apropos of nothing, goes up to the poor man, seizes him by the nose and pulls him a few paces across the floor. This scandal leads to a second and greater scandal, mentioned above, as Stavrogin, called to account by the provincial governor for his nose-pulling prank, makes as if to whisper a speech of explanation in that worthy's ear, but in fact seizes it firmly between his teeth. Why? The author never gives any authoritative explanation, and in any case it is known from his preliminary work on the novel that Stavrogin was explicitly intended to be a mystery man. All Dostoyevsky will concede is the deliciously teasing comment 'people said afterwards that, at the actual moment of carrying out the [nose-pulling] operation, he looked rather thoughtful.' [15]

Such actions, inexplicable or disproportionate, are considered by Russians to exemplify a phenomenon which they term *proizvol,* of which no closer translation than 'arbitrariness' suggests itself. Viewed 'from a safe distance, *proizvol,* as liberally attested in Russian life and letters, helps to explain the special fascination which the Russian mentality has always exercised over the foreigner. He feels plunged into a world more vivid and dramatic than his own: a sort of moral 'no-go area' where normal restraints and conventions do not apply. Here is a people—the relatively hidebound Briton, German or American may be tempted to feel—more vital, more spontaneous, more dynamic in every way than his own, a people liberated from customary taboos. And yet this very consideration at once raises one of the major paradoxes with which a study of the Russian mentality is beset. For the fact is that, despite all these impressive claims to have pioneered new and exciting areas of human behavior, no feature of the country is more commonly attested by the united witness of its memoir-writers, poets, critics and novelists, and of foreign witnesses too, than that of supreme boredom: boredom crashing, inspissated, abysmal.

A succession of identical villages and towns set in an endless featureless plain: such is the picture which witness after witness paints. Fleeing through Russia from Napoleon in 1812, Mme. de Staël complains that the houses in the sparse villages are all built to the same model. No less depressed is a visitor of 1839, the Marquis de Custine: depressed by the monotony and gloom of the villages through which he has passed, 'two lines of log cabins placed along a road which seems unnaturally wide.' Every twenty or thirty leagues along the route Custine comes to a town, but he complains that it is always, in effect, the same one. Nor did the Scottish journalist Mackenzie Wallace fare better during his prolonged visit of 1870–75. To him all Russian towns were little more than villages in disguise, with their straight, wide, unpaved or potholed surfaces. He speaks of 'an air of solitude and languor,' no street lighting, few or no shops. From these criticisms he exempts two cities only, St. Petersburg and Odessa—both major ports, incidentally, and as such diversified by a large variety of foreign visitors and residents. As for Moscow, the Empire's second city, Mackenzie Wallace was by no means the only nineteenth-century visitor to disparage that metropolis as little more than a sprawling Russian village writ large. Native witnesses give a similar picture. Chekhov, one of the most reliable, considered all Russian towns pretty well interchangeable. 'Yekaterinburg is just like Perm or Tula. It's also like Sumy and Gadyach.' [16]

More recent developments have tended, all too often, to replace one form of monotony with another. Moscow is now anything but an overgrown village. The replacement of moldering log cabins, there and in the provinces, with rectilinear concrete-and-glass tenements has improved the amenities and raised the level of the skyline—but has also tended to import a new and not necessarily more pleasing brand of uniformity. And it is still the ancient churches rather than the extravagances (most common in Moscow) of wedding-cake architecture from the Stalin period which succeed most effectively in providing visual relief. The same function of diversifying and lending magic to the immense spaciousness of Russia's plains has long been performed by the onion domes of innumerable village churches, often visible from afar, often flashing gold in the sunlight. Nor, even when lacking a domed skyline, does the rural scene present the spectacle of monotony unrelieved. There is the variety of central Russia's hills, woods and streams; there are the great prairies in the south; there are Siberia's majestic mountain ranges, lakes and taiga.

That Russia's monotony has never been narrowly confined to matters architectural seems the almost united witness of its great nineteenth-century novelists, who have collectively pioneered picturesque tedium as a fictional theme. One thinks of the 'superfluous men' immortalized by Pushkin and lesser scribes. There is his blasé Eugene Onegin who, tiring of city life, moves to the country only to discover that rural solitude also palls, and after a mere two days. There is Lermontov's Pechorin in *A Hero of Our Time*—a more energetic and enterprising figure than Onegin, but an experimenter with other people's emotions whose utter boredom and disillusionment can only be relieved by creating synthetic crises in the lives of his mistresses and other associates. Above all, there is Oblomov, that supreme emblem of listlessness, hero of the novel of the same name by Goncharov, and renowned as the only, or at least the first, character in fiction to spend roughly a hundred pages getting out of bed. And there are also Chekhov's superb depictions of frustration, of spiritual unease, of inability to come to terms with life.

That these traits by no means disappeared, but rather increased, with the advent of the twentieth century may be shown from a variety of witnesses who include Maurice Paléologue, French Ambassador to Russia during the First World War. No society was more prone to ennui than the Russian, he declared. He speaks of indolence, lassitude, torpor, bewilderment; weary gestures, yawns; an extraordinary facility for easily tiring of everything; a horror of solitude; the perpetual exchange of purposeless visits and pointless telephone calls; fantastic immoderation in religious fervor and good works; facile indulgence in morbid imaginings and gloomy presentiments.[17]

To Paléologue's catalogue of depressive attributes may also be added the intense gloom which Russian literature has often seemed to generate even in the titles of some well-known works: *Dead Souls, Memoirs from the House of the Dead* and so on. This aspect of the national literary ethos has been most memorably caricatured in Stephen Leacock's parody 'The Russian Drama: New Style.' Here, in a dimly lit underground lodging in Pinsk with water oozing through the walls, a thief, an imbecile, a homicidal maniac, an 'immoral woman' and a murderer proceed to kill each other or expire by slow stages between gulps of vodka out of dirty glasses and so on, the action terminating with the imbecile giggling over the corpses. 'In other words,' Leacock comments, 'it's a regular Russian scene.' [18] His main target is obviously Gorky's doss-house drama, *The Lower Depths,* but there are echoes of Dostoyevsky and other authors too. These aspects of Russian literature, its squalor and exotic melancholy, appealed to Western readers of the early twentieth century and were taken to reflect a comparable degree of squalor and melancholy in Russian life. Nor need such an impression be entirely misleading provided that one does not lose sight of Russian life as a complex affair. To concentrate unduly on any specific aspect of it is to distort it.

The same may be said of the allegedly transformed post-revolutionary era when, by contrast, intense optimism ('saying yes to life') has become an article of officially imposed faith for the happy milkmaids and jolly lathe-operators, all wreathed in smiles, who figure in such illustrated magazines as the Moscow-published *Ogonyok.* Do these phenomena reflect a genuine collective euphoria? Or is the obligation to pretend that all is for the best in the best of all possible worlds merely another form of regimentation—and not even a modern one, for the milkmaids of Russian eighteenth-century fiction were often depicted in accordance with similar idyllic conventions? There is, alas, no technique whereby a statistically valid answer could be obtained. If it could, one suspects that neither tedium unrelieved nor euphoria unalloyed would prove to constitute the true state of Russian affairs, but an atmosphere in which individuals are still prone at any given moment to embrace the one or the other more wholeheartedly than are the representatives of many another ethnic group.

So far, then, this argument seems to have landed in an impasse. Here, it began, is a people supremely alive, exciting and stimulating because of its penchant for incongruity, its neglect of conventional taboos, its flair for the spectacular un-provoked sally: a race, in other words, of life-enhancers. But here, it added in the next breath, is a nation supremely dull and drab, sunk in torpor, apathy, boredom and gloom: a breed, rather, of life-deniers. Manics? Or depressives? Per-haps this very dichotomy, this very contradiction between total inactivity and excess of activity, may provide the first clue to the Russian mind. The second element may less contradict the first than complement it. These slaughtered elephants, bitten ears, massacred canaries and the like—may they not be, in es-sence, a protest against a background of ineffable tedium? If so, it might be correct to invoke, as an explanation of the Rus-sian mind, the immortal words of Herzen: 'The stifling emp-tiness and dumbness of Russian life, curiously combined with its vitality and rumbustious character, provoke all sorts of crackpot outbursts in our midst.' [19]

Herzen's splendidly phrased formula has the advantage of seeming to explain all the problems so far propounded: of seeming to explain, though, rather than of fully explaining. The present investigation is, after all, only just beginning, and it is far too early to announce, at the end of the first chapter, any triumphant solution to a problem of such baffling com-plexity as the Russian mind. Crackpot outbursts punctuating periods of trancelike torpor—these may seem typical of the Russian, but are after all only one facet of the problem. Other very different, no less typical-seeming phenomena will be en-countered, such as the following, in which the elements of sudden violence are wholly absent. 'A man falls in love with a married woman, and they part and meet, and in the end are left talking about their position and by what means they can be free from "this intolerable bondage." "How? How?" he asked, clutching his head.' Such is Virginia Woolf's account of Chekhov's story *A Lady with a Dog*, of which she speaks as arousing her bewilderment. 'What is the point of it, and why does he make a story out of it?' [20] Perhaps the very pointlessness *is* the point. The story certainly does have one factor in common with the various 'crackpot outbursts' invoked above: an element of seeming irrationality. But, here again, might it not be unwise to make too much of the irrationality and of the tendency toward apparent mental imbalance which can so easily be read into Russians by non-Russians, especially if interpretations are based too exclusively on literary sources?

There are times when it may be salutary to remember the words of an English reviewer, Gerald Gould, writing in the *New Statesman* of 8 April 1916: 'My Russian friends are without exception perfectly sane; yet almost all the Russians I read about in books are mad as hatters.'[21]

## *PROBLEMS OF PERSPECTIVE*

The present study is the latest in a long series of attempts by non-Russians to investigate the Russian mentality. They go back to the early sixteenth century and to the first systematic account of the country by a visitor from Central or Western Europe, Baron Sigismund von Herberstein.

After twice serving, in 1517 and 1526, as the Holy Roman Emperor's ambassador to Muscovy, the usual name for Russia at the time, Herberstein returned home to publish his description of this realm, not so long emerged from the quarantine of alien, Mongol-Tatar overlordship. Since then literally thousands of accounts of Russia, brief or voluminous, have been contributed by European, American and other travelers, explorers, diplomats, businessmen, doctors, spies, soldiers, journalists, scholars and the like, among whom many a wise man and many a talented eccentric has been numbered along with the inevitable bores and repeaters of platitudes. Russophobes have sought to portray the Russian as a devil incarnate; russophiles have idealized him; Russia-fanciers have patronized him as a 'holy fool' or jolly buffoon. Fortunately, though, there has been no lack of other, subtler observers who have had the wit to discern Russians as a phenomenon considerably more complex.

Not a few of these foreign commentators have sought to analyze or explain Russian thought processes. Yet the enigma of the Russian mind seems to retain some of its secrets to this day. And still, four and a half centuries after Herberstein, the world's thirst for insights into the Russian psyche remains unslaked. Nor will the present study triumphantly unwrap some oracular riddle from its enveloping enigma and present it neatly solved in a brief, crisp, unambiguous formula. It is, however, hoped that readers may begin to find Russian behavior, often so baffling to the outside observer, considerably less puzzling than it may previously have appeared.

To inquire into the Russians' or any other people's mentality is to accept a challenge. Here is a collection of so many hundred million human beings whose ways of thinking, both past and present, must be ransacked for common denominators simultaneously typifying them while differentiating them from the rest of mankind, dead or alive. In an inquiry so broad, a knowledge of the country, a command of source materials, and a grasp of statistics, literature, history and thought are essential; but they are not enough. A study such as this must, in the last analysis, be a somewhat impressionistic personal statement. It must depend a great deal on 'hunches'—a consideration which in turn imposes on the investigator the duty to cultivate modesty and caution, yet not to the extent of being deterred from stating the truth as he sees it.

While delving into the complexities of a single national psyche the investigator must also try to do justice to the wider picture. It has, accordingly, been helpful to forget from time to time that I happen to be an English student of Russia, and to think of the many studies, entirely outside the Russian-English sphere, of one nationality contributed by the representative of another. They all tend to possess one particularly significant feature: the emphasis which the alien observer is apt to place on the uniquely paradoxical and self-contradictory nature of the national mentality under review. No one, perhaps, could be much further removed from myself in background and outlook than a Spanish duke. And few peoples, surely, offer fewer superficial points of resemblance to the Russians than the Dutch. Yet here is the Spanish Duke de Baena's excellent study *The Dutch Puzzle* (1975) making the following points about a nation which has been the object of his profound scrutiny as ambassador to their country: 'Never in my long and adventurous life have I known a people so riddled with paradoxes as the Dutch.' The Dutch are, according to the duke, 'passionately fond of freedom and equally servile to convention . . . tender and sentimental in [their] feelings, and also rude in [their] . . . manners . . . both tolerant and fanatic . . . both grand and petty . . . excessively cautious and madly indiscreet . . . strongly materialistic and extremely religious, both sensuous and puritanical.' [1]

It chances, as will emerge from much of the material below, that every word in this summary of the eminent Spaniard's assessment of the Dutch closely echoes my own assessment of the Russians. Can it then be human nature in general rather than Russian or Dutch, Spanish or English nature which is so riddled with incongruities? Can it, even, be human nature in general which the representative of Nationality A tends, unconsciously, to have in mind when he thinks that he is focusing his gaze exclusively on Nationality B? This is, surely, a useful consideration to keep in mind. I have accordingly attempted, when examining Russia's many paradoxes, to consider whenever possible whether they may not be universally human rather than exclusively national. Still, one does acquire a certain patriotism by adoption about the object of one's most extensive observations. And though I can readily concede that the stolidity so misleadingly projected in Amsterdam or The Hague is a mirage, I still find it downright impossible to believe in my heart that the Duke de Baena's Dutchmen can even begin to compete with my Russians when it comes to the generation of paradoxes.

Another difficulty presented by the investigation of a national mind—any national mind—is that which confronts an inquirer whose philosophical approach is as unfashionably individualist as mine happens to be: one whose natural instinct is never to find his own or anyone else's chief significance in his function as the representative of some class, income group, color, race, creed or other category, including that of nationality. 'My attitude as a housewife, teenager, window-cleaner, ordinary this, average that . . .': such self-categorization, frequently accompanied by the smirk of the inverted snob and so sadly encouraged nowadays by the pomposities of the media, seems to be on the increase. This is regrettable if so, since to think of oneself primarily as a status-geared unit typical of other, identical units, is surely to take a step toward adopting the mentality of a slave, cipher or automaton.

Fortunately contrary currents may also be observed, suggesting that typicality is not universally accepted as admirable. Such a disparaging streak may be traced in the language of insult. 'How typical of a man; how like a woman; I know your sort; I've met your kind before': the use of such formulae in an angry or disparaging sense is encouraging. It shows that ordinariness, averageness and typicality, though by no means necessarily disgraceful characteristics, need not always be automatically invoked as causes for complacency and self-congratulation. The existence of this disparaging attitude toward group allegiances suggests that there is no great harm in having a collective phenomenon like the Russian mind scrutinized from an avowedly non-collectivist viewpoint. There may, on the contrary, be something unusually stimulating in surveying from such an angle a culture's characteristic structure of mental grooves, verbal patterns, conventional responses—its thought formulae, its facial and other gesticulations, its unconscious or largely unconscious taboos. These phenomena owe part of their fascination to the potential danger which they represent; for what can pose a greater threat than the consolidated prejudices of 'ordinary people,' especially if harnessed by political manipulators and officious do-gooders? Nor are such manifestations necessarily a less valuable or absorbing subject for study simply because they are less admirable and striking than are the achievements of remarkable individuals in overcoming their own national or other group limitations.

Great minds, whether they operate on Russian, American, British or any other soil, are surely far from 'thinking alike,' as the proverb so mistakenly claims. On the contrary, they are exceedingly prone to think unalike. It is, rather, minds of smaller caliber which incline to the processes of mimesis, conformism and taboo-acceptance. To study a nation's psychology is therefore, in a sense, to study its clichés, its conventions, its inhibitions—to wander along the beaten tracks of the foothills rather than to scale the heights. But the heights, too, are part of the landscape. Indeed, it has not been found possible to calculate the various Russian intellectual common denominators without taking frequent sightings from the peaks and trig points represented by the country's many creative nonconformists—by such men as Pushkin, who ignored; Chekhov, who rejected; Dostoyevsky, who carried to extremes, and thereby transcended, the national norm. Nor will it be forgotten that an ability to rise superior to collective limitations is no monopoly of exceptionally gifted individuals. Many a more modestly endowed Russian has achieved such freedom of spirit, as any sensitive person who knows the country will readily confirm. Moreover, even the dullest conformists have an importance which one would be foolish to deny: they contribute to a society, for good or ill, that element of cohesiveness and stability without which there might not be any Russian or other collective mind to analyze. A community consisting solely of individualists is, happily, never likely to arise; but may heaven preserve mankind from a society which entirely lacks them.

There are those who believe the investigation of any and all national characteristics to be mischievous and foredoomed, since it must inevitably become bogged down in vague generalizations which can neither be proved nor disproved, and which may turn out both misleading and offensive to the nation concerned. Much respecting this objection, I have tried to meet it in two ways. First, this study has been made as concrete and precise as possible, rather than abstract and portentous. And, secondly, an attempt has been made to observe one simple rule of etiquette which should arguably be accepted as a cardinal element in civilized behavior in any context: never to assume in advance that an unknown citizen of Russia or any other country will necessarily exhibit even a single characteristic, however minor, from among any amalgam which may be claimed as typical of the group as a whole.

To turn from the general to the particular difficulties of the subject is to be faced above all by the need to distinguish between the overlapping concepts of Russian and Soviet. The nationality which dominated the Tsardom of Muscovy and later the huge, multi-national Russian Empire, was transformed, in the years 1917–22, into the leading partner in the allegedly federal and to some extent notionally denationalized USSR. At the same time the Russian words for *Russia* and *Russian* fell more or less under an official ban as smacking of the previous regime. That ban has long been lifted and national pride has been admitted, since the mid-1930s, as a legitimate and indeed obligatory element in the litany of institutionalized

Soviet Russian self-praise. And yet, at the same time, the official claim is also made that a new and superior generalized
psychological type—Soviet Man—has been evolved on the soil
of the USSR. How much weight can be attached to this claim?
To what extent is there a Soviet as opposed to a Russian mentality? These are not the least intractable among the many
problems on which glosses will be offered in the course of this
study. At the same time a decision has been taken not to give
undue prominence, in what is intended as a survey of Russian
attitudes throughout the ages, to the Soviet period. Post-
revolutionary phenomena will indeed be considered below in
some detail. But they will not dominate a review which ranges
through the centuries with a tendency to find the last six decades of the Empire (1855–1917) the most fruitful source of
inspiration.

Another difficulty is to decide precisely who the Russians
are. In so far as they have a national territory it is now that of
the Russian Soviet Federated Socialist Republic (RSFSR). This
is the largest by far of the fifteen Union Republics into which
the USSR is divided—so large, indeed, that it spans the entire
six-thousand-mile stretch from Smolensk to Vladivostok. But
many non-Russians inhabit this territory too, some of them
encapsulated in large Autonomous Republics of their own.
Russians also abound as sizable minorities in the other fourteen Union Republics: the Ukraine, Belorussia, Moldavia,
those of the Caucasus and Central Asia and the formerly independent Baltic states. Then there are also Russian *émigrés*,
millions of whom have enlivened the non-Russian scene in
both hemispheres, and many of whom were originally refugees from the 1917 Bolshevik Revolution or the Second World
War. Though they and their descendants have become increasingly assimilated in their countries of domicile, not a few
still consider themselves thoroughly Russian, and their mentality cannot be left out of account in the present survey.

Such are some of the difficulties of defining the subject in the present century. To them must be added the complexities of the nation's evolution during an entire millennium. Should this investigation be taken back to A.D. 862—in which year, according to tradition, the Russian state was originally founded? What degree of attention is to be given to Kievan Russia: the first East Slav state, that loose confederation of competing principalities which was converted to Christianity in the late tenth century, and which flourished considerably before subsiding into insignificance and being finally destroyed by Tatar invaders in 1240? The subject is a tempting one, if only because of various tidbits of Russian lore lodged in the early chronicles. There is the original invitation extended, according to legend, by the East Slav ancestors of the Russians to the Viking chieftains and raiders known as Varangians: 'Our land is large and there is no order in it—come and rule over us.' This probably apocryphal episode was to be invested by nineteenth-century Slavophile philosophers with deep symbolic significance based on the alleged voluntary as opposed to compulsory symbiosis of Russian rulers and Russian ruled throughout the ages.[2] Such speculations may safely be ignored, but there yet remains a kernel of symbolic truth in the story of the invitation extended to the Varangians. Russia indeed is large, far larger now than in Varangian times. Moreover, as will be noted, there always has been a tendency for lack of order to require correction by the imposition of excess of order, and often through the importation of non-Russian rulers, of whom—from the Varangians through the Mongol Khans and the German Catherine the Great to the Georgian Stalin—Russia's history has known not a few.

Despite such elements of continuity, there are yet reasons why Kievan Russia will not loom large in this investigation. The Kievan state, having a civilization advanced by the standards of its own day and possessing intricate dynastic links with many another medieval kingdom, was less differentiated from contemporary Western European society than Russia has ever been since: for which reason the early medieval Russian mentality has less significance here than it otherwise might. There is also the consideration that Kiev was the cultural, national and institutional ancestor not only of Russia itself, but also of two other important East Slav peoples: the Ukrainian and the Belorussian. Leaving the three nations to argue about which of them is the true heir of Kiev, the present investigation will concentrate on more recent times, only noting in passing that the strict differentiation of the three East Slav peoples is a twentieth-century phenomenon. Before 1917 the term *Russian* tended—decreasingly and in the teeth of growing nationalist objection—to cover all three, with *Great Russian* as a semi-specialist term used in contexts where it was necessary to distinguish what are now called 'Russians' from the Ukrainians (then officially called 'Little Russians') and the Belorussians.

The decline of Kiev in the twelfth and thirteenth centuries was accompanied by persistent Russian colonization of a forested mesopotamia to the northeast, in what is now central Russia. The earlier Finnic settlers were gradually ousted or assimilated as the small fortified settlement of Moscow, first mentioned in the Russian chronicles under the year 1147, gradually grew to be a minor and then a major principality. Here, far more than in Kiev, does one seem to recognize the cradle of the Great Russian people, whose physical features tend to include the high cheekbones and slanted eyes associated with the Finns—a characteristic not inherited by the Ukrainians and Belorussians. It also happens that the Great Russian people was, while yet in early process of formation, almost strangled at birth through the first and greatest of many appalling disasters. The invasion by Mongol-ruled Tatar cavalry hordes in and around the year 1240 devastated the country and subjected it to overlordship until roughly 1480, the year in which Muscovy is traditionally regarded as having ceased to pay tribute to the Tatars. To compute the effects of the Tatar yoke on the Russian mentality, and with special reference to the key theme of Russian attitudes to authority, is another complex problem which must be faced later. For the moment it is important only to note that the Russia with which this study is chiefly concerned is that which developed after the collapse of Tatar overlordship at the end of the fifteenth century: first as Muscovy; then, from 1721, as the Russian Empire; and later, from 1917, as the predominant Russian component of a new revolutionary state.

Though Muscovy threw off Tatar dependency in about 1480 and went on to the offensive in the following century, itself conquering many of the lands of its former masters, the Tatar peril had by no means been liquidated. Centuries of acute and devastating harassment by slave-trapping Tatar raiders and freebooters were to follow, an appalling and ever-present ordeal which only ended with the conquest of the Crimea under Catherine the Great in the late eighteenth century. The Tatars were, accordingly, the scourge of Russia from roughly 1240 to roughly 1783—more than half a millennium. The need to maintain a large standing army and a fortified line of outposts against Tatar marauders placed an excessive strain on Russia over many centuries, especially as the country was also exposed to many another foreign enemy. Wars on and for her western frontiers, notably against the Poles and Swedes, were frequent from the sixteenth to the eighteenth centuries. More recently a series of major collisions of increasing severity—the Napoleonic invasion of 1812, the Great War of 1914–18, the Second World War—have helped to ensure for Russia an experience of mass suffering notably more extensive than any other large modern occidental or partly occidental state has experienced—so extensive as to create yet another barrier to the understanding of Russians by non-Russians. Russians make the most of this. They are still systematically seeking to enlist visitors' sympathy, not to mention negotiating and propaganda advantages, by the endless retailing of German atrocities committed between 1941 and 1945. No attempt will be made to minimize these, or the appalling Russian losses in the First and Second World Wars; but it must also be pointed out that the ordeals imposed on Russia by foreign enemies have not fallen far short of those imposed on Russia by her own rulers, or, for that matter, on occupied foreign countries by Russian invaders. Of Russia's tyrants Joseph Stalin has been the most destructive, largely through casualties inflicted by concentration camp conditions, which led to so many million fatalities. But Ivan the Terrible (ruled 1547–84) rivals Stalin in the percentage of the then much smaller Russian population which he liquidated. And Ivan outdid even the Georgian dictator in the element of apparent irrationality underlying the massacre of his subjects. Nor do these two names exhaust the tally of Russia's despots, among whom Ivan the Great in the late fifteenth and Peter the Great in the early eighteenth century were outstandingly ruthless; but they appear to have concentrated more effectively on confining the slaughter of their own subjects to contexts linked with the strengthening of state power.

Though Russia's traditional sufferings owe so much to human agency, whether foreign or native, they have also derived in no small degree from environmental factors. The country's excessively cold climate has captured the imagination of the world ever since the days when travelers from Elizabethan England were reporting home that a man's spittle was liable to hit the ground as a solid gob of ice, and where the all-too-common drunks were apt to freeze to death in the street. But it is not so much the discomforts and dangers of long, severe winters as the associated poor agricultural conditions which have made the climate a source of special hardship. Since even the best agricultural land, the Black Earth belt of central Russia, lies in an area of unfavorable precipitation, harvests have tended and still do tend to be both poor and unpredictable. Terrible famines, in which the food-producing peasant has usually been the worst sufferer, have punctuated the country's history. And though the most recent occurred as long ago as 1932–33, agricultural conditions—additionally hampered by the notoriously inefficient system of collective and state farming as forcibly imposed from 1929—have made it necessary for Russia to buy American and Canadian wheat extensively in the 1970s. Furthermore, quite apart from the hardship imposed by famine conditions, Russia's inability to produce an adequate food surplus has all along hindered the growth of her economy in general—notoriously primitive until the late nineteenth century, even when compared with that of some less advanced European states.

Sheer territorial size has been a dominant factor conditioning the Russian mentality for many centuries. Consisting largely of a vast plain with no significant natural barriers between its western frontiers and the far-distant mountain ranges of central Siberia, the country has always lacked defensible frontiers such as might have saved it from becoming embroiled again and again in so many long, exhausting armed conflicts with its neighbors. Despite a vast network of navigable rivers, for centuries the main arteries of communication, immense distances have rendered travel and transport difficult, slow and hazardous: a further hindrance to the development of the economy and a handicap to effective administration. At the same time the availability of apparently infinite expanses of unused space in the southeast and east has contributed to a nomad psychology in the Russian peasant. Feeling less solidly grounded on his own particular plot of soil than the traditional peasant of other lands, he has stood poised to uproot himself and seek his fortune in what has been called Russia's wild east. This had its own dangers and hazards, but was for several centuries relatively free from interference by the increasingly authoritarian central government. Hence the obsession with untrammeled spaciousness which has often been cited as a feature of the Russians. They are said to dislike rooms with low ceilings, and when visiting the city of Oxford they have expressed a strong emotional preference for the wide-open reaches (small enough by their own standards) of Port Meadow over the willow-enclosed, claustrophobia-inducing banks of the River Cherwell. This same obsession with space once induced a Russian parish priest—one Father Vasily, a native of the central Russian plain—to complain during a visit to the spectacular Caucasus range that there was 'no scenery' in these parts; to those who found the statement difficult to understand he would explain that the wretched mountains got in the way.[3]

Space, expansiveness—these, surely, provide a vital key to the Russian character, since they have played such a great part in the country's evolution. After shaking off Tatar dominion Russia has expanded, as the United States and Canada were later to expand, over an enormous integral territory rich in natural resources. Both territorially and in terms of population increase the expansion rate has been phenomenal over the centuries, when the area of the country has swelled about fiftyfold, while the population—by conquest as well as by natural growth—has increased almost as much. As might be expected, the boost in territorial growth preceded the peak demographic explosion. In the century and a half between 1550 and 1700 Moscow was *annually* adding to her territory an area equal to that of modern Holland.[4] Thereafter territorial expansion proceeded at a much slower rate, a mere 50 percent having accrued since 1650, unless the 'satellite' states of eastern Europe are to be regarded as part of a greater Russian empire.

During the years of greatest territorial expansion demographic growth was comparatively modest: in the two centuries between 1550 and 1750 the population barely doubled, from roughly 8 million to roughly 17 million. But then it quadrupled in a century, to about 68 million in 1850; doubled again by 1900, to 126 million; and has now, in the 1970s, doubled yet again to top the 250 million mark. The figures reflect expansion by self-colonization within an integral sovereign territory which has been the largest in the world since 1650. They also help to show how a feeling of space and potential mobility—accompanied, since this is a land of extremes, by the contrary sensation of being hampered, constricted and hemmed in—are so prominent in Russian psychology throughout the ages.

To feel freer, and yet somehow more cramped, than other peoples is one of those general Russian characteristics, including not a few other such polarized opposites, on which more must be said later in the argument. Fuller treatment will also be given at a later stage to further special Russian features which are now briefly invoked with the aim of completing this short preliminary review of major factors hampering East-West understanding.

Not least among these factors is Russia's abiding consciousness, surprisingly little modified in recent years, of its own backwardness when compared to the advanced nations of the West. Culturally, economically, industrially and above all administratively, owing to the two archaic institutions of serfdom (abolished 1861) and hereditary autocracy (abolished 1917), Russia long lagged behind. Hence the Russian love-hate hysteria about the West and other manifestations seeming to betray an inferiority complex, such as extreme national boastfulness combined with extreme self-deprecation.

Another feature differentiating Russia from the more advanced West is that of class structure and a slow rate of urbanization. Throughout most of its history the Russian and even the Soviet Russian Empire has been a predominantly peasant society, so much so that despite intensive industrialization over three quarters of a century, the urban population did not begin to preponderate over the rural until about 1960. At the end of the nineteenth century, when Russia's industrial revolution was already well under way, four-fifths of the population were still registered as peasants, while only 13 percent rated as town dwellers. In earlier times the proportion of town dwellers had been negligible: just under 4.5 percent in 1812. Towns were thus a rarity in imperial Russia, and large cities even more of a rarity. At the end of the nineteenth century, when London numbered about 6.5 million and New York about 3.5 million inhabitants, neither of Russia's two largest cities had gone far beyond the million mark.

These two metropolises, Moscow and Leningrad (formerly St. Petersburg) occupy a special place in Russian attitudes. In 1897 each was more than twice as large as the nearest Russian rival, the Black Sea port of Odessa, and their character and history were in striking contrast. Moscow was the ancient capital of the Tsars of Muscovy, the stronghold of Russian nationalist feeling and of the Slavophile movement; whereas St. Petersburg was the artificial creation of a single potent individual, Peter the Great, set up by a gigantic act of will on a remote misty marsh in the northwestern corner of his empire as a symbol of his determination to modernize and europeanize his country. With the restoration of Moscow as the Soviet Russian capital in 1918, and the two renamings of St. Petersburg (as Petrograd in 1914, as Leningrad in 1924) the former capital has fallen into second place, but without losing the intense local pride which is what presumably led Stalin to single out the city for discriminatory persecution outstanding even in an age of general severe oppression.

Another special feature is that of separate cultural and religious development. Unlike most of Europe, Russia never formed part of the Roman Empire and inherited neither Roman law nor Roman Christianity. Nor did Russia's adoption of Christianity in its Eastern, or Greek, form involve any consequential influence of classical Greek civilization. Perhaps, as a recent Russian philosopher has splendidly suggested, it would indeed have been desirable for his country's leading minds to have been suckled on Aeschylus rather than on that (ultra-dreary) early Marxist thinker Karl Kautsky.[5] But it was not to be, since Greek civilization, together with Roman, was to become the creative basis of the West's—not of the East's—cultural heritage, and to play its role in the Renaissance. For that development no parallel is to be found in the evolution of Muscovy, which was still struggling with the Tatar menace in the days of Michelangelo, da Vinci and Erasmus. Nor did Russia ever undergo any phase comparable to Europe's Reformation.

Above all, Russia's development has diverged from that of the West in the evolution of state authority. While authoritarian rule has, however unevenly and sporadically, steadily declined in the West over the centuries, a marked contrary trend is to be observed in Russia from the fifteenth century onward—and that despite occasional phases, the early reign of Alexander II (from 1855) being the most striking, in which official regimentation was in retreat. The introduction of totalitarian rule under Lenin, and its consolidation under Stalin, did nothing to reverse the trend. Now, after so many years, the country still lacks any tradition of civil liberty, of rule by law binding on rulers as well as ruled. It has never possessed a politically influential upper, middle or any other class; never any powerful corporate body able to exert irresistible pressure on central authority. Thus Russia has presented its sons and daughters with features markedly different from those conditioning their Western brothers and sisters. And this remains true however acutely conscious one must be that 'the West' is far indeed from forming any integral entity, and that generalizations such as the above strictly speaking require a host of caveats and reservations which the reader has been spared.

## THESIS OR ANTITHESIS?

Since the Russians have already been observed veering between the extremes of life-enhancement and life-denial, it will not be surprising if they also exhibit other opposed characteristics. Broad, yet narrow; reckless, yet cautious; tolerant, yet censorious; freedom-loving, yet slavish; independent, docile, tough, malleable, kind, cruel, loving, hating, energetic, lazy, naïve, cynical, polite, rude—they will be found veering in all these directions at some time or other; as what people will not? The Russian specialty is a tendency for a single individual or group to alternate between one extreme position and its opposite; or even, somehow, to occupy two or more seemingly mutually exclusive positions simultaneously.

A close examination of some of these pairs of polarized opposites may help to define the conditions in which one extreme rather than the other tends to become operative.

Are Russians energetic or lazy? Abundant evidence can be quoted to show them as both. Where one highly qualified observer stresses their 'dynamic energy' and 'enthusiasm for work,' another says that Russians cannot bear to exert themselves, and tend to 'be plagued by the curse of laziness.' [1] That 'Soviet Russians have . . . a far greater aversion than Americans to manual labor' is the opinion of an experienced American observer. A similar view was evidently held by that premier regimenter of Russians, Joseph Stalin; urging his subjects to cultivate 'a businesslike American attitude to work,' he pointed out at the same time that mere Russian exuberance was not enough.[2]

That the Russian tends at any moment to be a very monster of laziness or of energy—that he works, if at all, in spasms of momentary enthusiasm—is a common observation.[3] This pattern is often plausibly linked to the peasant psychology of a nation largely consisting until recent years of farm laborers ac-

customed to toil in a northern latitude where field work is concentrated within a short period, thus demanding efforts more
intense than more clement climes impose. To his brief, violent
spurt of annual labor the Russian peasant long ago gave the
name *strada* (etymologically, 'suffering'). And it is from the
*strada,* according to the historian Klyuchevsky, that the people
derives its talent for 'short, concentrated bursts of excessive
exertion. Hence the routine of brisk, frenzied, effective labor
followed by autumn's and winter's enforced idleness. No other
nation in Europe can put forward such concentrated spasms
of labor as the Russian. Nor, however, shall we find anywhere
else in Europe such inexperience of steady, disciplined, evenly
deployed work as in this same Russia.' [4]

So much for the national mentality as grounded in pre-
revolutionary peasant tradition. But what of the peasant's
master? He was all too easily visualized as a rural Oblomov.
Sunk in torpor never relieved by spasms of application, he was
apt to begin 'the labours of the day by resuming his seat at the
open window and having his Turkish pipe filled and lighted
by a boy whose special function is to keep his master's pipes in
order.' [5] As for mental work, the Russian intellectual has been
censured again and again for his inability to generate the kind
of solid, unremitting application which forms the basis of a
professional man's activities elsewhere; and for seeking to balance out this lack of persistence by developing a superficial,
frothy brilliance. 'For these people the enthusiasm of the moment is all that counts; they term it inspiration and nothing
else matters to them. . . . They call work pedantry.' [6]

The active-inactive polarization has also communicated
itself to Russia's rulers, at least during the monarchy, when individual autocrats tended to be either active or passive—in either case to excess. Thus was the egregiously energetic, indeed
frantic, sixteenth-century sovereign Ivan the Terrible succeeded by that saintly and sluggish nonentity, his son Theo-
dore I. With the Emperor Nicholas I, monster of despotic

energy and scourge of early nineteenth-century revolutionaries, may be contrasted his namesake and great-grandson
Nicholas II, that pious, unassertive but stubborn mediocrity
butchered on Lenin's orders. As for the intervening eighteenth century, 'This polarizing trend affected the ladies too,
among whom Catherine the Great was the outstanding trail-
blazer, while Catherine I, Anne and . . . Elizabeth belonged
rather to the quiescent order of rulers.' [7] Since many of these
sovereigns were barely if at all Russian by descent, here is confirmation of one thesis which seems to suggest itself: that it is
less some pervasive Russian racial gene than the Russian environment which provokes Russian-type reactions.

To the general routine of rustic life as a factor illuminat-
ing Russian psychology along the above lines may be appended, for the sake of the curious, an ingenious rider
whereby behavior patterns are derived more specifically from
a single detail in the life cycle of the muzhik ('peasant'). This is
the swaddling of babies, a practice of the lower orders rather
than the privileged classes, and one still widespread, though
now said to be on the decline. Constricted and enshrouded
during most of his day, when he can move only his eyes and
must bottle up emotions of rage or joy, the mummified infant
is periodically unwrapped for a delicious romp during which
he can briefly kick his legs about and relish a temporary ec-
stasy or tantrum. Thus, according to the swaddling hypothesis, is the Russian programmed for life to oscillate between
emotional extremes. The theory has been argued amusingly
and with some scholarly reserve by the anthropologist Geoffrey Gorer; but he has not, unfortunately, proceeded to any
systematic global diaperological survey which might conceivably have related the mentality of the Russians to that of other
swaddled nations, while distinguishing it from that of the
collective unswaddled. Nor has he demonstrated which categories of Russian babies have been swaddled, at what historical periods, and in what parts of the country. For these

reasons his study may be accepted as a stimulating speculation which is far indeed from proving its point.[8]

True or false, the swaddling theory is a reminder that the drive to express emotions forcibly, while switching easily and rapidly from one surge of feeling to its opposite, is a characteristic of the human infant in general, Russian or non-Russian, rather than of the human adult. Is the adult Russian, then, 'always a great, big grown-up child'?[9] He has been so described by the early twentieth-century British publicist and Russia-fancier Sir Bernard Pares, and one wonders in passing whether Pares's 'ordinary Russian' received a similar impression of his sometimes embarrassing observer. Still, though this witness may exaggerate, he does have a point—one perhaps better attached to the neutrally descriptive word 'childlike' rather than to the insulting 'childish.' 'It is in the expression of emotion that the childlike aspect of Russian adult behavior becomes most apparent,' writes a more recent observer, Harvey Pitcher. 'Russian adults are at liberty to express their feelings in a way that we would find more appropriate and acceptable in the behaviour of a child.'[10] But here again one finds the quintessentially Russian qualities best expressed, as often, by that Russian of Russians, Dostoyevsky. Himself so addicted to strong sensations, at least until his middle forties, that he often seems to have preferred—as he most certainly courted— violent unhappiness rather than mild happiness, he created in his fiction a gallery of formidable, emotionally oscillating characters whose behavior patterns, in adulthood, mirror those of children rather than of adults as commonly conceived outside Russia: 'What . . . is the emotional age of a typical character from Dostoyevsky? The parent of young children who is also a reader of his work might be inclined to put it at the two-year-old stage or even at that of the infant in arms.'[11] Such are the torrents of uninhibited emotion, such the love-hate oscillations to which Dostoyevsky's brainchildren are prone. And if, as seems possible, Dostoyevsky's appeal to his readers derives partly from his skill in causing them to relive the sensations of the cradle, thus performing on themselves a kind of psycho-analytical therapy, then something similar may account for the fascination which the allegedly childlike adult Russians also seem to hold, even outside the pages of Russian novels, for the perhaps prematurely senile Western adult intellectual.

It is in the context of the capacity—whether or not inspired by intensive harvesting and swaddling routines—to concentrate enthusiasm and superhuman efforts on a limited, selected target, that one special Russian institution, here termed the prestige project, may be understood. Its pioneer was Peter the Great, and the most notable Russian prestige project still remains St. Petersburg, now Leningrad. It was by imposing an autocratic whim of iron that the Great Tsar caused this fine city to be erected from 1703 onward, contrary to all logic and good sense, on an uninhabited swamp in a disputed corner of his realm. In this, the very battle area of a war which he seemed to be losing, he drove to work tens of thousands of conscripted peasants, many of whom perished on the job. An act of grandiose folly? Or of prodigious statecraft? It is still possible to argue either case, and Russians themselves have done so endlessly.

Other prestige projects have included the wholly frivolous. Such was the great palace of ice erected at the behest of the Empress Anne on the River Neva during a particularly cold mid-eighteenth-century winter. Complete with its columns of ice, its statues, its balconies, its ingenious lighting effects created by blazing oil, it was over a hundred yards long and contained among other absurdities a life-sized ice elephant mounted by an ice man in Persian dress. The whole folly was designed as the venue for a marriage which the Empress had decided to arrange, to while away the winter's tedium, between two of her court jesters: a hideous Kalmuck woman and a titled buffoon, one of the many Princes Golitsyn. Bride and groom were locked inside for the night, with sentries posted to prevent escape; and 'It says much for their fortitude and ability to take a joke that both survived the nuptial slab.' [12]

Then again, long after the grotesque hymeneal edifice had slumped and slid into the thawing Neva, the same city was the scene for another great assertion of imperial will. In December 1837 the huge, splendid, ornate Winter Palace, which had taken eight years to build from Rastrelli's plans in the previous century, was gutted by fire; whereupon the reigning monarch, Nicholas I, decreed that the whole vast structure should be restored in its original form within twelve months. Through haste and appalling labor conditions, the undertaking caused the traditional high incidence of mortality among Russian workers engaged on a prestige project. But completed on time it was. 'So you see,' a contemporary French visitor was told, 'in your country people spend three years arguing about how to rebuild a village hall, while our Emperor restores the largest palace in the universe in a single year.' [13]

In the twentieth century similar boasts have been made on behalf of various exercises in ostentation, including not a few which must be conceded to possess more utility and rational purpose than the prestige project in its purest form— boasts made by Russians themselves, but also by observers as dissimilar, albeit united by a love of sweeping false generalizations, as Bernard Shaw and Adolf Hitler. Stalin had 'solved' Russia's agricultural problem by collectivization, Shaw incorrectly maintained, adding less misleadingly that the Soviet dictator had been 'founding new cities and colonies in two continents much faster than we can get a private bill through Parliament for a new tramline.' And Stalin, said Hitler, had constructed railways which were not even on German maps (some were not on Soviet soil either), and with more than Teutonic efficiency, getting the job done when mere Germans would still be arguing about the price of the tickets.[14]

Though many of Stalin's projects went far beyond showy

prestige operations, in matters architectural he stuck more closely to that concept. Grossly neglecting basic housing, he poured building resources into the all-too-eyecatching 'wedding cake' monstrosities of his capital city: Moscow State University, the Ukraina Hotel, the Ministry of Foreign Affairs. But his main monument in this area must be Moscow's underground railway, the Metro: a symphony of veined marble, tinted granite, stained glass and glittering mosaics—part folly, part efficient public amenity. Nor did such mixed prestige projects end with Stalin, for they have included the post-Stalinist space program, which combined serious technological research with status promotion, and was outstandingly successful until overtaken in both respects by American efforts. At the time, though, Russian achievements in space shook the world, beginning with the launching of the first sputnik in October 1957 and continuing less than four years later with the first manned orbit of the earth.

Gifted as they are in areas as varied as chess, rocketry and athletics, Russians are often successful when they turn their combined efforts to prestige projects, many of which are functionally effective as well as impressively decorated. One important secondary aim is usually to capture the imagination of foreign observers in the hope that some of them may be sufficiently dazzled to overlook the poor living conditions endured by the average citizen; for though the Russian is 'wonderfully sensitive to the seductive influence of grandiose projects,' he is by no means unique in this respect.[15]

Spectacular as Russian prestige undertakings can be, and formidable as is the concentrated energy which they can focus, no one familiar with the country could miss the antithetical and no less characteristic qualities of vagueness, laziness, casualness, unpunctuality and the like. The usual complaint 'of people who have to work with them is that they are chronically unpunctual, wasteful, careless, and so on.'[16] To these defects many Russians will cheerfully own, sometimes making a virtue of them by contrast with the soulless efficiency of the German. They have their own word for all this: *bezalabershchina,* 'sloppiness,' of which the prefix means 'lacking,' while the root seems to derive ultimately from the Latin *elaborare.* Thus the word expresses an inability to 'work things through.' Hence typical Russian strictures on their own habit of doing things 'any old way'; hence the insistence on the need 'to get rid of dreaminess and vague ideas . . . devoid of everything but the crackling and smoke of an over-heated imagination.' Referring to the 'utter slovenliness of everyone,' the nineteenth-century memoirist and literary censor Alexander Nikitenko adds that 'all our enterprises begin with words and evaporate in words.' [17]

A similar point of view is attributed to no less a figure than Lenin as his thoughts are reconstructed by the twentieth-century Russian novelist Alexander Solzhenitsyn. Why, oh why, the unhappy Bolshevik leader is made to ask himself, had he been doomed to originate in so uncouth a land? And why, he continues, had fate hitched him to the 'ramshackle Russian rattletrap' when 'nothing in his character, his will, his inclinations made him kin to that slovenly, slapdash, eternally drunken country'? Lenin knew of nothing more revolting than 'back-slapping Russian hearties, tearful tavern penitents, self-styled geniuses bewailing their ruined lives.' [18]

These harsh judgments of an imaginary Lenin are echoed by the twentieth-century French ambassador to Russia, Maurice Paléologue, when he refers to the fluid, vague and inconsistent character of Russian schemes and notions. 'There is always a lack of coordination or continuity somewhere. The relationship between facts and ideas is hazy; calculations are merely approximate and perspectives blurred and uncertain. . . . Russians see reality only through a mist of dreams, and never have precise notions of time or space!' [19]

That these remarks are not of universal application is vividly illustrated by the success of so many prestige projects as invoked above: imperial as well as post-imperial and including such enterprises as the Trans-Siberian Railway begun in 1891, together with the various hydroelectric stations, nuclear submarines and the like of a later age. These are no ice palaces. Yet, in spite of so many impressive Russian achievements, precision seems hard to attain, particularly where figures and dates or other time contexts are involved. The disease has grown more acute since Stalin apparently sought to correct it by issuing floods of detailed economic statistics. Relating to such achievements as the over-fulfillment of work norms and the tonnage of pig iron produced, they turned out on examination to be incantational rather than informative, being virtually uninterpretable except by astrologers.

Wherever the concept of time arises in a Russian context, one seems to be in the presence of the occult. For the fact that, in 1917, Russia's 'February' Revolution took place in March, and its 'October' Revolution in November, a rational explanation may be found: the thirteen-day lag between the Julian calendar then used in Russia and the Gregorian calendar, then used in much of Western Europe and adopted by Moscow in 1918. Still, the apparent date blur is somehow typical, recalling to those with long memories the appalling complications which took place before and around the year 1700. At that time Russia, far from lagging thirteen days behind most of humanity, was no less than 6,508 years ahead—until Peter the Great readjusted the date with typical decisiveness, while happily ignoring contemporary predictions of the imminent end of the world.[20]

Of the many changes to be noted in Russia since Peter the Great none has perhaps been more striking than the inculcation of a sense of time, which the German Russia-watcher Klaus Mehnert believes to have been effected by the Bolsheviks. At the beginning of the twentieth century, according to him, young Russians were more or less unaware of time; but they have since become thoroughly sensitized to the chronological dimension: 'For this the Bolshevik training has been less responsible than the facts of life in an industrialized society with its piece-rate wages.' Elsewhere Mehnert refers to the establishment of a feel for time as the field in which the Bolsheviks have attained more success than in any other: he calls it a 'profound and apparently permanent transformation.' His opinion always commands respect; and yet, to the excessively time-geared Westerner, Russia still seems to operate in an atmosphere relatively emancipated from the clock, resembling Spain rather than Germany, Britain or America in this respect. Here, indeed, is one of the country's most attractive features, well evoked in symbolic form so far as British parallels are concerned by the acute observation that it is not the teapot, as in England, but the samovar which rules in Russia.[21]

Is the Russian kind or cruel? Both, naturally; and both, naturally, to excess. 'Of his [the Russian muzhik's] spontaneous kindness towards strangers there are innumerable testimonies,' according to the historian Richard Pipes. There was the peasant habit of bestowing gifts on exiles bound for Siberia, not out of sympathy for their cause or crime but because they were thought of as unfortunate. 'In the Second World War, Nazi soldiers who had come to conquer and kill met with similar acts of charity once they had been made prisoners.' Even when drunk, Russian peasants only became tender and maudlin instead of fighting and killing each other like drunken Frenchmen; such, at least, was the testimony of a nineteenth-century French nobleman generally considered hostile to the Russians.[22]

Contrary witness—that the Russians, as a people, are exceptionally cruel—is not lacking either. In his essay 'On the Russian Peasantry' Gorky has characteristically overstated his case. Published in Berlin in 1922 in the wake of the appalling horrors of the Russian Civil War, this hair-raising pamphlet has been suppressed in its country of origin, and for many obvious reasons. Gorky thinks that a 'special sense of cruelty, cold-blooded and seemingly devoted to probing human endurance of pain to the limit' is a quality as distinctive to the Russians as their much-advertised sense of humor is to the English. Drawing on the Civil War for atrocity stories which are indeed blood-curdling, Gorky asks which were the more cruel, the Reds or the Whites, and answers that there was probably nothing in it. 'After all, both are Russian. . . . I ascribe the cruelties of the Revolution to the exceptional cruelty of the Russian people.' [23]

Here Gorky, carried away by natural revulsion, showed himself poorly attuned to the rhythms of history. That he no whit exaggerates the horrors of the Civil War, the appalling and well documented atrocity record of that conflict fully confirms. But the unpalatable fact is that non-Russian wars, civil or not, have produced so many atrocities and horrors, both before and after Gorky's day. No one nation can conceivably claim any monopoly in cruelty. Not that Russians can claim any special credit in the other direction either, however commonly Russian kindness may also be attested. One Western observer ascribes Russian cruelty to indifference and lack of imagination, rather than to the dedicated sadism which Gorky claimed to discern. 'It seems comprehensible that people who pay so little attention to their own physical sufferings should also ignore those of others. . . . A good deal of behaviour which, if performed by occidentals, would be deliberate cruelty, should rather be described as indifference when performed by Russians.' [24]

To the Russian capacity for great kindness as well as great cruelty must be added a penchant for exhibiting both characteristics in turn. Such switches can often strike foreigners as dramatic or surprising, owing to the Russian tendency to execute a sudden volte-face. The same point is expressed in different words by the anthropologist Margaret Mead when she writes of the Great Russians that 'in attitudes towards individuals an expectation that friends could behave like enemies was combined with an expectation that this behavior could also be reversed.' [25] And the tendency to oscillate between expressions of good will and hostility, which often alternate with bewildering rapidity, has helped to create that minor yet significant type, the malign buffoon or *faux bonhomme*. Of these, Russian literature and life have each provided one outstanding representative in Dostoyevsky's Fyodor Pavlovich Karamazov (of *The Brothers Karamazov*) and in a recently deceased statesman, Nikita Sergeyevich Khrushchev.

Of Khrushchev in his role as a sinister clown it has been well pointed out that Western journalists and politicians were far too ready to praise him as shrewd, jovial, human, candid and the like, while all the time the jolly, chubby little chap was bloodily suppressing the Hungarian uprising of 1956; saber-rattling during the Suez crisis; manufacturing crises in the Congo and Berlin; indulging in Russian nuclear roulette over Cuba. [26] One still remembers this genial, clubbable, sweating, folksy autocrat as he mocked foreign ambassadors at Moscow receptions; disrupted the United Nations by banging his shoe on the table; and, at home, hobnobbed with allegedly norm-exceeding pigmen, his face contorted in a rictus of simulated good will. Beloved of foreign journalists because his 'colorful' behavior made such excellent copy, poor Nikita Sergeyevich was less popular at home, where his manners were considered compromisingly uncouth; and where his successor, the stolid Brezhnev, has proved in many ways more acceptable.

As for Fyodor Pavlovich Karamazov, that other malign buffoon or treacherous clown, one remembers him best for the scandal which he creates near the beginning of Dostoyevsky's novel, in the monastery where he has agreed to meet his estranged eldest son Dmitry with a view to reconciliation. After crossing himself before the icons with already suspect zeal, Fyodor Pavlovich kneels—again with a parade of fervor unnerving in the context—in front of the local holy man, Father Zosima, and asks, 'Master, what must I do to inherit eternal life?' Soon the clowning monster is parodying the biblical Russian in which the monks address each other, and eventually rounds on them, accusing them of hypocrisy and 'attempting to save their souls by living on cabbage.' Then he tells an anecdote, highly unseemly in these pious surroundings, about a man who was murdered in a brothel and nailed up in a box while prostitutes sang comic songs—all this as a prelude to threatening his son Dmitry with a duel instead of extending his fatherly forgiveness, the ostensible purpose of their meeting.[27]

That Russians have the capacity for friendliness and hostility, and both in extreme degree, does not distinguish them from non-Russians so much as the apparent ease with which they can make the transition from one condition to the other. And the capacity for such 'breadth' of behavior, alike unusually oscillatory and unusually intense, is one of the qualities for which they are inclined to claim credit with foreigners whenever conversation turns, as turn it inevitably must if the more typical kind of Russian is involved, to the problem of comparative national psychology. 'It was an article of faith for the intelligentsia (not entirely unfounded in fact), that the Russian people were endowed with a "broad nature," expansive and generous, a nature which it was impossible to restrict within the narrow confines of legalistic formulae.'[28]

The same generosity of soul was lavishly bestowed by Dostoyevsky on the above-mentioned Dmitry Fyodorovich Karamazov, whose broad Russian nature is much emphasized throughout the novel. This 'breadth' includes the elements of recklessness, exuberance, panache, verve, commitment, wholehoggishness and general enthusiasm, as covered by the commonly invoked term *razmakh,* which embraces all the above qualities. From displaying *razmakh*—or 'letting himself go'—the more hidebound foreigner is temperamentally disqualified; or so the Russian will often 'tactfully' imply. Nor, if the same miserable, limited manikin of a foreigner should ever be persuaded to embark on a drinking bout, is he likely to do so with sufficient *élan* to qualify the operation as a sample of *razgul:* a real full-blooded orgy *à la russe*. Nor yet will the foreigner be credited with the capacity to appreciate another of these *raz*-prefixed words: *razdolye,* that sense of spaciousness which the Russian feels to be far beyond the limited ken of the inhibited alien. From the special function of the *raz* prefix, suggesting vigorous expansion in all directions, the Russian mentality might be characterized as centrifugal and extrovert by comparison with that of the inward-turned, self-restricting, strait-jacketed, centripetal non-Russian.

Russian generosity of spirit extends, naturally enough, into the financial sphere. The Russian is liable to lend or give away his last rouble, and to borrow or take someone else's—both with equal unconcern. To this must be added a sense of property so alien to the non-Russian mentality that the very language does not possess a proper verb for 'to lend' or 'to borrow,' so common in English, and that the translation into Russian of such a phrase as Shakespeare's 'neither a borrower nor a lender be' therefore presents certain linguistic problems. 'A Russian student does not expect to *ask* if he can borrow something—he just takes it. He will go into a friend's room and immediately start rummaging for the cigarettes, whether the other student is there or not.' [29] As for ever saving money, the mere notion strikes clean against the Russian's ideal conception of himself, being more suitable to the calculating, despised yet admired German.

In this connection I recall a conversation in which I once took part when visiting the country on a journalistic assignment, briefed to discover how the 'ordinary' Russian lives. Striking up conversation with a well-dressed youngish man in a restaurant, and learning that he was an engineer, I soon profited by the convention whereby such inquiries are rarely resented in Russia to discover how many roubles a month he earned; and then went on to ask whether he ever managed to save. This question did arouse mild resentment. What did I take him for? A lousy German or Englishman? The very suggestion was insulting. A little later, though, relations having been reestablished in accordance with the conventions of volte-face, I asked how much my new friend had paid for the impressively well-cut suit which he was wearing; whereupon he named a sum roughly equal to his monthly salary.

'But how could you afford it, Vyacheslav Mikhaylovich?'

'Saved up, of course.'

At this point interrogator and informant remembered the latter's robust earlier denial that a true Russian could ever demean himself by *saving,* and the conversation dissolved in mirth, having reached one of those cruces where the English, Russian and perhaps other senses of humor coincide. This trivial episode well illustrates a tendency of the Russian which must be further examined below: to keep two entirely separate mental account books, the one for ideal, the other for actual, transactions.

Apt to see and project his personality in terms of an idealized image, the Russian will particularly emphasize among the traits which he attributes to himself a reckless, devil-may-care attitude. Hence the rejection of saving money as a characteristic unworthy of a full-blooded man. Hence too a style of hospitality which, though it may be kindly intended, is apt to run adrift or even amok; and of which one cannot positively assert that it is in every case inspired by unalloyed benevolence.

In the nineteenth century 'the hospitality of the great Russian houses could probably not be duplicated anywhere else in Europe,' what with Russian grandees keeping open house and consuming more champagne each year than was produced in all the vineyards of France.[30] This was all very well for the numerous jesters, buffoons, parasites and hangers-on who attached themselves to the same great houses. But what of guests less willing? Many are the tales of bored country squires who would waylay passing strangers and force food and drink on them, having first immobilized them by removing, for example, a wheel from their tarantass. One such incident, attributed to the year 1871, involved an unwilling guest being kidnaped, incarcerated and plied with food and drink for forty-eight hours by a man whom he had never seen before. In the end the conscripted guest only escaped by bribing the servants of his tyrannical—and by now no doubt incapacitated—host. Another skeptical view of Russian hospitality is that of Custine, who reckoned it very largely an excuse for spying on the suspect foreigner. 'They refuse you nothing, but they accompany you everywhere. Politeness is here a surveillance technique.' [31]

That the use of hospitality as a nerve-warfare weapon has not died out, many a recent visitor to the country can testify. Genuine kindness may remain the dominant impression, but it is difficult to forget other occasions when visiting 'delegations' to the USSR have been plied with food and drink by all means short of intravenous injection. These operations have a way of turning into competitions in national prestige whereby 'the honest, hearty, all-embracing Russian stomach' is, so to speak, held out for comparison against its 'squeamish and etiolated' non-Russian counterpart.[32] Can it be that to cause a guest to vomit, or to suffer an acute hangover, qualifies a Russian host to collect bonus points on some award scheme? Certainly there are those among them who seem to confuse hospitality with hospitalization. To such over-zealous dispensers of good cheer nothing short of their guests' collective expiry through surfeit of alcohol, caviar and suckling-pig could, it seems, be accepted as an adequate response. Here, not for the first time, excess of zeal must be recorded as a feature of Russian *mœurs*.

While thus competing with foreigners in what can almost be a duel to the death by food and drink, the Russian male often seems from his general posture to be confusing ingestive with sexual athleticism. Is the whole operation, one sometimes wonders, inspired by that classic symptom of insecurity, the need to mount a public demonstration of superior virility? To

reflect on this aspect of East-West conviviality is to be reminded of a notable libel directed, with admirable impartial-
ity, against both the Persian Orient and the Greek Occident in
425 B.C. through the dialogue of Aristophanes' *Acharnians.*

ENVOY: Only the greatest gluttons and boozers are proper
    men, according to the barbarians.
DIKAIOPOLIS: Now, with us Athenians it's always the buggers
    and the fornicators.[33]

Yet, while admitting gross excess of Eastern hospitality to
be more exceptional than Western sexual misdemeanors, one
may well sympathize with the German woman whose husband
has written that 'When we were among Russians she always
felt rather ill at ease, because they seemed to expect her to
demonstrate openly and enthusiastically the same good fellow-
ship that came naturally to them.' If she sat somewhat
bewildered and unintentionally stiff in her chair, someone was
liable to rush up and ask, 'Why don't you like us?' [34]

Russian recklessness and addiction to extreme sensations
finds characteristic expression in what some have regarded as
the nation's chief hobby: the consumption of alcohol. Though
it must be conceded that hard liquor also plays a prominent
part in the routines of many non-Russians dwelling in comparable northern latitudes with their long, harsh winters which
somehow have to be endured, there yet does seem to be a
special relationship between Russians and alcohol—and that
from earliest times. Back in the tenth century Grand Prince
Vladimir of Kiev is said to have rejected Islam as the infant
nation's religion on the ground that the proto-Russians of his
day enjoyed drinking and couldn't do without it. Yet it was not
until the sixteenth century that Russians learned the craft of
distilling spirits—from the Tatars, perhaps the most lasting
and significant legacy of so many harsh years of Russo-Tatar
symbiosis. That the nation as a whole at once took to imbibing

hard liquor with characteristic *razmakh* has been the impression of many a foreign traveler from the early sixteenth century onward.

'Drinke is their whole desire, the pot is all their pride, The sobrest head doeth once a day stand needfull of a guide'—such is the verdict of the versifying diplomatic secretary George Turbervile on his visit of 1568. Another English envoy, Giles Fletcher, who visited the country a few years later, has described a typical Russian meal as one at which all concerned drink themselves speechless; it was quite usual for them to get drunk every day of the week. The seventeenth-century German scholar and traveler Olearius calls Russians the tipsiest people in the world, describing drunkenness as a universal vice to which clergy and laity, men and women, all ages and stations, were equally prone, so much so that they commonly dropped dead in public from overindulgence.[35]

Early developed, too, were those elaborate technical devices, some still operative to this day, whereby the hospitable Russian toper ensures that his foreign guest should drink himself into a condition of comparable insensibility. Herberstein records the custom whereby each banqueter must invert his goblet over his head after a toast has been drunk, as proof positive that every drop had been drained. But this faint-hearted envoy contrived on occasion to escape the fate allotted to him. 'I had no alternative but to assume the appearance of being drunk, or to say that I was too sleepy to drink any more.'[36] It was to thwart such cowardly evasions that Peter the Great, two centuries later, introduced his special drinking horn, as now exposed to view in the Moscow Kremlin's Armory. This vessel was so devised that it could not be placed on the table without falling over, a safeguard against any evasion of responsibility by the Great—and insatiable—Tsar-Emperor's often conscripted guests. I once had to interpret a long explanation of all this while suffering (the word is not used lightly) from a hangover induced by the kind of trick which the wretched vessel itself so aptly symbolized: a quintessentially Russian situation, if there ever was one.

For centuries what is in effect an official campaign to promote drunkenness has run in double harness with an official campaign to eliminate drunkenness—yet another example of the principle of polarized opposites. For instance, a ban on the private retailing of vodka and beer—ineffectual, like most Russian bans—was declared by Tsar Alexis and the Patriarch of Moscow in 1644; [37] and similarly the sale of spirits, as prejudicial to collective martial effectiveness, was prohibited on the outbreak of war in 1914. Nowadays, as the most superficial reader of the press must be aware, official campaigns against drunkenness succeed each other with the inevitability of the sea's waves. On the evils of the 'green snake' (alcohol) the newspapers publish innumerable moral tales, often describing the ingenuity with which addicts succeed in evading attempts to restrict their supply. Some high-minded doctors have even refused treatment to people injured on the roads, on the grounds that the mutilated victims' breath smelled of alcohol: the offense was so grave, one infers, as to have suspended the operation of the Hippocratic Oath.[38]

No statistics are available on the present-day Russian consumption of alcohol, but this might well turn out less impressive than a reading of the press would suggest. In the late nineteenth century, when statistics were available, the per capita consumption of alcohol was amazingly low compared with that of France, Britain, Germany and Denmark.[39] The point then was, and perhaps still is, not so much that the Russian regularly consumes more alcohol than anyone else, as that he tends to proceed, as in other walks of life, in a series of spasms or peristaltic jerks. When he does get drunk he likes, with characteristic recklessness, to make a thorough job of it and he particularly likes—as will be further noted below—to be seen to be drunk. But he may well plunge into his intervening bouts of abstinence with equal zeal.

To these attitudes toward drunkenness must be added the high regard, respect, tenderness and even affection with which the average sober Russian seems to regard any intoxicated person. One would think, sometimes, that to achieve a condition of helpless alcoholic befuddlement was a feat not only meritorious, but also extremely arduous and only attainable after years of unremitting self-sacrifice and dedicated apprenticeship. In minor criminal cases, such as assault and 'hooliganism,' drunkenness may—though not during one of the successive intensive anti-drunkenness campaigns—be put forward as a plea in mitigation, rather than being considered an aggravation.

A tolerance of such minor or not so minor vices as alcoholism may perhaps be invoked as a further example of the Russian breadth of mind, especially as addiction to this peccadillo is sometimes implied by Russians to constitute evidence of possessing major virtues such as charity, generosity, compassion. This way of thinking is linked with another tendency: to depersonalize such concepts as crime and sin, while claiming that a specific criminal or sinner should not be regarded too harshly on the grounds that 'we' are all guilty in some manner deeply felt yet rarely specified. Hence a nineteenth-century Scotsman's comment that 'One constantly meets in Russian society persons who are known to have been guilty of flagrant dishonesty, and we find that men who are themselves honourable enough associate with them on friendly terms.' [40] Times change, and this kind of tolerance—less laudable, it may be thought, than some—seems, like so many of the qualities pioneered by nineteenth-century Russians, to have extended itself to the world in general.

Allied with breadth of character and generosity is the special degree of acceptance and understanding of others which Russians repeatedly claim for themselves. In his novel *A Hero of Our Time*, for example, Lermontov writes that he 'couldn't help being struck by the Russian's ability to adjust to the customs of the peoples among whom he happens to live. Whether this quality of mind is deplorable or praiseworthy I don't know; but it does show the Russian's extraordinary adaptability, and a lucid common sense which forgives evil when he sees that it can neither be dispensed with nor eliminated.' [41]

Dostoyevsky makes the same point more extravagantly when he claims that the Russian is endowed with a unique ability to get 'inside the skin' of foreigners. Whereas, for example, Shakespeare's numerous Italians are all Englishmen in disguise, Pushkin's *Stone Guest*, set in Spain, might actually be mistaken for the work of a Spaniard were it not for Pushkin's signature. So, at any rate, Dostoyevsky has claimed; but purely on the basis of feel, since he advances no evidence. He ascribes this adaptability to that special 'universality' and 'omni-humanity' which, he claims, distinguishes the Russian from the non-Russian.[42] Though this is surely the merest mumbo jumbo, the Russians may yet be credited, in their foreign contacts, with a degree of flexibility perhaps derived from centuries of experience in managing a multi-national empire. That other peoples may practice different religions, have different complexions and facial appearance, talk a different language—these things may be said to surprise, dismay and shock them less than peoples more insular in outlook. Their tolerance has also been traditionally extended to the religious sphere. Early nineteenth-century English Quakers who turned up in Russia, stolidly refusing to remove their hats in the presence of the Tsar and even of holy icons, were in no way ridiculed for these outrages, but treated with the greatest respect; perhaps they were mistaken for the foreign equivalent of that traditional native phenomenon, the *yurodivy*, or 'holy fool'? As was noted by one early nineteenth-century observer, J. G.

Kohl, Russian priests were then 'distinguished for their tolerance in religious matters.' [43] And in modern times high officials—Party members committed to militant atheism as part of their political philosophy—are not thereby precluded from speaking with affection and respect of the Christian faith practiced by their dear old grandmothers.

That the people is comparatively free from malice and vengefulness in relations with its enemies seems confirmed when one contrasts the striking vindictiveness of a Stalin (no Russian, but a Georgian reared on the traditions of the blood feud) with the cruelties of ethnically Russian rulers—far less directed to revenge on individuals against whom a grudge has been harbored over the decades. Even Ivan the Terrible, who contravened this generalization more than a little, may have been acting out paranoiac fantasies rather than working off old scores à la Stalin, when he engineered the painful death of so large a section of his population. Lack of grudge-bearing, as imputed to the Russians, receives confirmation from witnesses whose general record exempts them from the charge of Russia-fancying. Speaking of an 'inability to bear malice,' Pitcher adds that 'Russians have long memories of the last war, which is not surprising when one remembers the depth of their suffering, but it is an abstract kind of hatred seldom extended to flesh and blood Germans.' To this the stolid, by no means vengeful, reaction of the Russian public to a parade of 55,000 German prisoners through Moscow in the summer of 1944, bears witness. And Mackenzie Wallace, perhaps the most level-headed, judicious and well-informed of all nineteenth-century foreign observers of Russians, admits that they can be very violent when their patriotic feelings are aroused; but he also claims that they are, 'individually and as a nation, singularly free from rancour and the spirit of revenge.' [44]

Are the admittedly broad, generous, reckless Russians liable to lurch into equally extreme narrowness, meanness and calculation? Naturally this element can be traced too, and it seems particularly evident where government and administration are concerned, whether one thinks of the cold and often sadistic practices of a Nicholas I or of a Stalin (neither being Russian by descent); or of the caution and calculation imposed on many of their subjects by the hosts of bureaucrats who have made the pre-revolutionary term for official—*chinovnik*—a synonym for petty, officious interference. The work of Michael Saltykov, Russia's most renowned nineteenth-century satirist, abounds in such figures, immediately recognized as lifelike by his many readers. There must evidently be something small and niggling as well as something broad and impulsive about the Russian soul if such characters as Plyushkin and Korobochka (in Gogol's *Dead Souls*) could so readily be accepted as symbolic of a common psychological type. The same may be said of Chekhov's hidebound, spoil-sport schoolmaster Belikov (the tyrant of a provincial town in the story *A Hard Case*) and of his Sergeant Prishibeyev, from the story of the same name, a prototype of the future concentration camp guard. That these figures also, alas, exemplify a common human type is another consideration which may be worth adding. One thinks, too, of those thin-lipped, self-righteous Soviet matrons who are so often found ordering people about and interfering, Belikov-like and Prishibeyev-like, in their affairs. But though such narrowness of spirit as one detects in Russians is certainly not confined to the political sphere, where it looms particularly large, the dominant impression remains that, in their contacts with their fellows, typical Russians err if at all rather from an excess of generosity or pseudo-generosity than from pettiness of spirit.

# II

# COMMUNICATION
# SYSTEMS

## *SIGNALING DEVICES*

The workings of a mind, whether individual or collective, can only be studied in terms of the signals—words, grunts, gesticulations and so on—which it transmits, and it is therefore necessary to consider the techniques whereby Russians communicate with each other. Do they put out different signals to foreigners? Are there areas in which they communicate with particular freedom? And others in which their lips are sealed? To what distortions, deliberate or otherwise, and in what contexts, are these messages liable?

Personal names are usually the first feature to attract the foreign reader of Russian novels as peculiarly Russian. That every Russian possesses three basic names soon becomes apparent. There is the first name, which it becomes increasingly anachronistic to call 'Christian'; then the patronymic, consisting of the father's first name with an attached suffix (usually *-ovich* or *-evich* for men, *-ovna* or *-evna* for women); and finally the surname. Hence such triple combinations as 'Dmitry Pavlovich Karamazov,' 'Anna Arkadyevna Karenin,' or—by no means unknown—'Ivan Ivanovich Ivanov.' But who are all

( 57 )

these 'Mitenkas,' 'Annushkas,' 'Vanyas' and the like who also crop up all over the place? Any reader with a talent for elementary code-breaking soon gets the hang of them too, learning to equate a 'Sasha' with an 'Alexander' or 'Alexandra,' and even a 'Dunechka' with an 'Avdotya'; and deducing correctly that these are affectionate ways of referring to someone who may elsewhere figure as an 'Alexander Pavlovich' or an 'Avdotya Romanovna.' The trouble, then, is not to understand the system, but simply to retain in one's head the identity of characters of whom there seem to be far more than necessary, and to distinguish in each case the numerous and various names under which they are known.

Of the different admissible combinations, that consisting of first name and patronymic is perhaps the most significant. To address someone in this way, for example as 'Ivan Ivanovich,' is to achieve an intermediate point of cordiality between, on the one hand, the familiar 'Ivan' with its still more familiar derivatives 'Vanya,' 'Vanichka' and so on; and, on the other hand, the relatively curt or formal 'Ivanov,' 'Comrade Ivanov' and the like.

Much of the interest of Russian name usage lies in such atmospheric nuance, but no less in the sheer frequency and persistence with which—even when no third party is present and there can be no question of mistaken identity—two Russians will incessantly address each other with their 'Nikolay Gavriloviches,' their 'Marfa Timofeyevnas,' their 'Antoshas,' their 'Lizochkas' and the like, for all the world as if these were radio call-signs. It is as though each speaker had contracted to confirm the fact of the other's existence in return for a similar courtesy. This habit of repeating an interlocutor's name in dialogue is often considered characteristic American usage too: not least in conversation between comparative strangers, who are apt to find themselves repeatedly addressing someone or being addressed by someone as 'Mr. Smith,' 'Dr. Jones,' 'Bill' or 'Charlene' in contexts where neither speaker seems in any real danger of forgetting his identity. In effete England this custom has tended to be confined more rigorously to salesmen and others with a professional public relations interest in communication. Such mateyness is possibly less welcome the more densely populated a country is, belonging properly to the lands of prairie, steppe and other wide-open spaces.

Russians and Americans are akin in this usage, then, but the Russian variation places more strain on the memory. To observe decent etiquette with even the most casual Russian acquaintance two names must be retained as well as the surname, since to call a Timofey Matveyevich 'Matvey Timofeyevich' is a grave solecism. It is not enough to know that the same man is surnamed 'Kuznetsov' or 'Sidorov'; whereas a Smith, a Jones, a Robinson might work in an English-speaking office all his life without any of his colleagues learning what his father's first name is. But, though Russian usage places a strain on anyone with an extensive acquaintance, the national mind is conditioned to such special efforts from birth; and necessarily so, since it may be socially unacceptable for a Russian to write to another Russian unless he has a firm grip on his addressee's name and patronymic. He may therefore need to send another letter first, to some common acquaintance with a known name and patronymic, in order to obtain the necessary particulars.

That phenomenal mnemonic feats are expected from readers of Russian novels is notorious. Reviewing Solzhenitsyn's *August 1914* a few years ago, I wrote that I was 'saddened to find myself yet again expected to remember some Zhenya who resurfaces on page 551 after nothing has been heard of her for five hundred pages—expected, moreover, to distinguish her from some equally unremarkable and long-neglected Ksenya.'[1]

Denseness of allusion can be just as grave an obstacle as sparseness. In the first thirty-three pages of his novel *Dr. Zhivago*, Pasternak introduces no less than thirty-three differently named characters. Nor is the seeming perversity over names confined to such technically limited practitioners of the art of prose fiction as these. It is also cultivated by more impressive craftsmen. The first ten lines of Chekhov's story *The Russian Master* name three horses (Count Nulin, Giant and Mayka); an elderly man, old Shelestov; and his daughter, Masha Shelestov. Of her we further learn, not only that she was known under the pet names Manya and Manyusya, but also that, when a circus had been in town, she had enjoyed it so much that her family had nicknamed her 'Marie Godefroi' after a celebrated equestrienne of the era. By now, line 12 of the story, the reader is already judged fit to meet other characters: Masha's sister Varya, a 'Nikitin,' various officers. Nor is this an isolated aberration. Another of Chekhov's finest stories, *A Hard Case,* introduces within a comparably short space a village, Mironositskoye; a village elder, Prokofy; and two hunters: 'Ivan Ivanovich, a veterinary surgeon, and Burkin, a grammar-school teacher.' All very well so far, but was it really necessary for the vet to have 'a rather odd and quite unsuitable surname: Chimsha-Gimalaysky'? At this point the non-Russian reader or critic might be apt to dismiss the passage as incompetently written, were he not usually so bemused by the Russian atmosphere as to suspend judgment on the grounds that the sequence must possess some incantational or occult significance. But to the Russian, schooled as he is in proper names and their variations, it is all straightforward and acceptable.

Another refinement in the use of names, the atmospheric variations obtainable by change of suffix, is delightfully illustrated by Yekaterina (Catherine) Maslov, heroine of Tolstoy's novel *Resurrection.* We learn that the child Yekaterina's domestic status had been ambiguous, neither that of a maid nor that of a daughter; 'so they called her by the half-way name of Katyusha: not Katka or Katenka.' [2] That Katka is coarser and Katenka more genteel than the intermediate Katyusha, Tolstoy can assume as evident to his Russian reader. Then again, there is the folksy practice of referring to someone of mature years or senior status by the (when possible) abbreviated patronymic alone: for example, as 'Ivanych.' This implies a peculiarly Russian combination of respect and familiarity, resembling the English use of 'the Gaffer,' 'the Boss,' 'the Old Boy' or even 'His Nibs.' Lenin is accordingly referred to in certain contexts (for example, if reported as conferring with dear old peasant women) as 'Ilyich,' a locution which carries a strong emotional charge of respectful affection, whether genuine or simulated for propaganda purposes. In the case of the grim Stalin, by contrast, since his oppressions were even more extensive and spread over a far longer period than Lenin's, no such cozy, folksy atmosphere could be generated even for propaganda purposes. In other words, no dear old crone is likely to have addressed that feared tyrant with the semiplayful 'Vissarionych.' Stalin, indeed, even disliked being called by the relatively neutral 'Joseph Vissarionovich,' preferring the distant 'Comrade Stalin.' As for top men of intermediate status in propaganda-registered popular affection, Khrushchev figured most naturally as 'Nikita Sergeyevich,' not as the cozy 'Sergeich.' Brezhnev is a 'Leonid Ilyich'; and for reasons of copyright, as it were, could not conceivably be referred to by the patronymic Ilyich alone, since that would be to claim for him parity of status with the sanctified Lenin.

Children may address adult strangers as *dyadya,* 'uncle,' corresponding in context with English 'mister,' and as *tyotya,* 'aunt,' or, with the addition of the wheedling suffix *-enka,* as *tyotenka* and *dyadenka.* Adults may accost coevals as their little brothers, tending to reserve the no less affectionate 'little mother,' 'little father' for those senior in age. For a man to call his wife *mamasha,* 'mother,' as Dymov does in Chekhov's *Butterfly,* is paralleled in English regional usage. But in Russian a man can call another man by a variant of the word for mother, *matushka;* for that matter, he may well call him his 'little pigeon' (*golubchik ty moy*) without this being in the least interpreted as a form of 'camp' or homosexual endearment.

The prime function of such locutions is splendidly defined by Mme. Jarintzov. Listing certain affectionate and other variants on the first name Dmitry as 'Mityusha,' 'Mityushka,' 'Mitik,' 'Mitenka,' 'Mityunchik' and 'Mityunya,' she correctly if quaintly points out that 'You only have to select this or that ending . . . and your feelings, your attitude at the given moment towards the addressed person is sun-clear!' [3] This well emphasizes a significant point: elusive Russians may be in some ways, but in their special field of emotional response they are correspondingly anxious to make their feelings, or what they wish to be thought their feelings, abundantly manifest. That a non-Russian might positively prefer, at least in casual contact with comparative strangers, to keep his emotional responses to himself, to have them fog-blurred rather than sun-clear, they may not understand—for which reason they can feel ill at ease among the restraints of a non-Russian milieu. 'On coming to live here [in England], we [Russians] sometimes feel quite awkward in being spoken to as if we were nonentities, without any names or personalities. . . . With us . . . something or other is always there, besprinkling the speech, so that you feel sure that it is you whom the speaker keeps in his mind and not the general public.' [4]

So much for personal names. But what about the total stranger whose name is unknown? The Russian is apt to hail him or her by some improvised label: 'Hey, girl' (*devushka*) or even 'Hey, spinster' (*devitsa*). And an unknown male is liable to be loudly accosted in the street—especially if he wears sandals or a beard, or is in breach of some other taboo—either as *molodoy chelovek*, 'young fellow,' or as *starik*, 'old man.' But why is it *young* men who are commonly accosted as *starik*, whereas many a *molodoy chelovek* might easily be, from his appearance, at least an octogenarian? I do not know. Nor, in general, am I able to explain this Russian insistence on repeating names and labels. Is it just a need for repeated assurance that they are heeded and appreciated? Or do they crave something more basic: the constant confirmation that they exist in the full ontological sense and possess a discernible identity? Whatever the basic urge underlying the cult, it seems to minister to some drive from which representatives of many other nationalities are relatively immune.

The desire to repeat proper names may be further stimulated by a craving for stability and the special need for mnemonic aid created by a marked lack of continuity in designations of persons and places. Was there ever a nation so addicted to changing labels, often suddenly, often for reasons of policy or decorum? That a town called Black Muck (Chornaya Gryaz) should have been renamed as the more ennobling Empressville (Tsaritsyno) seems perfectly understandable, and might have happened anywhere. Less universal, though, is the evolution of a similarly named city, Tsaritsyn, which first became Stalingrad for a political reason (Stalinization) before relapsing, again for a political reason (de-Stalinization), into the neutral and safer Volgograd—Volga-town—which it remains at the time of going to press. Similarly, the ancient city of Perm became Molotov (in 1940) before reverting to Perm (in 1957) with the disgrace of the honorand. That Vyacheslav Mikhaylovich Molotov, the key figure in this peripeteia, was born a Skryabin and that Stalin, the person who inspired the now suspended town names Stalino, Staliniri, Stalinogorsk and many another such as well as Stalingrad, was born a Dzhugashvili: such details further emphasize the mobility which the Russian climate seems to impart to names, both native and colonial.

Then again, the same bridge may be Holy Trinity Bridge, Equality Bridge and Kirov Bridge in bewilderingly rapid succession.[5] What more natural in a city which has itself progressed from St. Petersburg through Petrograd before being named Leningrad—and that after Vladimir Ilyich Ulyanov! As this example reminds one, Lenin and other Russian revolutionaries almost all adopted synthetic names, and sometimes a whole string of such aliases, in the pre-1917 period—partly for security, partly as a matter of style. Lenin, Gorky, Trotsky for the original Ulyanov, Peshkov, Bronstein—these are only a few among legion. This practice of name variation makes the reading of a map, gazetteer or telephone directory—assuming, which may prove over-optimistic in the Russian context, that one can obtain such a thing—a more difficult operation than it is in countries where the labels for things and people are handled in a more humdrum, less volatile fashion.

To turn from the Russians' use of proper names to their general use of language is to find a similar emphasis on emotional nuances. Like ordinary Russian first names, ordinary Russian nouns tend to possess diminutive and other similar forms, exploiting a wide range of suffixes to express variations of mood: for example, not only *domik*, 'a dear little house,' but also *domishche*, 'a bloody great house.' The term *diminutive* is misleading if taken to refer solely to size; rather does its use reflect the speaker's mood. To call someone a *durak*, 'fool,' is offensive; but to call him a *durachok*, 'a bit of an ass,' can be affectionate. In many cases diminutives are indeed 'really meant to imply smallness,' admits the pioneer English grammarian of Russian, Nevill Forbes; but he adds that they are often used 'merely as a means of expressing affection, politeness, or good humour, and as such they are difficult, if not impossible to translate into English.' And Forbes admirably points out that when a train conductor asks to see your *biletiki*, 'little tickets,' this does not imply that the tickets are small, merely that he would not refuse a drink.[6]

As for the ever-sensitive topic of liquor, and also food, the appropriate diminutive is practically compulsory unless the speaker wishes to emphasize that he is out of humor. *Kak nashchot vodochki?* ('How about a spot of vodka?') The diminutive *vodochka*, rather than the balder *vodka*, is the natural form for a convivial Russian to use. And he will similarly refer to another drink as *chayok* rather than *chay*. *Chayku by mne*, 'I'd like a spot of tea.' Similarly, a relaxed Russian will demonstrate the casual national attitude to time by saying that he will be ready *chasika cherez dva*, 'in a couple of hourlets.'

Similar emotional flexibility is made possible by the existence of two forms for 'you' when reference is to only one person. *Ty*, 'thou,' is used when addressing intimates, small children, animals, lunatics, drunks and God; *vy*, 'you,' is the more formal mode of address, which foreigners are recommended to employ unless they are sure of their ground. But one foreign grammarian of Russian misrepresents usage when he invokes the use of *ty* in converse with servants, peasants and other inferiors as a 'grave social error' in present-day Russia.[7] It is in fact normal in that highly stratified society for an official to address, say, his chauffeur as '*ty*,' while requiring the respectful *vy* in return. He will happily do so in the presence of foreigners too, showing that in this context the preservation of hierarchic differences takes precedence over the contrary urge: to treat, or to pretend to wish to treat, all men as equals. In this matter Russian usage differs from that of French and some of the many other languages which also preserve the distinction between an intimate and a polite form of the second person singular; for here of course English, with its single undifferentiated 'you,' is the exception among the world's leading tongues, and it is Russian which follows the norm.

It is less this fairly generalized feature of the Russian language than another, more specialized, phenomenon which has captured the imagination of non-Russian dabblers in the arcana of Russian linguistics: the so-called aspects, imperfective and perfective, of the verb. For this feature English and the other major Western languages furnish no close parallel, in that the typical Russian verb has two distinct sets of verbal forms—the aspects, perfective and imperfective—where other tongues tend to have only one. The perfective aspect lays emphasis on the result of an action, the element of achievement;

whereas to use the imperfective is to stress the process of the action together with its accompanying emotional resonance. The perfective describes what was done, the imperfective how it felt—which obviously makes the imperfective, broadly speaking, the more 'Russian' of the two. This point has been well brought out by an early English student of the subject, that authority on ancient Greek religion, Jane Harrison. In a pamphlet published in 1915, *Russia and the Russian Verb,* she claims outright that the aspects furnish 'one clue to the reading of the Russian soul.' It is the imperfectiveness, she says, which readers seek and find in the Russian novel, especially in Dostoyevsky, because the imperfective is the aspect of emotion and sympathy. Pointing out that the Russian verb is relatively weak in its tense structure, she relates this deficiency to Russian vagueness about time, whereas 'the Latin languages love order and are precise as to time.' [8]

Miss Harrison is soon denouncing a group of people whom she terms 'we' and who seem to be equated in her mind with representatives of Western, non-Russian civilization in general: 'We draw sharp lines, we circumscribe, we leave no open field for imagination and sympathy, and here we may well learn from the Russian.' Miss Harrison also adds: 'I want to use these aspects, I long to be able to, I need them, they feed me spiritually.' Here is a remarkable case of the transfer of *umileniye,* 'gush,' across national barriers, in view of which it may seem heartless or soulless to point out that the statistically scrutinized Russian employs the perfective more commonly than the imperfective: out of every hundred verbs 53.1 percent of those used in conversation and 57.5 percent of those used in non-conversation have been recorded as perfective. [9]

A contemporary reviewer of Miss Harrison's work congratulated her on the rich experience which would await her 'when she arrives at the stage of attempting the translation of a really skilled artificer in imperfective aspects, such as Chekhov.' [10] Though she never seems to have embarked on this form of self-indulgence, I have myself translated a million-odd words of Chekhov; but without, it now occurs to me for the first time, ever consciously considering the aspect of aspect. On reflection I feel that Chekhov, like many other Russian authors, makes particularly skilled and characteristic use of the past tense of the imperfective aspect to describe actions which are conceived as typical or repetitive without the author necessarily committing himself on whether they even took place or not. It is consistent with Miss Harrison's findings to link this usage with that habitual vagueness and imprecision which, in certain contexts, seems typical of the Russian and which can be so stimulating or so infuriating or both. The imperfective can also be regarded as the aspect of the ruled in Russia, and of the more inactive among its rulers. That 'most gentle' seventeenth-century Tsar Alexis Mikhaylovich may well have mooned through his reign in an unremittingly imperfective state of mind. But a Peter the Great and a Stalin were more inclined to express themselves in the perfective, with its emphasis on results. To these monstrous social engineers the aspect of emotion, of savoring the process rather than of achieving the goal, was of no interest at all.

Not that these two rulers left the niceties of Russian usage unaffected. Peter the Great temporarily reduced the language to a 'hideous jargon,' [11] through the importation of imperfectly digested Polish, Dutch, English and other loan-words and calques. And Stalin, who spoke Russian with a strong Georgian accent all his life, was not thereby prevented from developing his own brand of Russian linguistic chauvinism. In his celebrated article 'On Marxism and Linguistics' he describes Russian as a victorious language: one of those which has always absorbed the other languages with which it has come in conflict, and which is therefore destined to influence the world language of the remote Communist future.[12] Meanwhile, though, this linguistic imperialist was ordering the arrest of anyone ever known to have expressed an interest in another candidate world-language, Esperanto—blithely disregarding the fact that he himself had once been an unsuccessful student of that synthetic tongue.

Since this brief survey of one language, Russian, is couched in another, English, it is worth considering claims put forward about the comparative merits of these two major tongues as vehicles of expression. To Mme. Jarintzov Russian is much to be preferred: 'The luxuries of speech which we possess and you don't are so numerous that they overwhelmed me.' That there are many words in English for which Russian has no equivalent, she admits, but she finds it instructive to consider just what these words are. Russian has no word for 'kick,' for instance. Nor can something be described as 'shocking' except by use of the obviously borrowed verb *shokirovat*— and this, clearly, because the urbane and supremely tolerant Russian is not subject to the inhibited timidity and shockability of the typical Anglo-Saxon. Still less does the Russian—emancipated, devil-may-care, un-bourgeois, with soul unbuttoned— have a word for 'respectability.' ('We don't need this characteristic, somehow!') To fill the gap another ludicrous borrowing, *respektabelnost,* must be made to serve. Nor, she further points out, does Russian possess native words for 'job,' 'business,' or 'weekend.' [13]

Fascinating as Mme. Jarintzov's arguments are, and not least for the grotesque brand of English in which she couches her claim that English is an inferior language, a more authoritative view is that of the *émigré* Russian writer Vladimir Nabokov, who has used both tongues with panache and subtlety in his novels and other works. Many of his writings are especially instructive through having appeared at different times in both languages in the author's own version. A comparison of parallel English and Russian passages in Nabokov is a particularly rewarding process for the light which it sheds, not only on the author's own psychology, but also on the languages, native Russian and adoptive English, which he uses. And it may be significant that, after writing his best-selling novel *Lolita* in English, the language in which it was first published, he later proceeded to render it into Russian while expressly confessing, in a postscript, that he considered the English version to be the better. The exercise of back-translation had convinced him that Russian was a green and immature tongue, whereas English resembled a succulent plum, ripe or over-ripe with the wisdom of the ages. He defined the main advantage of English, over Russian, as its ability to flick at meanings in contexts where the Russian must make things painfully explicit.[14]

To suggest that Russian cannot flick at meanings seems unkind, especially from an author such as Nabokov, who at his best can practically make his native language sit up and beg. Nor is it borne out by such an author as Chekhov, arguably one of the greatest flickers in literature—so much so that one often despairs of rendering his subtler nuances. However, the English language seems to come out of this test quite well; where the flicks remain unrendered a translator's unresponsiveness may be more to blame than the inadequacies of the English language. On the other hand, long experience of the opposite process, that of teaching advanced Russian prose composition, suggests that a richly allusive and intonationally subtle English author—an Anthony Powell, an Evelyn Waugh, a Norman Douglas—can, by dint of hard work and sympathy, eventually be rendered into suitably sensitive and responsive Russian. As between the opposing views of the two Russians, Jarintzov and Nabokov, I therefore find it hard to adjudicate, and would be more inclined to declare a dead heat.

## *DISPLAY POSTURES*

Does the Russian reveal, as a communicator, the tendency to oscillate between extremes noted above? So it appears from the evidence of many witnesses who have him flashing across the screen in one of two diametrically opposed guises: either as a truthful, open, sincere, frank, extrovert, delightfully natural human being; or else as an obsessively secretive, devious, cynical, mendacious creature whose every word must be scrutinized in case it may not mean even the opposite of its purport. Never, according to one section of the evidence, was there anyone more delightfully self-revealing and open to inspection. 'It is the best part of a Russian,' writes a Russian of an earlier generation, 'that you always know where you are when you have to deal with him.' 'Russians behave,' writes an Englishman of a later generation, 'so much more openly and naturally than we do.' A second English witness testifies to the 'natural frankness in the Russian's approach to his fellow-beings,' while a third speaks of honesty as a quality for which the Russians are unmatched by any other nation. A young American woman loves the Russians' 'incredible lack of artifice'; a German of maturer years speaks of their 'uninhibited naturalness and candor.' [1]

Contrasting such testimony with the enigmatic, sphinx-like, inscrutable qualities which others (including Winston Churchill) have no less sweepingly attributed to the Russian, a simple—perhaps over-simple—hypothesis suggests itself. Can it be that the Russian's secretiveness is confined to the mundane world of mere fact, which he finds boring and fundamentally unreal; whereas, where emotion—the true stuff of life—is concerned, he delights in communicating his reactions to all and sundry on every possible occasion? Should a foreigner stop him in Moscow's Gorky Street and ask the way to Red Square, he might (according to an extreme extrapolation of this hypothesis) blur or refuse to disclose the information as belonging to the world of fact and therefore lacking significance. Yet he might immediately explain that the inquirer closely resembled his deceased father, son, brother, aunt or mother-in-law whom he passionately loved or bitterly hated under circumstances on which he will readily supply detailed information. Such a theory would, if valid, help to explain the psychological impasse which so often exists between a Russian and a typical Western citizen, since the latter tends to be more at home exchanging information than emotional responses, at least with comparative strangers. It is not, according to this theory, that the Russian is more or less tight-lipped or more or less communicative than the non-Russian; but that the areas within which these qualities are displayed tend to be mutually exclusive.

This hypothesis would also help to explain the frequent claims made by and on behalf of Russians that they are peculiarly spontaneous, 'warm,' natural, sincere and the like. On first meeting someone, 'we frequently burst out with something . . . omitting even the word of greeting,' writes a Russian, also claiming credit for an unusual capacity to get to know complete strangers. 'How often we make thorough acquaintance in the course of the first conversation with a stranger who appeals to us, telling and asking each other with equal straightforwardness dozens of things of a personal nature.' The Russian 'allows himself to be openly angry when he feels angry,' just as he allows his heart to go out to people when they do appeal to him. We are not capable of concealing fermentation, whether with wrath or exaltation.' Not that Russians can be said to wear their hearts on their sleeves, the same informant adds. It is just that 'some power, without asking our permission, has concealed little X-ray cameras against our hearts.' [2]

Nowhere is the emphasis on the projection of emotions more characteristically displayed than in the genre of the memoir and autobiography, to which the Russians have made many outstanding contributions, as well as some on a mediocre level. In such works one is liable to read that father 'positively exuded secretions of sincerity' (*ot ottsa tak i iskhodili flyuidy serdechnosti*). There is often, in the less tasteful of these documents, an over-insistence on the vitality, dynamism and gleeful panache of the main characters, and of the world in general: a hearty, all-jolly-Russians-together atmosphere which seems to generate an effect contrary to that apparently intended. 'Life at Skuchishchevo was always a-bubble' (*tak i kipela*); Uncle Gleb 'literally sprayed everyone [*bukvalno opryskival vsekh*] with merry witticisms and lighthearted puns'; Cousin Boris 'simply spluttered with *joie de vivre*' (*ot nego tak i pryskalo zhizneradostnostyu*). Such is the common coin of Russian memoirists—that is, if one is unkind enough to pick out some of their more undignified effusions and translate them perhaps too literally. And what a mood of impending doom or inspissated lugubriousness an excess of such heartiness can create in the reader.

These examples have been deliberately chosen as grotesque and exceptional, however, and one can go too far in reacting against exposure to such frantic insistence on the exuberance of all and sundry. Nor need too much be made of the references to the soul with which Russian speech abounds. A Russian will address his friend or spouse as 'my soul' (*dusha moya*); or refer to a particularly close friend as *zadushevny*, 'a behind-the-soul one.' One is struck, too, by the extraordinarily concrete images in which the Russian soul can figure. A comic writer can express anguish, whimsically, by saying that 'Cats were scratching at my soul.' Then again, the Russian frequently refers to himself as wearing his soul, as one may a shirt, 'unbuttoned' (*naraspashku*).

The Russian soul is no longer the target for the non-Russian's indiscriminate admiration which it once was. Nor is the decline surprising when one notes that hard statistics show the use of *dusha* to have declined in Russia by about 50 percent since 1918. But this concept, never closely defined, was much in vogue in the West during the First World War—the years when an epidemic of cultural Russomania swept the world. During this period an illustrated miscellany of articles, *The Soul of Russia,* was published as a book in London in aid of Russian refugees, and the concept much exercised English critics and writers of the period. While Jane Harrison, as quoted above, was seeking its essence in the aspects of the verb, Virginia Woolf was magisterially identifying the soul as the chief character of Russian fiction: 'this perplexed liquid, this cloudy, yeasty, precious stuff, the soul.' She also says that 'in reading Tchekov we find ourselves repeating the word "soul" again and again. It sprinkles his pages.' And not surprisingly if, as one Russian has it, there is 'a passionate love for the soul of Nature which radiates human warmth and sympathy winding its way through the whole of Russian literature.' [3]

As the last quotation reminds us, the Russian is rarely overinhibited by fear that the word *love* may become debased by overuse. 'Russians love to love. . . . What a power of loving there is granted to the Slav.' [4] To such characteristic claims can be added those of a non-Russian witness: 'Chekhov loved people. He crammed his life with them. . . . Wherever he went he knew everybody, talked to everybody, listened to everybody, liked everybody.' [5] Thus reads the introduction to a translation of Chekhov's selected stories into English—a statement which reference to almost any page of the author's correspondence immediately and devastatingly refutes. Chekhov was no misanthrope, lacking any generalized *a priori* attitude to humanity; but he had a rare gift, repeatedly exercised, for rasping comment at the expense of the innumerable individuals who caused him acute irritation.

It is well to bear such possibilities in mind since one might otherwise judge the Russians to be all mush, all dedicated to the cult of *umileniye.* For this common but notoriously untranslatable word, the dictionaries have some such rendering as 'tenderness,' but one is tempted to render it 'gush,' 'emotional self-indulgence.' I have also heard it rendered 'the self-congratulatory jactitation of simulated emotion,' but that is going too far. That *umileniye,* however defined, indeed is a common feature in their projection of feeling, cannot be denied. But is it as universal as some pretend? By no means, thank heavens. Nothing could be more misleading than to regard all Russians as the emotionally incontinent beings of popular misconception. They can be dry, austere and reserved as the most tight-lipped or strait-laced Anglo-Saxon of legend, since there is as much scope for variety in Russian as in any other national psychology.

As for the overworked soul, there is at least one forthright opinion to set against the mush-and-gush brigade. According to Custine, an 'absence of soul' betrays itself in all Russian contexts.[6] It might be hard to substantiate that extraordinary claim, but at least one may defuse the sentimentality so falsely fathered on the restrained Chekhov. For instance, the frequent occurrence of the word 'soul' (in the versions of his works presumably read by Virginia Woolf) was simply due to coarse translation; for where Russian *dusha,* conventionally rendered 'soul,' is used, some other rendering such as 'heart' is often nearer to English usage. Thus *ot vsey dushi* usually goes better as 'with all my heart' than as 'from the bottom of my soul.' When I was first translating Chekhov I stated outright that it was not 'necessary to bring in the soul wherever the Russian has *dusha,* since the use of the English word "soul" is now almost confined to theological contexts.'[7]

So far was Chekhov from wallowing in the soulfulness often falsely attributed to him that he rejected such sentimentality even when its source was the person with whom he was most intimate. His wife, the actress Olga Knipper—herself of German parentage, incidentally, but Russian by upbringing—once wrote to him that 'My soul aches when I remember

the quiet anguish which seems so deeply seated in *your* soul.'
The husband's reply was brief, to the point and spectacularly
un-Russian in the conventional sense: 'What nonsense, dar-
ling.'[8] Turning from domestic to literary emotions, one yet
again finds Chekhov running true to form when he considers
the widely admired sentimental heroines of Turgenev's fiction. Those pure, idealistic young women were 'intolerably affected and bogus,' he once said.[9] He even wrote a telling literary parody on that common Turgenevesque situation whereby
such a pure young girl was liable to 'drop everything' at any
moment and follow her—usually highly unsuitable—lover to
the ends of the earth. As such a young woman Chekhov's
heroine Zinaida, in his *Anonymous Story,* is revealed when she
suddenly 'drops everything' by dutifully leaving her husband
and joining her lover. But that cynical, ironical and urbane
character, one Gregory Orlov, is no Turgenev hero, and he
spoils the pattern by treating his mistress's unheralded arrival
in his home as a major disaster, not as the prelude to a New
Life. Far from conveying the intruding Zinaida to the utter-
most ends of the earth, he is chiefly concerned to disembarrass
himself of an intolerable encumbrance. 'Yes, old boy,' he wryly
interprets his situation to a crony, 'the prescription is Turgenev's, but it's me who has to take the bloody medicine.' 'I am
not a Turgenev hero,' he later complains, adding that 'should
I ever require to liberate Bulgaria I could dispense with any
female escort.' Here is a dig at Turgenev's *On the Eve,* which
describes the Bulgarian freedom-fighter Insarov as being followed part of the way to the 'ends of the earth' by his devoted
Helen.[10]

In the context of Turgenev's novels it is instructive to find
an Englishman, not a Russian, displaying emotional incon-
tinence. 'This pure girl, with passionate courageous soul,'
oozed Edward Garnett, writing of *Virgin Soil*'s heroine
Marianna, 'is in fact the Liberty of Russia. . . . In her figure is
personified the power of the Russian youth.'[11] 'What non-

sense, Garnett,' Chekhov might well have replied, had this exercise in *umileniye* ever been brought to his notice.

As Chekhov's comments on Turgenev remind us, it is nearly always a Russian who proves the most effective correcter of the typical Russian faults—if, that is, one is indeed justified in assigning over-emotionalism to the category of defect. But Chekhov's corrections went largely unheeded. Nor could he protect himself against the false reverence and automatic piety which leading writers always seem to attract, by no means only in Russia. But here again it is another Russian— another writer, Chekhov's personal friend, the even more caustic, the even less sentimental Ivan Bunin—who comes to the rescue of good taste. Criticizing commentators for going on and on about Chekhov's tenderness, sadness and warmth, Bunin remarked that he could just imagine what Chekhov's own feelings 'would have been if he had read about the tenderness. As for the warmth and the sadness, they would have disgusted him even more.' [12]

From Bunin on Chekhov, and bringing this review of unsentimental Russians into modern times while advancing ever further from *umileniye,* one may turn to the novelist Vladimir Nabokov on Bunin. In his autobiography, *Speak Memory,* Nabokov describes how the elderly Bunin, flushed with the recent award of a Nobel Prize, invited him, the then-youthful Nabokov, out to a meal at a time when both authors were living in Parisian emigration. In issuing the invitation Bunin had been unaware that this young man, whom he rashly sought to patronize, had a morbid dislike of restaurants and cafés; besides which, 'heart-to-heart talks, confessions in the Dostoyevskian manner are . . . not in my [Nabokov's] line.' Nabokov describes Bunin as a spry old gentleman 'puzzled by my irresponsiveness to the hazel grouse of which I had enough in my childhood and exasperated by my refusal to discuss eschatological matters.' [13] Such is the English version. In the earlier, Russian, rendering of his autobiography, Nabokov had put this last phrase differently. There Bunin is portrayed as 'irritated by my refusal to unbutton my soul.' Nabokov thus showed in both versions of this episode a stalwart refusal to indulge in—nay, a robust and total rejection of—*umileniye* in any shape or form.

If, then, Russians have sometimes been prone to overdose themselves with the poison of emotional self-indulgence, let them also have the credit for having evolved their own antidote. Nor are the Chekhovs, the Bunins and the Nabokovs by any means as rare as foreign Russia-fanciers often pretend. Not least among such unsentimental and emotionally restrained Russians is Alexander Nikitenko. Such a witness, simply because he can also be so caustic about his fellow-countrymen on occasion, commands great respect when he makes the kind of statement which seems so unacceptable on the lips of a Pares, a Jarintzov or any other mush-and-gush artist. If the restrained Nikitenko claims, as he does, that 'In our hearts and emotions we Russians are more richly endowed than all other European peoples,' the most hardened skeptic will be well advised to heed his words. 'What an amazing people the Russians are,' Nikitenko has also written. 'They are pretty well impossible to live with. Yet you feel drawn to them by something so kind, intelligent and enchanting that no German, Frenchman, *or even Englishman,* can compare with them.' [14] Disarmed by the anglophile phrase here italicized, I should have liked to leave Nikitenko with the last word on the Russian tradition of communicating emotion. However, it is also necessary to cover certain serious reservations to which Russian emotionalism and its prophets can give rise. It has, or can have, disturbing qualities not yet discussed. Though sufficiently exceptional not to invalidate Nikitenko's favorable verdict, these elements are yet obtrusive enough—and above all, sufficiently neglected by other commentators—to demand their place in the reckoning.

How different from Nikitenko's witness is the common insinuation that emotion, as expressed by a Russian, is automatically not only stronger, but somehow on quite a different and more laudable plane than that to which the mere non-Russian can aspire. For example, Mme. Jarintzov writes of a poor Russian peasant woman during the First World War 'with large tears standing in her eyes as she hands a pot of milk to the wounded on a passing train, calls them *rodnyye* [darlings] under her breath, for each of them is as much *rodnoy* to her heart as the one boy who is fighting somewhere far, far away.' [15] There seems a strong suggestion in such passages that no 'simple' woman of any other nationality could be moved by compassion for her wounded menfolk, or at least that, if she were, such a feeling must somehow rate as immeasurably inferior to that of the, by definition, super-sincere Russian.

The Russian, this same informant elsewhere stresses, loves passionately: other people, snow, frost, natural scenery, lying on the grass. No doubt. But the main urge behind the purveying of these data seems a wish to deride the miserable repressed Englishman, here portrayed as glumly taking part in organized games and solemnly going round in his woolen underwear while the Russian is lavishing love in all directions. If Mme. Jarintzov's Englishmen use the word *love* at all it is to speak of a lovely dinner or a lovely piece of bacon.[16] Here is a shrewd dig at certain traditional features in English behavior, and it would be humorlessly unconvincing to pretend that the charge was unfounded. What one must reject is, rather, the underlying assumption that Russian exuberance and self-revelation are necessarily always preferable. And though I find Mme. Jarintzov's long-buried denunciations of the British or English amusing, I am unwilling even at this distance in time to capitulate abjectly in the Russia-fancying manner.

Her far-too-common kind of nationalistic bitchiness seems designed to convince the bemused alien that it is all somehow 'charming,' a key word in the context; he is to be indoctrinated with the patter and sent forth repeating it as his own independent judgment. Thus may the uninstructed non-Russian be found bewailing his own inferiority, his incapacity to feel true emotion by comparison with the vivid, colorful, uninhibited, outgoing, extrovert Slav. And how rarely such Russia-fanciers confine their self-abasement to the first person singular. Influenced, again, by Russians, they have a strong tendency to speak of themselves as representatives of a group which most certainly never elected them as its spokesmen, causing their confessions of emotional atrophy to embrace not only their own persons, but 'the West,' 'the British,' 'Americans' or some never-defined community called 'we.' A recent English witness is found praising the absence, in Russia, of what he has been taught to call *hypocrisie anglaise*. Virginia Woolf goes further. Speaking of the Russian writer's simplicity and absence of effort, she contrasts the stilted and self-conscious Anglo-Saxon: '*We* become awkward and self-conscious; denying our own qualities, *we* write with an affectation of goodness and sincerity which is nauseating in the extreme.'[17]

Another such propaganda casualty has described the tragic première of Chekhov's *Cherry Orchard* in Moscow on 27 January 1904, when the dying, jubilee-detesting author was dragooned into attending a celebration enacted on stage in honor of the twenty-fifth anniversary of his literary début. Of that moving—but to Chekhov acutely painful—experience, the following comment is made: '*It is difficult for anyone except a Russian to appreciate* the warm personal feeling with which he was greeted that night.[18] But is it really so very difficult for a moderately sensitive person, however ethnically preconditioned, to make this empathetic leap? Have the Russians indeed cornered the higher sensibilities, as is here implied? The author of the above lines was, alas, myself in youth. When, therefore, in the present study, I chide various Russia-fanciers and propaganda casualties for mindlessly repeating the patter taught to them by Russians, I am also criticizing myself—or at least myself of the year 1950.

If Russians are quick to volunteer information on aspects of their lives which others would regard as private, they are no less quick to demand similar information in the opposite direction. Hence the impression of inquisitiveness which they can make on those schooled in other social conventions. One early nineteenth-century foreign observer found this kind of insistence downright offensive: Dr. Robert Lyall, who spent several years in Russia after 1812 and who married a Russian woman. 'With as much ease as they say, "How do you do?" [they] . . . ask the most impertinent questions, with respect to your connections and family, your property and revenues, and your secret affairs and private opinions. An evasive answer only prompts their curiosity.' [19] This trait has by no means evaporated over the centuries, as foreign visitors to the Soviet Union can readily testify. *Zachem, pochemu, otchevo, dlya chego, chego, na koy chort:* the language seems to possess, and to need, an infinite number of words for 'why.' Why, why, why? Why do you not grow a beard, why do you not shave off your beard? Why do you never say what you mean? Why did you learn Russian, why do you not learn Russian? Why don't you like me? Why do you like me? Do you love your wife, hate your children? What are your impressions of Soviet Man? Such questions can, to a sensitive ear, become a considerable irritation—particularly since, as Dr. Lyall also noticed, a polite evasion will not usually be accepted. As for inter-Russian communication on home soil, this native inquisitiveness has been further encouraged by official insistence, in the totalitarian period, that every civic-minded person must directly concern himself with such matters as his neighbor's efficiency at his work, together with his attitudes to topics as varied as art, literature and his mother-in-law. Thus is the Russians' innate 'inquisitiveness of big children,' [20] as Pares defined it, further reinforced as part of the officially inculcated Soviet ethos.

Concerning the projection of emotion one further clutch of points must be made; perhaps the most important of all, though I do not recall seeing them put before.

To concede that the Russians are unusually prone to utter emotionally charged statements in the presence of strangers—this is not necessarily to accept certain corollaries which are commonly assumed to follow. Among them is the imputation that the expression and the feeling of strong emotion are necessarily closely correlated, whereas surely the very opposite can sometimes be the case. The second assumption is that to express strong emotion is a meritorious activity in itself, somehow placing the emotion-displayer on a pedestal of moral superiority irrespective of such considerations as context and good taste. Then there is, thirdly, the common assumption that something called 'sincerity' can be automatically assessed, in a Russian or anyone else, by persons who present no credentials of competence in performing so complex an act of divination; and who never seem to recognize that the accurate assessment of an individual's—still more a nation's—collective sincerity would (even assuming it to be possible) be an operation of the utmost delicacy and difficulty. A Bernard Pares, a Virginia Woolf, may lecture the world on Russian 'genuineness,' 'naturalness,' 'simplicity' and so on. But how, oh how, did they acquire such supreme confidence as arbiters of these elusive qualities? Does the 'sincere' man somehow splutter, does he work his facial muscles, his intonational pitch, his gesticulations in some specially 'genuine' way which can at once be recognized—if only by some other, equally sincere, genuine individual? Such judgments would be far more convincing if some of those who make them presented more credible evidence, as for example Nikitenko and Bunin so splendidly do in the context of their writings as a whole, that they possess the precious gift of sensitivity and good taste.

To deny that the over-projection of emotion *à la russe* is

necessarily more laudable than its under-projection *à l'anglaise*
is most emphatically not to assert the opposite. Believing neither that all Russians over-project, nor that all non-Russians
under-project, I would not pose as an arbiter in the comparative evaluation of these practices. I would suggest, though,
that if a person of whatever nationality prefers not to express
his feelings in public, no conclusions whatever may be legiti-
mately drawn by total strangers as to the strength or quality of
those feelings; nor are they the rightful concern of anyone but
the individual in question and those with whom he chooses to
be intimate. Conversely, if someone chooses to express his
feelings more openly, he is fully entitled to do so. And let neither type seek constantly to claim credit points for exercising
its own particular option. Over-projectors or under-projec-
tors—what does it matter? Stimulating and boring, kind and
callous, sensitive and crude individuals may be found in both
categories; and these qualities surely count far more than reserve or effusiveness. As for the proportionate distribution of
these relatively significant virtues and vices between persons of
restrained and of exhibitionist habit, one suspects it to be on a
roughly equivalent basis.

The point is, then, not at all that restraint is always good
and lack of restraint always bad; merely that the reverse
assumption, all too common in the present context, is not
justified either.

To features in the communication of emotion already discussed must be added a passion for self-dramatization. Histrionically gifted, the Russians tend to keep an eye and ear
constantly cocked for audience reaction. Where 'Western civilization has bred in us an aversion to being conspicuous in
public, a horror of being involved in "scenes," such reluctance
is not . . . found among Russians.' Making this point, Mehnert contrasts the readiness of a typical woman shoplifter in
Germany to 'go quietly' when apprehended, and to attract as
little attention as possible, with some Russian woman whom he

once chanced to see arrested in Moscow for illegal street trading. She 'screamed like one possessed and fought tooth and nail until the police finally threw her bodily into an open truck.' [21] Such too was the robust attitude to public disgrace displayed by 'Grandma' in Chekhov's *Peasants*. Far from hiding her head in shame when her treasured samovar was carried off by the village elder in lieu of unpaid tax arrears, she rushed after him shrieking in a sobbing chant, and beating her breast more in the style of a heroine from Greek tragedy. 'Good Christians and believers in God! Neighbours, they have ill-treated me! Kind friends, they have oppressed me! Oh, oh! dear people, take my part.' [22]

Self-dramatization often seems present whenever Russians undertake, as they so often do, the consumption of food and drink on a scale far beyond their means. A lower-paid worker will go to a restaurant on the weekend and order black caviar with his vodka—not, according to Harvey Pitcher, because he can really afford it, or even necessarily because he likes caviar, but *to show that* he is as capable of doing this as the next man, and as an example of the broad, expansive nature on which Russians have always prided themselves.' [23] It is not enough for him, that is, to indulge in such recklessness privily: he must be manifestly seen to do so, whether he happens to be Pitcher's worker or one of Dostoyevsky's fellow-convicts from the prison at Omsk a hundred years earlier. As described in his *Memoirs from the House of the Dead*, they were often able to smuggle liquor into jail, and then to indulge in solitary drinking bouts—but solitary only in the sense that the lucky toper would keep all the precious fluid to himself. Audience reaction was of the essence on these occasions, when the celebrant 'would get as drunk as an owl and make a point of staggering and blundering round the prison, trying *to show everyone* that he was drunk, that he was "on the binge"—and thereby to earn general respect.' [24]

Dostoyevsky has also noticed the Russian tendency to 'fall

in love with the injuries done and insults offered to them'
(*polyubit svoyu obidu*), and to whip up self-pity as a basis for theatrical behavior. His tempestuous heroine Nastasya Filippovna, once seduced in youth by a middle-aged roué, thus
proceeds (in *The Idiot*) to build her entire life-style around the
dubious thesis that she is a 'fallen woman.' And on a more
trivial level such histrionic self-pity, very much *à la* Dostoyevsky, is regularly called into play on the occasions when
some well-meaning foreign visitor chances to offer a tip to a
self-respecting citizen of the modern age. This can be a delicate maneuver in a society where tipping, on the one hand officially considered to have been abolished as inconsistent with
the dignity of Soviet Man, is on the other hand a fairly widespread practice. An Intourist official once told me how an
American visitor had insulted him in this way, by proffering a
one-rouble gratuity in return for some service or other. But
however tactless the original *faux pas* may have been, the injured party did seem to be protesting, and to be enjoying protesting, rather too much. He seemed, like Nastasya Filippovna
before him, to propose building his whole future emotional
life around this petty incident. And yet, somehow, the entire
protest was obviously, *au fond,* little more than a joke, game or
charade to him, as will become clearer below, where the
neglected phenomenon of the Russian leg-pull is to be
scrutinized in depth.

Such a contretemps can erupt on a grander scale, as
witness the similar incident of 1959, when Richard Nixon visited the Soviet Union as Vice President of the United States.
Believed, probably through some misunderstanding, to have
offered a tip or bribe to a humble meat-weigher, one Smakhtin, encountered during a good-will tour to 'meet the people,'
Mr. Nixon found that he had alerted the media and plunged
the entire country into an orgy of Dostoyevskian self-pity.
Meat-weigher Smakhtin, having thus had greatness thrust
upon him, appeared on Moscow radio to bewail the insult of-

fered to an 'ordinary Russian working man' and sent a letter to *Pravda* describing how he had proudly thrust aside the wallet of the transatlantic gentleman.[25] This episode, which shows Russian self-dramatization enthusiastically harnessed by the department of agitation and propaganda, was allowed to smolder on for an unconscionable time. Soon afterward, on a still higher level, Nikita Khrushchev was directing similar 'They can't treat me like this' tantrums at President Eisenhower at a summit conference held in Paris in the wake of the U-2 spy-plane scandal—a real connoisseur's specimen of the hammed-up disproportionate reaction.

Politics everywhere tend to involve a strong element of play-acting and buffoonery such as has certainly not been confined, in Russia, to the totalitarian period. The Emperor Nicholas I could never forget for a second who he was. 'He postures incessantly, with the result that he is never natural even when he is sincere.' And a similar claim has been made for that emperor's, and his successors', bitterest foes: Russia's pioneer revolutionaries. 'All you want is to play a part and posture to the mob for the sake of applause'—thus Nikitenko apostrophizes the followers of his *bête noire*, the radical publicist Herzen. And again, 'These ultra-progressives . . . want to posture on the stage, they want to play at making history.' But Nikitenko does not go so far as another authority, who once dismissed the whole of Russian civilization as pure play-acting: 'They are much less interested in being civilized than in making us believe them so.' [26]

This histrionic tendency helps to explain the national love of *skandaly*, 'scenes.' 'A Russian takes incredible delight in every kind of scandalous public upheaval,' wrote Dostoyevsky when introducing what must be the greatest *skandal* sequence in literature: the scene (in *Devils*) where a gang of malicious semi-politically motivated hooligans or nihilists contrives to wreck an already preposterous public literary conference, thereby triggering the moral disintegration of the unnamed provincial town which is the scene of the action. Wherever, in general, the outward decorum of everyday life shows signs of breaking down, the average Russian still seems as much inclined as ever to foster such disruptive tendencies—no matter how trivial their origin, such as an argument about the quality of a single potato offered for sale in a collective farm market. Everyone in hearing joins in, accusations and counter-accusations fly about until sooner or later authority steps in, if only in the person of a humble militiaman, and decorum is restored—until the next *skandal* rears its always-enticing head. Indeed, the whole of Russian history can be plausibly related to the rhythm of the *skandal* and inevitable subsequent tamping-down operation or counter-*skandal*. *Zamyat*, 'to hush up,' is a verb which frequently occurs in this context.

Small wonder, then, that the rulers of a nation so histrionically inclined should have resorted to theatrical devices when seeking to bolster their own authority. The most spectacular example of this was the great trilogy of Stalinist show trials of 1936–38. The available surviving senior colleagues of Lenin were paraded in court, where they vied with each other in confessing to espionage, economic sabotage, assassination plots and other forms of terrorism—all or virtually all fiction, and all part of an elaborate script taught to them at the behest of the producer-in-chief, Stalin, by various forms of persuasion, including appeals to Party discipline, threats to relatives and torture.

Similarly, on a humbler level, use is still made in factories, universities and other institutions of 'boards of shame' on which delinquent individuals are pilloried for failing to have their hair cut, cheating in examinations, seducing girls, neglecting to follow prescribed safety regulations—and of course, above all, for getting drunk. There are also show trials of a kind, still: the semi-public self-criticism sessions or kangaroo courts at which an erring individual may be called to order by his self-righteous workmates. One may read in the press many a cautionary tale, such as that of a certain worker in a match factory who had been detected listening to foreign broadcasts. Hailed before a meeting of his mates, he was bullied until he broke down, confessed his sins, bowed to his fellow-workers and thanked them for standing bail for his future conduct and thus showing their trust in him.[27] Such episodes are obviously rigged from start to finish by local Party officials, activists and busybodies, but even so they could probably not take place at all but for the Russian love of self-projection, particularly where highly dramatized repentance and contrition is involved. In this way the aggressively secular state has harnessed traditional Russian religious reactions, a topic which must be considered in a later chapter.

The same histrionic urge perhaps explains the people's fondness for political demonstrations—no matter that, under totalitarian conditions, they are often organized by and for the authorities; far less commonly against them, as in less effectively regimented societies. 'Set a collection of Russians down in a street, tell them to start walking in the same direction, and in no time they will all be singing together and smiling.' Moreover, the fiction that these officially rigged demonstrations are spontaneous can the more easily be sustained since it involves injecting the element of leg-pull, always an acceptable spicing, into a situation already distinguished by its theatricality. Such are the occasional spontaneous (that is, officially rigged) demonstrations sometimes staged by 'ordinary workers impelled by elemental righteous indignation' (that is, those detailed by officials to take part) against foreign embassies in Moscow in order to point up some international squabble. One such performance was mounted outside the British Embassy in 1956 at the time of the Suez crisis, when a well-regimented shouting 'mob' flourished placards ('Dirty Hands off Egypt') on the perimeter. But the obliging fur-capped major general of police who was in charge was able to inform an inquiring embassy official of the exact hour at which the spontaneous explosion of the people's wrath was scheduled to end.[28]

An example of similar 'spontaneity' on an individual level is to be found in Pitcher's acute analysis of 'Kolya,' an enthusiastic young Party member with whom, as a visiting student, he shared a room in Leningrad. Considering it his duty to project *bodrost* (a buoyant, optimistic approach to life), Kolya would switch on his ideal personality when required. 'Whenever a stranger came into the room—whether a Russian or a Westerner—Kolya's "liveliness index" would immediately shoot up several points.' He would become instantly livelier, more talkative and cheery. ' "You'll be able to go back to England and tell them how jolly Soviet students are," he would comment after this sort of performance.' [29]

Such posturing is a significant national characteristic. 'Just you watch me being spontaneous' is the formula which most effectively covers it. But there is, of course, something highly paradoxical about the kind of 'spontaneous,' sincere, natural and so on behavior which is not merely ostentatiously labeled as such by those who stage it, but can also be announced in advance as being about to be put on show—and even timed to end at a predetermined moment. And all this becomes somewhat less than acceptable when accompanied, as is not unknown, by 'tactful' allusions to the alleged lack of spontaneity of the American, German, et cetera, person who has sometimes been chosen as audience or target for the exhibition. The same point is made in a less irreverent and more Russia-fancying way by another observer: 'The Russian . . . displays that naturalness which has so often enchanted foreigners.' [30] *Displays!* Precisely.

And yet the Russian somehow manages to 'display' all this elemental jactitated naturalness without really possessing a word for 'spontaneous' or 'spontaneity.' Indeed, he has had recourse to borrowing in this area the forms *spontanny* and *spontannost*—than which, etymologically, nothing could be less Slav. Why does the language lack the terms? It is typical of the problems posed by Russians that two mutually exclusive explanations simultaneously suggest themselves. Either the Russian is so spontaneous and natural that the very concept can be taken for granted and needs no words to express it. Alternatively, or simultaneously, the very possibility of any human reaction *not* being dictated by deep-laid guile is so totally excluded as to have exempted the language from filling what, in any other tongue, might be found a serious lacuna.

In any case the Russians are obviously not the only people given to the sin or feat, however regarded, of self-projection. Nor can all Russians be accused without discrimination of constantly seeing themselves on stage with the spotlight playing on them. Chekhov, for example, least of all men sought to cultivate an 'image,' as he showed when someone accused him of betraying, in his story *The Party*, a fear of being considered a liberal. 'I think that I can be accused of gluttony, drunkenness, frivolity, frigidity, or of any crime in the calendar rather than of wishing to seem or of wishing not to seem something.' [31]

Then again, though Russians can appear a little comic when going through the carefully prescribed and pre-scripted motions of self-criticism in kangaroo courts and the like, it should not be forgotten that they also have, as a nation, a remarkable record for detecting and analyzing their own shortcomings in a more dignified yet hard-hitting style wholly free from paranoia and ostentatious self-disparagement. Even Custine, one of their severest critics, admitted this when he wrote, 'Fundamentally they judge their country more harshly than I.' [32] And so indeed they do. One thinks here of the shattering pictures of provincial life conveyed in Gogol's *Dead Souls* and *Inspector General;* of Chaadayev's wholesale denunciation of Russia's past, present and future in his *First Philosophical Letter;* of Saltykov's scathing picture of Russian officialdom; of the critique of the Russian intelligentsia in the symposium *Land-marks* of 1909; of Gorky's above-quoted diatribe against the Russian peasantry. And one also thinks of the satire of the 1920s: that of Zamyatin, of Ilf and Petrov, and of many another. As these instances show, one may accuse the Russians of many crimes, not excluding the occasional orgy of bombastic self-glorification. But one cannot accuse them, as a nation, of ignoring their own defects—which indeed, as so much else, they seem on occasion to exaggerate with their usual exuberance and *razmakh*.

## CAMOUFLAGE DRILL

Few analyses of the Russian psyche so much as mention one key concept: *vranyo,* the national brand of leg-pulling, ribbing or blarney. It is defined by one dictionary as 'lies, fibbing, nonsense, rot,' and by another as 'idle talk, twaddle.'

*Vranyo* is the more innocent of two distinct terms denoting the dissemination of untruths, its more serious equivalent being *lozh.* To impute *vranyo* involves little more than the affectionate charge of possessing a lively imagination: *vryote,* 'You're kidding.' But to accuse someone of *lozh* is harsh: *lzhosh,* 'You bloody liar!' The roots of both words are rich in derivatives such as *zaviratsya:* crudely translated, 'to prevaricate oneself into a condition of trance.' Indeed, Russian may possess almost as large a vocabulary of terminological inexactitude as Arabic has for different kinds of camel.

The distinction between these two brands of prevarication is drawn in a notable essay, 'Pan-Russian Vranyo,' by the pre-revolutionary short-story writer and dramatist Leonid Andreyev. He claims outright—unfairly perhaps—that Russians have no talent whatever for *lozh*, calling this more serious brand of misrepresentation 'an art, difficult and demanding intelligence, talent, character, stamina.' A good *lozh*-type liar is Shakespeare's Iago—whose skill is beyond any Russian's, says Andreyev. 'Yes,' he continues, 'the Russian is incapable of telling downright lies [*lozh*]; but seems equally incapable of telling the truth. The intermediate phenomenon for which he feels the utmost love and tenderness resembles neither truth nor *lozh*. It is *vranyo*. Like our native aspen, it pops up uninvited everywhere, choking other varieties; like the aspen, it is no use for firewood or carpentry; and, again like the aspen, it is sometimes beautiful.' As an example Andreyev quotes someone who, after conversing normally for a while, suddenly announces that his aunt has died—and this though the good lady, 'far from being deceased . . . is about to turn up in half an hour, as everyone knows. He has no way of benefiting from his aunt's supposed death, and why he uttered the *vranyo* is a mystery.'[1] To this may be added Potugin's story (in Turgenev's *Smoke*) of the sportsman who, while beating an unfamiliar countryside for game, was directed by a helpful rustic to a nearby marsh offering a vast profusion of wild fowl helpfully waiting to be shot. The huntsman trudged on, only to discover, alas, that both marsh and birds were pure mirages.[2]

Such is *vranyo* at its simplest, in which form it has outlived the nineteenth century. I was once present when a USSR-domiciled Russian visitor to England spoke to a British host about a Russian *émigré* known to both of them. According to the visitor, one of the *émigré*'s sons had recently returned to Moscow after a stay in Paris; had published a book of which the exact title was given; had changed his name; had undergone various other adventures. The host listened to this rigmarole with a straight face, thus preserving the conventions, though he was a close friend of the family concerned

and knew that every word was untrue. Did the narrator realize, then, that his game had been rumbled? Yes and no. That,
as will be seen below, is the very point and nub.

Here, then, is the kind of fantasy in which Andreyev
claims a Russian monopoly. As his country's true representative he singles out Khlestakov, that ingenious hero of
Gogol's *Inspector General* whose skill lies in juggling fantastic
improvisations, and who, according to Andreyev, constitutes
something uniquely Russian, 'like a samovar.' [3]

On so quintessentially national a phenomenon as *vranyo*
that arch-patriot Dostoyevsky has inevitably made the most
memorable contributions of all. He has magnificently spouted
it himself, not least in his famous 'Pushkin Speech' of 1880.
He has acutely analyzed its theory, especially in the article 'A
Word or Two about Vranyo,' published in his *Diary of a Writer*
in 1873. And he has created many a notable *vranyo*-monger-
ing brainchild in his fiction. Among these General Ivolgin of
*The Idiot* holds pride of place. Most readers remember Ivolgin
for his account of an alleged experience in a railway compart-
ment which he had once purportedly shared with a woman
and her lapdog. Objecting to his smoking, she had, according
to Ivolgin, snatched his cigar and thrown it out of the window,
whereupon Ivolgin had forthwith avenged himself by tossing
her lapdog after his cigar. Unfortunately a member of
Ivolgin's audience, unsympathetic to *vranyo,* then broke the
conventions by remarking that this same incident had recently
been reported in a Belgian newspaper, from which the inevitable inference followed that the general had not been concerned in it at all.

As the episode confirms, *vranyo* at its best represents an
art form, not a means of gaining personal advantage. Its function is to provide light amid the encircling gloom. This point is
also made in Andreyev's essay, where he has one of his imaginary *vranyo*-purveyors say that he does not in the least mind
being caught out. 'It's only right that truth should triumph—I

value truth and respect it. But before you're found out *you do seem to come to life for a moment.'* [4] Indeed, *vranyo*'s continuing late twentieth-century vogue may well derive from its function of enlivening the drabness of modernity, since the official doctrine that totalitarian Russian life is somehow more exhilarating than life elsewhere is itself so extreme an example of creative fantasy.

To invoke totalitarian Russian fantasy-mongering is to be reminded that the subject has so far been considered only in a relatively private or intimate context, as it develops in *tête-à-tête* dialogue or small social gatherings. But what of public *vranyo*, as developed by Russia's rulers, statesmen and official spokesmen, not merely since 1917, but throughout the ages? Here the Russian claim to a monopoly is less firmly founded, since public *vranyo* tends to become fused with and indistinguishable from public political bombast in general—for instance, with that found incised on the obelisks of the Pharaohs; with the grandiloquent addresses directed by such highly un-Russian figures as the poets Vergil and Horace to the Emperor Augustus. Yet how prosaic were these stolid Romans by comparison with the public *vranyo*-purveyors of a later, larger, more ebullient empire.

Among virtuoso pioneers of Russia-based *vranyo* was the Empress Catherine the Great, who, as has been said, 'erected self-advertisement into a system of government.' [5] One example was the elaborate *Instruction* framed by her in 1765–67 for the guidance of a specially summoned Legislative Commission charged with drawing up a new legal code. But there was, it seems, no prospect whatever of any practical outcome resulting from the harangues on the desirability of equality, justice and other abstract nouns with which the empress, versed in Montesquieu's *L'Esprit des lois* and other foreign sources, had adorned her *Instruction*. The operation was more of an incantational exercise in official *vranyo*. That this kind of operation, already detected in ancient Egypt and ancient Rome as well as Russia, has been pretty well universal throughout the ages, need hardly be argued. It was the nineteenth-century Church of England, not Catherine's Russia, which Samuel Butler most directly satirized with the 'musical banks' where all respectable citizens of his imagined state Erewhon kept accounts in a notional or ideal currency of purely decorative and symbolical significance—currency parallel to and entirely separated from the real coin of the realm, with which alone it was actually possible to buy things. Long before *Erewhon* this principle had been translated into visual terms by Catherine's most celebrated favorite, Potemkin, creator of those renowned 'villages' which remain to this day the prime emblem of Russian *pokazukha* ('bull') and *ochkovtiratelstvo* ('eyewash'). They were mere two-dimensional stage props erected in sight of the River Dnieper, being designed to impress upon the touring sovereign, as she glided downstream with a flotilla of notables, the comforting illusion that the wilderness around her was a prosperous and densely populated province of her realm. Well might Michael Speransky, the statesman who served the empress's grandsons Alexander I and Nicholas I, complain in another context that 'in no other State do political words stand in such contrast to reality as in Russia.' [6]

Though *pokazukha* on the scale of a Potemkin and a Catherine had somewhat receded in Speransky's day, the Russian nineteenth century by no means renounced her legacy. One observer lamented that 'Any traveler who let himself be indoctrinated by the locals could traverse the length and breadth of the Empire and return home having done nothing but tour a sequence of façades.' [7] Skipping another hundred years or so, one finds that many earlier façades have been hauled down, and also that far more new ones have been put up in their place. But only since Stalin's death has *vranyo* emerged as a key element in totalitarian public posture. One might oversimplify and call the age of Lenin the age of truth, since it was after all also an age of faith. When official spokesmen then promised the people that they faced a glorious future, that they would overtake America, and that revolution was about to erupt in Germany at any moment, they were speaking the truth in the sense that on the whole they believed the promises to be well founded. Then came the age of Stalin, that era of *lozh* militant, when a sincere belief in anything—especially in Stalin himself—could become a passport to disgrace and arrest. When Stalinist spokesmen referred to millions of peasants voluntarily joining the collective farms, this was no *vranyo*, but just a deliberate *lozh*-type lie. Not until the era of Khrushchev did *vranyo* come into its own as a factor influencing public behavior, partly through the personal example of the new leader, whose statements on cultivating maize, catching up with America and the like often carried so strong a whiff of fantasy, and were obviously made partly for fun. But the spread of *vranyo* then derived less from Khrushchev's own sterling example than from the relaxations over which he presided by enabling more communication to take place—both internally, between citizens; and externally, between natives and foreigners. This relaxation of controls released a torrent which had been dammed for decades, and which has since been expertly canalized and exploited under the leadership of Brezhnev, himself—by contrast with his predecessor and to humanity's loss—no great *vranyo*-monger.

*Vranyo* has changed considerably since Catherine's and Dostoyevsky's days, having become more of a ritual. Its subject matter now runs in prescribed grooves. Whereas your old-time purveyor of *vranyo* could merrily improvise about whatever came into his head, and enjoyed strictly amateur status, one now finds various officially licensed greeters or contact men—Intourist guides, members of delegations and the like—who bear all the signs of having been drilled in the gentle art of manipulating foreigners at some highly secret central school of *vranyo*. Approved topics include the frequent denial that begging, tipping and prostitution exist within the Kremlin's sway. But such are only fields for negative *vranyo,* an unimportant by-product of the genre, since it is hard for even the most experienced practitioner to embellish the *absence* of something with what is a vital element in the exercise, elaborate embroidery—especially when that something does not happen to be absent at all.

For embroidery purposes a positive topic is needed. One example is the fiction, widely propagated of late, that tens of millions of 'workers' may be observed every summer as they drive their families along the main roads of the country toward some Black Sea resort 'in their own cars.' When once listening to such a recital I must have committed what George Orwell called 'facecrime'—conveyed involuntary disbelief by my facial expression—because the speaker, a woman, quickly remarked that there were 'some workers who don't yet have cars of their own.' This comment brings out a modern refinement beyond the ken of Dostoyevsky's contemporaries, that of oblique *vranyo:* the various 'defects' or disadvantages of the country are 'frankly' admitted, an admission designed to underline, by implication, the reliability of the performance as a whole. The above episode also illustrates another difference between present-day and nineteenth-century *vranyo.* With double chauvinism Dostoyevsky claimed the practice as unique to the Russian male, which is no longer true; here as elsewhere the equality of the sexes has been robustly asserted.

The changes since Dostoyevsky's day have not been all gain, for it is now common practice to dilute *vranyo* with injections of truth. One finds this in the endless 'building stories,' one of the staples of modern *vranyo* which few foreign visitors to Moscow escape. The presentation is unrolled with traditional ceremony, with accounts about how there was 'nothing here, nothing' except swamp and shacks a few months ago, whereas there is now some vast suburb containing so many million square meters of living space. Such achievements are explained with certain accompaniments not yet mentioned;

expansive gestures, a piercing glance, a swelling neck, an empurpled face and that curious constricted voice which suggests that the speaker is on the point of choking. But something is wrong; for the apartment blocks—even if not built quite as quickly as indicated—are visibly present. Thus a fine old tradition has been adulterated and diluted in the modern age, though of course *vranyo*'s loss has been the Muscovite's gain. One should not underestimate the fantasy element in traditional construction stories, though. Precisely the same stories, told with precisely the same physical symptoms on the part of the narrators, had been put out by precisely the same spokesmen in earlier years when (they now 'frankly' admit) the building program had been grossly inadequate. It could of course be argued that this has involved no adulteration, but an even greater sophistication: in earlier times *vranyo* had to be untrue, but nowadays its connection with truth has become so obscure that it no longer matters.

To what extent does the *vranyo* artist believe his own fantasies? He obviously differs from the *lozh*-purveyor, who knows perfectly well that he is lying. But still less does he believe himself to be telling the truth, occupying rather an intermediate position. Can it, then, be that he simultaneously believes and does not believe the creative fictions which he disseminates? No. More probably, he does not believe them at all as he begins his harangue; but then he suddenly becomes convinced by his eloquence in mid-career, a phenomenon which may be termed the take-off. Such at least is Dostoyevsky's view. In his essay on *vranyo* he addresses a typical adept as follows: 'You have told such fantastic stories . . . that, though you have have started to believe in yourself halfway through your story (for one always does begin to believe in oneself halfway through a story), nevertheless when you go to bed at night and have enjoyable memories about the pleasant impression made on your listener, you suddenly pause and remark involuntarily, "Heavens, what rubbish I talked." ' [8]

It seems likely, therefore, that the typical *vranyo* dispenser at any given moment either believes or does not believe wholeheartedly in what he is saying, and that he oscillates between these two conditions. Since the more distressing physical symptoms—mentioned above as including the strained voice, bulging eyes and purple face—are associated with the period of take-off, during which he comes to believe himself, it seems possible that the recurrent gusts of clearheadedness are nature's way of providing relief.

To consider this question is to touch on a particularly elusive general problem, the nature of belief. It is a puzzle intractable enough anywhere, but doubly so in a totalitarian context, since too little is known about what happens to a man's brain when he is compelled year in and year out to repeat statements which he may know or suspect to be untrue. The evidence of refugees from totalitarian countries shows that many persons of high intelligence have emerged from years of conditioning surprisingly unscathed. Some have managed to adapt themselves to their environment by developing a form of controlled schizophrenia whereby private thoughts and compulsory official mendacity are, so to speak, confined in separate compartments of the brain.

In some cases, though—as observation of 'capitalist' politicians also richly confirms—the repeated acting of a false part seems to wear a groove in the actor's brain until he comes to believe propositions which he originally knew to be absurd. That this may prove dangerous is suggested, again by Leonid Andreyev, in his *Thought*. One of the most spine-chilling stories ever written, it describes a man who has decided to murder his wife, and who, wishing to evade criminal proceedings, cultivates an alibi in advance by faking insanity. He indulges, that is, in a series of carefully planned preliminary eccentricities—none serious enough to cause him to be confined in a mental home, but all sufficiently suggestive of an unbalanced mind as to make it appear obvious, after the murder, that he had been mad all along. But he unfortunately acts his part as a madman so convincingly that he eventually becomes a real lunatic, or something indistinguishable from one, an important point of the story being the impossibility of assessing his, or perhaps anyone's, true mental state. Now, a lifelong addiction to *vranyo* may well produce some similar dislocation in the brain, a possibility which discourages any temptation to regard the modern Russian adept as necessarily a comic character. He might instead be a *pagliaccio* or tragic clown, increasingly ill at ease each time he dons the motley. General Ivolgin, that grand master of *vranyo,* is in many ways such a tragic figure; but even Ivolgin was not compelled to indulge in *vranyo* by forces outside himself.

How much more painful, then, must be the predicament of an internally protesting Soviet *vranyo*-monger who is humiliated at being compelled to produce officially sponsored fantasies like a robot. Perhaps he wishes to protest and dissociate himself from the performance, yet he is not prepared to face the penalties for failing to produce *vranyo* at all—or, still worse, for substituting the truth in its place. And yet there is one kind of protest which he can make with relative safety. By subtly overdoing his performance, he can deride the whole process, separate himself mentally from his humiliating position and thus preserve a measure of self-respect. He is safe in doing so, for who can be certain that the exaggeration is deliberate? Moreover, though interfering 'activists' can easily embarrass someone who shows insufficient zeal, they are less favorably placed when confronted by one who shows an approved brand of zeal, however synthetic, in excess. In attempting to harass him, they might easily find themselves in trouble.

Soviet literature provides many examples of such counterfeit displays of excessive zeal by way of protest, perhaps none more striking than that at the deathbed of Professor Skutarevsky's son in Leonid Leonov's novel *Skutarevsky* (1932).

The son, implicated in counter-revolutionary activity, has attempted to commit suicide by shooting himself in the stomach.
As he lies in a hospital, dying and unable to speak, his father
directs at him an interminable enthusiastic political harangue.
Now, Leonov cannot conceivably have been serious in writing
this and other similar passages in his works; rather was he
mocking indoctrinational literature. This was daring, since
many of his presumably satirical sallies were published under
Stalin; but it was still fairly safe, for what censor would dare
suggest that they were written with tongue in cheek? Such
protesting mimicry may play a greater part in inspiring modern *vranyo* than one might imagine. It also calls to mind a
traditional practice of pre-1917 Russian revolutionaries which
will be further discussed below: that of supporting and attempting to intensify reactionary governmental policies with
the aim of discrediting the government through its own increasingly absurd measures, and thus rendering its violent
overthrow more likely.

Given the Russian's sensitivity to audience reactions, one
is not surprised to find *vranyo* incorporating this element. It
requires not only its purveyor or donor, but also its recipient
or recipients. *Vranyo* differs in this important respect from
*lozh,* which can operate through radio broadcasts and diplomatic notes no less than in the *tête-à-tête,* whereas the true
*vranyo* artist can only give his best in the presence of a partner
or straight man—the role in which the forgotten Marshal
Bulganin once served the ebullient Khrushchev. The fact that
*vranyo* is a two-way process is stressed again and again in the
literature of the subject; and, as the following key quotation
from Dostoyevsky's above-mentioned essay shows, facial expression has an important part to play. 'Have you never told
an anecdote, an alleged personal experience, to someone who
originally told that very same story to you about himself? Have
you really forgotten how, half-way through the story, you suddenly remembered this fact . . . also confirmed by *the suffer-*

*ing glance of the listener, fixed firmly upon you, for in such cases peo-*
*ple somehow do stare into each other's eyes with tenfold intensity?'* [9]

As this passage illustrates, the relations between purveyor
and recipient are of the essence. Perhaps the greatest passage
of *vranyo* in fiction is the scene in *The Idiot* where General
Ivolgin tells Prince Myshkin a tall story about his supposed
childhood experiences during the Napoleonic invasion of
1812. Ivolgin claims that Napoleon appointed him his page
during the occupation of Moscow, and the zenith of the *vranyo*
is attained when Napoleon is described as ordering the French
retreat on the infant Ivolgin's advice to 'Buzz off, General.'
Throughout this preposterous account Ivolgin studies Myshkin's expression. 'He squinted mistrustfully at the Prince, saying "You are smiling, Prince, you are looking at my face," ' and
so on. After Ivolgin had left, the recipient 'had a premonition
that he [Ivolgin] belonged to that category of liars who, al-
though they lie to the point of sensual self-indulgence and
even to a condition of trance, nevertheless suspect that they
are not being believed and cannot be believed.' Myshkin had
manfully heard Ivolgin's absurdities out with a straight face,
hoping thus to have ministered to the poor man's self-respect;
but he had not done well enough, for he received a note from
the general that same evening breaking off all relations.

Prince Myshkin's experience is a warning to all visitors to
Russia. When confronted with *vranyo* they should assume a
serious, respectful expression, thus avoiding 'facecrime.'
Surely that is not too much to ask. Many a *vranyo*-monger is a
decent enough man, after all; and if it is his official duty to
bemuse foreigners with misleading signals, that is no reason
for making him feel foolish by showing obvious signs of disbelief; still less by trying to catch him out. It may be irritating
to be told, as has often happened to foreign students in Russia, that all readers in Moscow's Lenin Library can easily obtain access to any book they want, including the works of
Trotsky, Zinovyev, Bukharin and—for such attempts have

been made—myself. But this, again, is no excuse for imitating those visitors who have been known to make the offending *vrun* show them all the various catalogues in order to expose the whole story as an invention. Of course it is; but some things do not need disproving. And those who seek to demonstrate the falsehood of a given piece of *vranyo* may unwittingly hurt some harmless craftsman by implying that it was a piece of *lozh* all along.

Given the vogue of Russian creative fancy-mongering it is no surprise that visitors from the country often imagine themselves exposed to an exhibition of Western *vranyo* when in fact they are not. I have noticed this when conducting Russian visitors around Oxford colleges. One has only to make an innocent remark of indisputable veracity, such as, 'Here is a typical undergraduate's room,' to see a change come over the visitor's face as he composes it in an attitude of respectful seriousness—which may not, however, entirely conceal his total disbelief. *The vryano has begun,* he has concluded; and, as one man of the world talking to another, he proposes to receive it with due solemnity. His own turn will come later, after all. There has to be some give and take in these matters; for, as Dostoyevsky enunciated nearly a century ago, 'A delicate reciprocity of *vranyo* is almost the first condition of Russian society, of all Russian meetings, parties, clubs, learned societies and the like.' [10]

While the *vranyo* artist does not expect to be disproved or otherwise shown up, and is entitled to this courtesy, a key question remains: Does he expect to be believed? Certainly not. There could be no greater error than to conclude that these creative effusions are meant to be taken seriously. They are intended to be accepted with a serious and respectful countenance, but that is a different matter. By believing, literally, a piece of *vranyo*—a phenomenon surprisingly common among more gullible Western visitors to Russia—the recipient gravely insults his host's inventive powers, implying in effect that they have not been called into play at all. There is no fun in feeding *vranyo* to an innocent who happily accepts it with an expression of beatific silliness on his face. Consequently official *vranyo* purveyors, when dealing with Western visitors, often prefer a tactful skeptic to a duped fellow-traveler. On Russian soil the latter type can easily seem far more sinister than he is; for there must be something wrong, it is felt, with someone who swallows official handouts while under no compulsion to do so.

Even in the totalitarian period some Russians have not hesitated to satirize certain aspects of official *vranyo;* for, despite all official controls, one may still find more than a few traces of that healthy early tradition whereby it is Russians themselves who most expertly deride and denounce the very incongruities and pretenses of their own society. Such protests are usually on a muted level at the present time, being linked to minor targets and restricted by the conventions of officially licensed 'self-criticism.' However, in phases of political relaxation anything may happen, and there have been occasions when the very basis of society has been called in question with a verve reminiscent of such as Radishchev, Chaadayev, Gogol and Saltykov, those scourges of the pre-revolutionary musical-bank network. Such an exceptional work was Alexander Yashin's famous story of 1956, *Levers.* Here members of a certain collective farm's Party organization are first found discussing the appalling condition of their fief: the widespread poverty, the shortage of livestock, the squalor, the mess, the meaninglessness of official catch-phrases. But then they suddenly pull themselves up, reverting with the ease born of long practice from real speech to the musical currency of official *vranyo,* and begin intoning those same meaningless catchwords which, in the previous phase, they themselves had been holding up to ridicule.[11]

Yashin's story admirably illustrates the two-compartment mentality which the Russian official has had to cultivate since long before the revolutions. It also illustrates my own long-standing contention that there are in effect two distinct Russian languages: the low-style or demotic tongue, based ultimately on peasant usage, in which ordinary events such as the loss of a collar stud or the price of a bottle of vodka may be discussed; and the priestly or hieratic argot, deriving partly from Church Slavonic, in which such matters as the notional fulfillment of notional norms, the 'achievements' of 'workers' and other—essentially liturgical or musical—material is traditionally couched.

## DECEPTION TACTICS

Now that the practice of *vranyo* has been reviewed, together with the kind of political duckspeak which so thoroughly exploits that national game of skill, the more serious kind of distortion must be considered: *lozh,* 'lies.'

To claim that all men are liars is to exaggerate; but it is not straining credulity to suggest that some Russians, like some Frenchmen, Englishmen or Greeks, do occasionally lapse into terminological inexactitude in a grosser form than mere *vranyo.* How far can one determine whether this is so? And, above all, do Russians exhibit any specific national characteristic when indulging, if they do, in the common human practice of affirming what one knows not to be and of denying what one knows to be?

That all Russians were hardened liars was a common impression of the earliest Western travelers to the country. The sixteenth-century British trader Antony Jenkinson referred to

them as 'great talkers and liars, flatterers and dissemblers.' [1]
His successor, the ambassador Giles Fletcher, made the same
point: 'From the great to the small (except some few that will
scarcely be found) the Russ neither believeth anything that
another man speaketh, nor speaketh anything himself worthy
to be believed.' Fletcher also contrasts the double-dealing Russians with their scrupulously honest Tatar subjects, repelled by
Christianity because of the utter duplicity of the Orthodox. [2]
An extreme statement or libel on these lines is that of a sixteenth-century Lithuanian traveler. Describing the sale of captured Russians, which regularly took place at Crimean Tatar
slave auctions, he asserted that the auctioneer always tried to
pass off his stock as Polish rather than Russian, 'for the Muscovite race, being crafty and deceitful, does not bring a good
price.' Hardly less severe is the verdict of the seventeenth-century traveler Olearius, who has described the Russians as
cunning and unscrupulous in dealing with each other, and as
even less sincere when dealing with foreigners. Incapable of
friendship, they would, said he, simulate good will only in
order to exploit another's benevolence for their own purposes.
Two centuries later Dostoyevsky, great Russian patriot though
he was, framed the all-Russians-are-liars case in language no
less forthright, even asserting that 'Among our Russian intellectual classes the very existence of a non-liar is an impossibility, the reason being that in Russia even honest men can lie.'
He then continues, slightly softening his harsh judgment, 'I
am convinced that in other nations, for the great majority, it is
only scoundrels who lie; they lie for practical advantage: that
is, with directly criminal aims.' Though this passage comes
from Dostoyevsky's essay on *vranyo*, mentioned above, it is the
*lozh* root which he employs here. [3]

That the Russia-baiter Custine should have voiced similar
sentiments will surprise no one; he speaks of members of all
classes conspiring with miraculous accord to bring about the
triumph of duplicity. 'They have a dexterity in lying, an apti-

tude for the bogus so effective that it affronts my integrity.'
Custine elsewhere denounced Russian mendacity as less than
dexterous; he felt insulted, he said, by the low level of the
deceits practiced on him, considering them 'infantile ruses.'
The same point is also made by Mackenzie Wallace, who
claims that 'When we [foreign visitors] happen to detect positive dishonesty, it seems to us especially heinous, because the
trickery employed is more primitive and awkward than that to
which we are accustomed.' Poor Russians: to be dismissed as
liars—and incompetent liars at that—not merely by the hostile
witness Custine, but also by one of their most sympathetic and
well-informed nineteenth-century observers. The same point
is put in a different way by a twentieth-century Russia-
watcher, Sally Belfrage, who, after noting Russians' 'incredible
lack of artifice' goes on to correct herself with 'or at least hopeless inability to put artifice over.' [4]

Miss Belfrage's perceptive comment conveniently strad-
dles the contrary witness of those quoted immediately above
who emphasize the supreme mendacity of the Russians, and
those whose witness was invoked on an earlier page as stressing their supreme honesty. Claims were there cited to the effect that one always knows where one is when dealing with a
Russian, that Russians exhibit a degree of honesty unparalleled among other nations and so on.[5] One might also have
added, had it not seemed premature before the phenomenon
of *vranyo* had been explained, the frequently voiced obsession
with *pravda* ('truth,' 'justice') on 'seeking' which Russians,
whether peasants or intellectuals, have constantly affirmed
themselves to be engaged, though just what they understand
by this quest is hard to say. Yet to a Russian, according to
Gorer, the gradual discovery and application of the Truth
(*pravda*) is the most significant activity of mankind. 'In the
Russian conception of the universe, their concept of Truth
holds an extremely important place.' [6] And the concept is all
the more vital to the Russian owing to his tendency, rein-

forced by exposure to a dogmatic ideology, to assume that, in any given situation, however complex, there can be only one Truth.

Bearing in mind such testimony, one may consider what inroads can be made in the extravagant claims of those many native and foreign witnesses who have found it practically inconceivable that a Russian should ever open his mouth except to tell a lie. At least it is only in earlier centuries that witnesses to Russian mendacity seem quite so outspoken and unanimous, which suggests that standards of truthfulness have improved over the ages. One must adjust one's aim very slightly, though, owing to the incidence in modern times of the Russia-fancier—the witness who, whenever he makes what might sound a disparaging remark on the country or people, is subject to an automatic urge to correct the balance, and display his own objectivity by some form of words designed to soften the impact of adverse criticism. From this kind of flaccid, mechanical fair-mindedness such robust witnesses as a Jenkinson, a Fletcher, an Olearius, a Custine, a Dostoyevsky, a Mackenzie Wallace and a Chekhov were refreshingly immune, living as they did in those happy eras when no one felt impelled to cultivate a personal image of this kind.

In what other ways can one modify the absurd yet so frequently advanced imputation that all Russians lie all the time? Certainly the incidence of mendacity can be shown to vary according to who is talking to whom, when, about what topic and—perhaps most important of all—in what mood. Owing to the usual emphasis on emotion and relative unconcern with fact, it is in the former area that one is more likely to encounter the kind of trenchant honesty which has impressed so many witnesses in the Russia-favoring camp.

In the nineteenth century, mendacity tended, according to some, to be far more widely cultivated among the privileged than among the unprivileged section of society. Though Nikitenko calls the muzhik 'almost a perfect savage' in his diary, adding that he is also a drunkard and a thief, he then goes on to say that the Russian peasant is 'incomparably superior to the so-called educated and intellectual Russian. The muzhik is sincere. He does not try to seem what he is not. . . . But the educated Russian is bogus through and through.' [7] A contemporary, the influential Russian political *émigré* Alexander Herzen, claims that all familiar with the Russian peasantry, as he himself unfortunately was only in limited degree, would agree that peasants rarely deceive each other; that they have almost unlimited trust in each other 'without need for formal contracts and written conditions.' [8] But where peasant relations with the authorities are concerned Herzen gives a different picture, describing some of the traditional subterfuges employed by the muzhik in the context of his undeclared war against landowners and officials. So does almost anyone else who treats the theme, by no means excluding Soviet-published authors. Sholokhov's collectivized rustics, in his novel *Virgin Soil Upturned*, tend to share the nineteenth-century muzhik's attitude toward authority, defined by Mackenzie Wallace as follows: 'Russian peasants, when dealing with the authorities consider the most patent and barefaced falsehoods as a fair means of self-defence.' It was only when the muzhik came into contact with the authorities that he showed himself an expert fabricator of falsehoods. 'In this there is nothing that need surprise us. For ages the peasantry were exposed to the arbitrary power and ruthless exactions of those who were placed over them; and as the law gave them no means of legally protecting themselves, their only means of self-defence lay in cunning and deceit.' [9]

If ordinary Russians have for centuries lied to their authorities, those authorities have been in no position to complain, owing to the high degree of institutionalized mendacity which they themselves have practiced and which has not been calculated to set a good example to the lower orders.

The regime of Nicholas I has been described as cynical

and seemingly based on the cultivation of a series of massive fictions: there were 'two images of Russian reality—the country as it actually was and as the authorities wished it to appear.' [10] And if 1839 should be compared with 1939 this impression would be much enhanced by the vast array of political fictions and myths in which Stalin's subjects were not necessarily expected to believe, but of which they were required to affirm their acceptance as a form of ritual obeisance. These included the claim that Bolshevik theory is scientifically based; that socialism had been achieved by the late 1930s; that the Soviet people was politically and morally united; that power was in the hands of the workers; and so on. 'By restricting the public utterances of . . . citizens almost solely to reciting parts of the theory and glorifying its creator, Stalin demonstrated the extent to which they were in his power.' [11]

Authority has always been fair game. But so too have foreigners—no doubt because, during so many years of Russian history, the foreigner has often represented or been equated with authority. From the Mongol Khans through the Tatar Tsar Boris Godunov, the German Empress Catherine the Great and the nineteenth-century Tsar-Emperors—increasingly and by the end overwhelmingly German by blood—to the part-German, part-Kalmuck Lenin and the Georgian Stalin, the country has often been ruled at the top by non-Russians endowed with absolute power. They have included some of the bloodiest of the country's many bloody tyrants. Meanwhile the local boss, from general and high official down to bailiff and factory manager, has often been some alien, or someone whom the muzhik considered a foreigner even if he was not. For these reasons foreigners have traditionally activated the self-protective evasive tactics of Russia's lower orders as much as any home-grown authority. This point must be borne in mind when one tries to assess the many alien witnesses who have for centuries furnished an amazingly high proportion of the source materials on the history of a people which long ago learned the unwisdom of volunteering evidence on matters of public interest.

That a foreigner who goes on and on about the truthfulness and sincerity of the Russian has all too often been fed this kind of talk for regurgitation as sort of automatic patter— this has already been noted. No less suspect, it must now be added, is the witness of those foreigners who stress the nation's inevitable unreliability, duplicity and general untruthfulness.

## SEALED LIPS

Ways in which the Russian arguably exposes himself, either excessively or misleadingly, have been scrutinized, and the time has come to examine those no less significant areas in which he assumes the opposite guise of compulsive undercommunicator.

Ever since Muscovy first became accessible to the intruding foreigner, there has been a strong tendency for information about the country to be kept a closely guarded secret, access to which must be denied to foreigners and citizens alike. Little did Ambassador Herberstein suspect this when he arrived in Moscow in April 1516, and naïvely set about seeking and imparting information. He offered, for example, to elucidate certain maps which he had brought with him; but which, as it turned out, aroused the gravest suspicions in his hosts. The result of this imprudence was that observers were quartered in his residence, and that he was permitted to receive visitors only under the eyes of these official scrutineers.[1] Far harsher was the treatment suffered by the learned foreign monk Maxim the Greek. Reaching Muscovy in 1518, only two years after Herberstein's first visit, to conduct a revision of liturgical texts at the invitation of Grand Prince Basil III, the poor man was never permitted to return to his native land despite strenuous attempts, spread over several decades, to secure the sixteenth-century equivalent of an exit visa. He died in a monastery near Moscow in 1556, after the reason for his detention had been made explicit in terms reflecting a dominant streak in his hosts' mentality: 'We are in fear: thou, a man of learning, comest to us and hast seen here of our best and worst, and when thou goest hence *thou wilt tell of everything.*' [2]

Such obsessive secretiveness has persisted throughout the centuries, ebbing or flowing according to the degree of relaxation obtaining at a given period. It was still in evidence when the Scottish scholar William Richardson, a visitor to St. Petersburg in the 1760s, lamented that he could obtain no information from the newspapers: 'Half of Russia may be destroyed and the other half know nothing about the matter.' Similarly, Mme. de Staël complained, when in Russia as a refugee from Napoleon in 1812, that she could discover nothing about the course of the Russo-French War.[3] And yet, little as foreigners may have been permitted to learn about the country, they have often enjoyed more privileged access to information than that conceded to nationals: 'No native could have been given the chance of visiting the prisons, hospitals, transport columns and barges that George Kennan was given, nor of holding conversations with political prisoners, even with police and governors.' [4] The reference is to the American journalist George Kennan, who toured Siberia's penal establishments in the 1880s, and whose description of them in his *Siberia and the Exile System* is an important historical source. The comment remains valid, even though it seems slightly exaggerated when

one remembers the by-no-means-niggardly facilities afforded
to that native student of Russian penology, Anton Chekhov,
when he visited the convict settlement on the Island of Sakha-
lin shortly afterwards. As this reminds one, the later decades
of the Empire, including even the notoriously reactionary
reign of Alexander III, were not one of those periods when
the flow of information was most rigorously restricted.

The general clamp-down on information has tended to
involve trivial and individual issues as well as matters more
portentous. For example, no accident or suicide statistics were
published in early nineteenth-century Russia. It was then possible for several hundred—or could it be thousand?—people
to perish in small boats in one particular storm in the Gulf of
Finland without the matter even being mentioned in the newspapers of nearby St. Petersburg, and also without the gaiety of
court celebrations being in the least affected. No one, indeed,
could be induced to talk of it at all.[5] Similarly, in the totalitarian period, such disasters as airplane crashes in which no foreigner is involved, and which can therefore more easily be
hushed up; the Tashkent earthquake of 1966; a forest fire in
the Vladimir area, followed by a local potato famine in
1972—all have been ignored by the media, and have only
come to notice long after the event.[6] And on the occasion of
Hitler's mass onslaught on the USSR on 22 June 1941, 'While
German planes and tanks were screaming into action in the
forenoon . . . Radio Moscow blandly ignored these irrele-
vancies for several hours—continuing to broadcast a routine
programme on physical training, and cataloguing the
"achievements" of Soviet workers in normal peacetime style.' [7]

For obvious reasons the pretense that Hitler's invasion
was not in the process of occurring could not, in June 1941,
long be sustained. But many another momentous event of the
past has been put into the cold storage of compulsory oblivion.
After Ivan the Terrible's private Mafia, the *oprichnina*, had
been wound up in 1572, the very mention of that defunct

body was forbidden on pain of death. Similarly, the assassination of the Emperor Paul, in 1801, was still officially a non-event forty years later; no reference to it might be made in public, and passers-by would avert their eyes as they hurried past the scene of the murder, the Mikhaylovsky Palace in St. Petersburg.[8] Another notable non-event was the Decembrist Rising which followed the death of Alexander I in 1825; all mention of it was forbidden throughout the thirty-year reign of the new monarch, Nicholas I, the executed and imprisoned rebels being relegated to the category of unpersons. Similarly, to take an eloquent example from the many suppressions of more recent years, it was possible for Stalin to deport an entire small nation of 200,000 persons—the Meskhetians—without this ever being officially admitted—indeed, without even the bare fact becoming known to the world at large for more than twenty years.[9] As for unpersons from Trotsky downward, recent history is littered with them. Trotsky himself, though second only to Lenin as the initiator of the October Revolution of 1917, is regularly denied an entry in Soviet encyclopedias published since his disgrace, though the abstract noun *Trotskyism* does tend to rate a heading.

A vivid monument to such liquidated or demoted phantoms could once, and for all I know still may, be observed in the colossal mosaics embellishing the roof of the Komsomol Square Station of the Moscow Metro. One of these panoramas depicted a notable scene of 1945, the surrender of captured German banners with their swastika emblems before a line of political dignitaries headed by Stalin. But of nine Politburo members portrayed, only three were still recognizable when I last visited the shrine in 1960. Six of them had suffered the whitewashing of their facial features, of which only the ghostly outline remained. There one could behold the spectral images of Beria, Molotov, Kaganovich and others who had incurred disgrace since Stalin's death—as indeed had Stalin himself in part, but without ever achieving unperson status. Just how durable an institution unpersonship is one may be reminded by the nineteenth-century comment, that 'in Russia, on the day that a minister falls from favour, his friends become deaf and blind. No one dares to remember that he is living, nor even to believe that he ever lived. A man is as it were buried the moment he appears to be disgraced.' [10]

Comparable elusiveness is found in the area of historical record, where one is, so to speak, repeatedly treading on a step which isn't there. In the first place, 'Most of the fundamental laws affecting Russia's system of government and the status of its citizens were never at all promulgated in any formal way.' These have included such basic institutions as the attachment of peasants to the soil and of urban inhabitants to the cities (serfdom), which had existed for more than two centuries before the emancipation act of 1861; the associated authority of landlords over peasants; the introduction of Ivan the Terrible's *oprichnina;* the system of automatic promotion by seniority within the civil service; the foundation of the first centralized political police organ, the Preobrazhensky Prikaz, under Peter the Great.[11] And, secondly, one may contrast with these institutions—existing *de facto* but apparently not *de jure*— the later, no less elusive, phenomenon of institutions which have existed *de jure* but not *de facto*. The most prominent of these has been the Stalin Constitution of 1937, whereby the population was guaranteed widespread civil rights which, far from being assertable in practice, were flagrantly contravened through mass arrests, torture and widespread relegation to concentration camps without due process of law. Bukharin, the main framer of this document, was himself framed and judicially murdered by show trial before the eyes of the world when the ink was barely dry on his signature to the draft constitution.

In this context of things turning out not what they might seem, it is no surprise to find a marked degree of dubiety in the area of Russian historical and literary documents. The greatest monument of Russian medieval literature, *The Lay of Igor's Raid,* commemorates a minor skirmish of the year 1185 in language admittedly memorable, but of what date? Is this oft-acclaimed work of genius a near-contemporary poem, and in an idiom of which no other specimen happens to survive, as patriotic Russian scholarship maintains? Or is the *Lay,* as some have maintained, an eighteenth-century forgery based on a fifteenth-century document, the *Zadonshchina?* Or was the *Zadonshchina* cribbed from the *Lay?* This is no place to offer solutions to a problem which has perplexed specialists for well over a century. Whatever the truth may be, the fact is that the document's authenticity is rejected by a number of reputable scholars. Its first publishers pointed with unconscious irony to the 'Ossianic Spirit' of the work, not realizing that the semi-mythical Gaelic bard Ossian was hardly even an unperson—a reminder that such episodes are no Russian monopoly.

Another historical document to fall under suspicion, and that only very recently, is the celebrated, purportedly sixteenth-century correspondence between Ivan the Terrible and a renegade nobleman, Prince Andrew Kurbsky. Long accepted as one of the most valuable and informative medieval Russian sources, extensively quarried for the light which it sheds or seems to shed on a vital epoch in Russian history and on a maniac ruler of fascinating psychological make-up, it is now claimed by Edward L. Keenan to be a concoction of the following century. His conclusions, though strenuously contested, have placed the Ivan-Kurbsky correspondence under suspicion which later researches may—but, given the elusiveness of matters Russian, very likely will not—decisively confirm or refute. Whatever the outcome of the debate, the fact remains that 'In the sixteenth and seventeenth centuries, forgery was used with the definite aim of improving a pedigree, giving an improved title to land ownership, and in political controversy.[12]

Dubiety of a different order attaches itself to an important document of the present century, the famous 'secret speech' delivered or not delivered by Nikita Khrushchev to a closed session of the Supreme Soviet of the USSR on 25 February 1956. It first became available in an English translation issued, without attribution of source, by the American State Department in the same year. Though official USSR sources have neither confirmed nor rejected the authenticity of this long pronouncement—the most important in the complex history of de-Stalinization—Western scholars have displayed more collective assurance of its genuineness than the more suspect *Lay of Igor's Raid,* and even the Ivan-Kurbsky correspondence, now enjoy. Still, authentic though the 'secret speech' surely is, its status as a historical document remains elusive in view of the failure of the authorities in the country of origin either to confirm or to disavow so widely disseminated a statement by their leading politician of the time. Khrushchev's name was to figure again when, in 1971, the first, huge, installment of his alleged 'memoirs' was sprung on the world by an American publisher without proper explanation of where they came from and with a great flurry of purported authentication which carried little conviction at the time. Could these seemingly senile babblings, by no means inconsistent in tone with what is known of their alleged author's character, indeed be his *ipsissima verba?* It was hard to decide. However, after the publication, in 1974, of a further massive installment of the mixture as before, at least one serious scholar has proclaimed the authenticity of the two-tier effusion as 'established beyond reasonable doubt.' He also adds that its 'value as a historical source remain[s] disappointing.' [13] The reason is, of course, that the Khrushchev material is too saturated with *vranyo* to be taken as evidence of much beyond its spouter's psychological condition.

To all this may be added another notable Russian twentieth-century document. The best-known novel of the Soviet period, Michael Sholokhov's *Quiet Don*, has been proclaimed in part a plagiaristic work filched from the writings of an obscure White memoirist of the Civil War. Whether the accusation may stand or not again remains obscure; one of its leading sponsors is another prominent writer of the Soviet period, Alexander Solzhenitsyn, whose opinions must command considerable respect.

All this is rather as if *Beowulf*, Magna Carta, the Gettysburg Address and President Eisenhower's memoirs should suddenly dissolve and enter a limbo in which their authenticity could no longer be established—nor yet impugned—while large parts of Hemingway's *For Whom the Bell Tolls* were suddenly revealed as possibly, but also very possibly not, lifted from the writings of some obscure war correspondent whose papers (if they ever existed) disappeared during the siege of Madrid. So much for certain literary and historical records. But what of non-records? The papers of Michael Speransky, perhaps the most gifted statesman and administrator of Russia's imperial period, who died in 1839, waited until the year 1961 to be published—an astonishing tribute to the security-mindedness of Tsarist and post-Tsarist Russia alike. It is also a reminder that Speransky himself had become, back in 1812, the victim of one of those sudden, volte-face disgraces which have characterized both major Russian regimes—when he left the Emperor Alexander I after a friendly chat, only to be arrested and taken straight off to Siberian exile while the monarch's affable words were still ringing in his ears.[14] True, Speransky was reinstated under Nicholas I, but there is something curiously enduring about Russian political disgrace, even when it has been nominally rescinded. Moreover, this gap of 122 years, not to mention three revolutions, between the man's death and the publication of his papers, prompts one to wonder how many other key documents may be moldering unread in the archives—documents touching perhaps on such bizarre episodes as the death of the uncooperative Tsarevich Alexis in 1718, knouted or not knouted out of this life on the orders of his father Peter the Great.

To speak of secrecy is to be reminded of censorship, that archetypally Russian institution with a history too complex to permit more than a few fleeting observations on its general character. In Nicholas I's reign Alexander Nikitenko, himself a censor, reckoned that the number of officials engaged in censoring books exceeded the number of books published in a year.[15] But these were comparatively easy times for the censored, compared with the situation a century later. A former Soviet editor now domiciled in the West, Leonid Vladimirov, has reckoned the total of censorship officials in recent times at seventy thousand. He also speaks of a three-hundred-page index of banned subjects, colloquially known as 'the Talmud,' with the aid of which the broadcast and printed word is kept free of reference, not only to such natural disasters as the above-mentioned Tashkent earthquake, but also to food shortages, price increases, the names of KGB operatives other than the head of that institution, the earnings of Party and government officials and also—not surprisingly—the very institution of censorship itself.[16]

Nor is such secrecy confined to domestic affairs. For example, the American Watergate scandal of 1973–74 was for a long time concealed by the Russian publicity media. Yet, in reflecting discredit on the United States, the traditional major target for hostile propaganda, the affair might have seemed one over which Russian publicists would have been allowed to lick their lips. Two considerations were probably operating here. As a sponsor of that modern form of appeasement misnamed *détente*, President Nixon was, in official Soviet eyes, one of the 'good guys.' Therefore his reputation must be bolstered as long as possible. And, secondly, if a figure as august as an American president could fall into disrepute, might not the sacred concept of authority in general—domestic as well as foreign—become devalued?

Foreigners have occasionally been enlisted in Soviet censorship or cover-up operations. As a subscriber to the Soviet Great Encyclopedia in the early 1950s, I recall being issued with a special page, largely devoted to supplementary material with which the entry 'Beria' in Volume 5 (1949) was to be replaced. The point here was that Beria, still honored in 1949, had since suffered execution and the imposition of unperson status, a grave embarrassment to librarians and archivists. Subscribers were accordingly instructed to gut the page containing the entry Beria 'with scissors or a razor blade, while preserving the margin near the binding.' To fill the generous space formerly allotted to the then in-person Beria, a diarist, Friedrich Berkholz, was rescued from perhaps unmerited oblivion, together with several pictures of dead whales and walruses as snapped in the no less alphabetically convenient Bering Sea. Here is the kind of topic with which the satirist Saltykov had been filling his writings nearly a century earlier. There is, too, more than a whiff of Gogol about the affair.[17]

Sounding such shoals of information—highly restricted at source, now filtered out, now suddenly withdrawn or disavowed—foreign Kremlin-watchers have long ago learned to gauge the hidden undertows of Soviet politics through analysis of such seeming trivialities as *Pravda*'s typographical house rules. Was Nikita Khrushchev properly described as a first secretary, a First secretary or a First Secretary of the Communist Party of the Soviet Union?[18] The man's influence could be seen waxing and waning as the honorific capitals came and went; and the tracking of such signals is even more vital to native officials (whose careers and livelihood can depend on them) than to foreign commentators.

It is in this context of official secretiveness that Russian imaginative literature has acquired its special status as a source of insights not otherwise obtainable into Russian life. The point has been made many times: for instance, in an English review, dated 14 September 1878, of Turgenev's novel *Virgin Soil*. Commenting on the difficulty of obtaining information on Russia's internal condition, the reviewer, Richard Littledale, wrote that 'It is only books like the present that enable outsiders to guess at it with any approach to correctness.' [19] The same point has been made for a later era by the economist Alec Nove. Noting the difficulty of obtaining information on agriculture in the Soviet period, he adds that 'the best material about the village appears in the literary monthlies.' [20] Often enough, then, one is compelled to treat imaginative writing as a historical source simply because all other evidence is so unsatisfactory. Once more, though, let it not be supposed that Russia is unique in this respect, for reference to the eminent Egyptologist Sir Alan Gardiner suggests a close parallel several thousand years ago in the land of the Pharaohs. 'If we ask where our best historical material is to be found our answer may seem to be almost a contradiction in terms; it is to be found in Egyptian fiction, where the authors were able to depict existing conditions and to vent their feelings with a freedom impossible when the predominant intention was that of boasting.' [21]

It is such considerations which have led to Russian history being described as part of the 'crown domain,' and as 'a state secret, one closely but by no means efficiently guarded.' [22]

# ❧ III ❧

# GROUP CONSCIOUSNESS

## *TOGETHERNESS*

After reviewing Russians as communicators the argument now focuses on their collective responses to various aspects of the world outside and inside their own country. These will include the wider affiliations of religion, political party, nationality and class, and also the intimate world of domestic, family and sexual relations. First, however, the Russian's general characteristics as a social being must be considered. Is he, as often claimed, the most gregarious of humans, is he endowed with a special gift for communion with his fellows? Or is he the opposite: a creature unusually ill-adapted for cooperation?

To find competent observers, Russian and foreign, making extreme claims on both sides is to be expected. 'The communal spirit is the basis, the foundation of all Russian history, past, present and future. The seed and the root of everything that appears on the surface lies buried in its fertile depths': thus the leading Slavophile Yury Samarin, in 1847.[1] But such sentiments are by no means confined to nineteenth-century pundits. Many are those who, like Klaus Mehnert, have since pointed out the special pleasure which the average Russian derives from the company of his fellows, even without the help of alcohol, and who have linked this sociability with the pre-revolutionary village commune, the *mir,* as also with the proliferation of various 'collectives' under communism.[2] Nor is it unusual to find Russians described as thinking themselves all members of one vast family. They 'do not seem to feel that enforced close company is [a] . . . threat to individual identity . . . the lack of physical elbow-room does not mean a lack of elbow-room for the spirit.' When a factory inspector visited a certain Russian sugar factory in 1903 he found the workers living in vast dormitories, and insisted that partitions should be put up so that each individual could enjoy some privacy in a small cubicle of his own. But this was not at all what they wanted. 'Are we cattle that we should be thus cooped in stalls?'[3]

A love of togetherness can be traced in many aspects of Russian life, and nowhere more than in the previously invoked *mir* or village commune. The institution consisted of an assemblage of heads of village households, meeting in an informal spirit and usually in the open air; and legally required, not merely empowered, from 1861 onward to take certain decisions regarding military recruitment, taxation and public order. But, informal though the atmosphere generally was, the *mir*'s discussions invariably ended, owing to some special ingredient in the Russian genius, in unanimous decisions: 'Peasants do not understand decisions by majority vote.' All members of the *mir* were required to engage on a united search for a true and just solution to their problems, and anyone unable to accept the consensus had no recourse but to leave his village and cut himself off from it. Similarly, in more modern times, a member of the Komsomol remarks, 'I say "my generation" all the time and not "I" because we never thought of ourselves individually, but always as a whole group.'[4] The compulsory unanimity of the *mir*'s decisions has been transferred to the totalitarian electoral system, but with the slight relaxation that a majority of, say, 99.23 percent is considered acceptable instead of the 100 percent conformity which stricter national tradition would demand.

In more violent contexts too the Russians have been credited with a marked tendency to react collectively. Gorky goes out of his way to identify the exceptional cruelty, in his view, of the Russian muzhik as a communal sport; he speaks of the peasantry enjoying the infliction of torture on a collective basis. Even in his atrocities, according to this witness, the Russian cleaves to his traditional togetherness.[5]

By many analysts the spirit of secular collectivism has been linked with the special communal spirit known as *sobornost,* 'community-mindedness,' often claimed as unique to the Russian Orthodox Church. One modern Russia-watcher speaks of the spirit of Orthodox Christianity combining with that of the *mir* to create in Russians a conviction that, in the common sharing of an experience—divine in Church worship, man-made in Communist achievement—'they preserve a truer humanity than a Westerner can partake of in his over-cultivation of the individual.'[6] Here once again is a modern, foreign authority echoing Slavophile doctrine of the nineteenth century. In this view the whole of Western culture has been corrupted by excessive rationalism deriving from the influence of classical Greece and Rome, while the Russian Orthodox Church owes its superiority to collective wisdom transcending that of any individual, however wise.

This special religious togetherness received eloquent expression in Dostoyevsky's voluminous polemical writings. An extreme traditionalist both in religion and politics, and one who liked to unite these two elements in his many impassioned harangues, he spoke of the 'spiritual indivisibility of the millions of our people, and their closest communion with the Monarch.'[7] During the Stalin period and thereafter such spiritual indivisibility has been expressed or simulated, not only by the officially rigged near-unanimous elections to which reference was made above, but also in endless pre-scripted political meetings or pageants at which the dragooned congregation is periodically induced to rise to its collective feet uttering tumultuous applause. When a twelve-sided phonograph recording of one of Stalin's speeches was issued, the whole of the last side was given over to the clapping and cheering which concluded the performance. A similar manifestation is reported in Solzhenitsyn's *Gulag Archipelago,* where a regional Party conference is found applauding a motion of loyalty to Stalin over a period of five minutes. They seem doomed to continue forever, since no one dares incur the charge of disloyalty by being seen to desist first. In the end, though, the director of a certain paper factory takes the initiative and sits down firmly, whereupon total silence follows. But the factory director is arrested that same night.[8]

Such collective responses are strikingly 'Russian,' and one could go on quoting them forever. But that would be to conceal another, less obtrusive feature: anti-collectivism. One modern observer bases his analysis not so much on the people's unique togetherness as on the tension between their admittedly strong centripetal urges and other—less obtruded but no less significant—centrifugal drives: 'the painful conflict between collectivism and self-assertion that the dualistic response to life was expressly designed to avoid.'[9] Looking back into history, this observer finds an even balance between the collective pull of the Church, which urged the peasants to sink their differences in common submission to God, and the individual pull of peasant behavior.

To accept, as is not unreasonable, Russian claims to be animated by a uniquely corporate spirit might naturally be to expect that this spirit would be expressed in some equally outstanding capacity for corporate action. In fact, though, the opposite seems to be the case. It is, for example, the relatively individualistic British who are able to sink their differences and combine to create that triumph of modern civilization, an orderly queue. To see the doors of a Moscow underground train stormed with much self-defeating shoving and fighting is to marvel at the Russian's capacity for collective counter-functional behavior. It is also to wonder at the good humor commonly preserved on these occasions, when no one seems to take offense at the odd fist in the ribs—perhaps because, as one witness puts it, they feel it to be the crowd which pushes rather than the individuals of which the crowd is composed.[10] Nor are these conflicts confined to the hectic metropolis. Even a judo Black Belt might hesitate before trying to catch a bus in Vladimir or Smolensk.

All Russian enterprises, great and small, tend to fall foul of this inability to cooperate. 'When three or four of us Russians gather together to promote some idea or common cause you may absolutely depend on it that we'll quarrel, play each other scurvy tricks and split up by day two or three.' Making this point, Nikitenko sagely adds that 'Our only salvation lies in the intervention of authority.' [11] In other words, though Russians may *feel* themselves at one with each other to an extent unusual among peoples, they yet seem exceptionally ill adapted for effective corporate *action* unless they can, in effect, sense a gun or a lash somewhere in the not-too-distant background.

Many impressive prestige projects, as discussed above—a St. Petersburg, a White Sea Canal, a Moscow Metro—were the work of conscripted or convict labor. One may therefore understand how, despite so many remarkable collective achievements effected under compulsion, it is yet possible for a well-informed observer to deny outright that the country possesses any corporate spirit.[12] Its corporate institutions, too, have tended to prove impotent except when used as channels for imposing control from above. Of the various pre-revolutionary social estates—gentry, clergy, artisans, peasants—only the clergy possessed a national organization, and that was headed by a lay government appointee: the Procurator of the Holy Synod, in effect a Minister for Religion. And though the totalitarian period has seen the establishment of numerous nominally autonomous collective associations, the taking of corporate initiative seems virtually ruled out by the technique of intermeshing them with Party and security bodies briefed from on high. An authority on the Soviet professional classes is not exaggerating, then, when he claims that 'Professional associations in the narrow sense of the term . . . are relatively unimportant in the Soviet Union.'[13] Many professions completely lack any national corporate association: lawyers, doctors, engineers, for example. One of the most active and politically important, the Soviet Writers' Union, remains essentially a docile instrument of the state. Yet it can acquire considerable significance on the not infrequent occasions when minor rifts are reported as occurring inside it: a sign, usually, of the temporary relaxation of official controls.

Togetherness thus turns out no less elusive than other aspects of the Russian mind. Tempted though one may be to make much of the ability to dispense with privacy (a privilege which many a Western citizen may regard as almost as important as the air he breathes), and encouraging though it may be to build inferences on the lack of any word for 'privacy' in their language, the fact yet remains that Russians do prize this privilege—and more, not less, than does many a philosopher of the subject. One may praise the Russians' ability to huddle together happily in communal flats and communal kitchens, and no doubt they do make the most of these disamenities. But there can be no doubt whatever that most of them vastly prefer, constantly seek and sometimes achieve a place of their own. To find foreign Russia-fanciers drooling from a safe distance over the communal cooking stove as an embodiment of the principles of *sobornost* and the village commune—this must be utterly sickening to such few Russians as are not mercifully unaware of the activities of these well-meaning patrons. The average Russian does not put up with queuing for use of the gas ring out of a talent for spiritual oneness with humanity.

He does so because he has no choice. He tends, moreover, to develop special skills in cultivating seclusion, living as he does in an ambience where every man tends to assume, and is officially encouraged to assume, that his neighbor's business is his own. A private Russian may, perforce, be comparatively rare; but he tends to be a very private person indeed.

As for the apparent conflict between the Russian corporate spirit and Russian corporate ineffectiveness, except under compulsion by all-powerful authority—at least the seeming contradiction helps to explain a difference of opinion over the interpretation of something as controversial as Chekhov's drama. I have always been impressed, along with many others, by the primacy of 'failure to communicate' as a Chekhovian theme. One may instance, for example, the refusal of his *Cherry Orchard*'s feckless owners to take notice, or even to listen, when the self-made man of action Lopakhin explains that their ancestral home will be auctioned around their heads unless they immediately adopt certain specific measures. Here is an absence of communication as complete as can be conceived—but only on the mundane level of information, common sense and practical affairs. For the fact is that Lopakhin and his feckless friends are as closely attuned as possible *on an emotional level*, as any sensitive production of the play must show. Communication is nil, but sympathy total, since Chekhov creates between his characters an 'interplay of emotion' or electrical field which transcends their many disagreements on practicalities.[14]

## SUPRANATIONALIST

No account of Russian collective responses can be complete unless it takes in the nation's relations to two supranational organizations, both of which make sweeping or absolute claims in the sphere of ideology, and neither of which possesses a unified global organization. These are the Christian Church and the world Communist movement. Each has played, each still is playing, a key role in the development of the Russian mentality.

Brief reference has already been made to the special place which Russia's religious evolution has given it in the history of Europe.

At the end of the tenth century the Russians began to adopt the Eastern form of Christianity, and thus joined a loose international religious community which became formally separated from the Western Church in 1054. It lacked any single center comparable to Rome, consisting of a group of autocephalous churches, of which the Russian Orthodox Communion based in Moscow became the most influential and extensive with the fall of Constantinople to the Turks in 1453. Under the already disappearing Tatar yoke, the Russian Church had enjoyed a marked degree of tolerance, including freedom from taxation, and had contributed much to the salvaging or creation of national unity and consciousness under alien oppression.

After the assertion of national independence the Church became an enthusiastic ally of Moscow's Grand Princes, soon entitled Tsars with full ecclesiastical blessing and encouragement. The Church promoted national self-admiration by sponsoring a campaign claiming Moscow as the Third Rome, but no effective attempt was—or, probably, could have been—made to assert ecclesiastical independence of a secular power itself not answerable to any extra-territorial clerical authority.

So it continued throughout the ages. In the sixteenth century Ivan the Terrible had a Metropolitan of Moscow and two Archbishops of Novgorod murdered by his minions. In 1589, during the next reign, the Regent Boris Godunov sought the Church's favor by securing the promotion of the sitting Metropolitan of Moscow to the highest Eastern ecclesiastical rank of all, hitherto held only outside Russia: that of Patriarch. One good turn deserves another, and seven years later the Patriarch Job is found successfully urging the feignedly reluctant Regent to assume the rank of Tsar. But the Patriarchate was to last little over a century. Peter the Great allowed it to lapse in 1700 (it was to be revived in wholly subservient form in the totalitarian period), replacing it by a corporate body, the Holy Synod. Thus casually, not even by a stroke of a pen, could a domineering sovereign overthrow the Church's constitution. And even a weak emperor, Peter the Great's grandson Peter III, contrived the seemingly portentous feat of sequestrating the Church's land during his six-month reign (1761–62)—again without evoking significant ecclesiastical protests.

The only notable believers' mutiny arose from concern with the minutiae of ritual and liturgy, matters always prominent in the preoccupations of the Orthodox. It was the state-supported decision of an unusually forceful seventeenth-century Patriarch, Nikon, to impose versions of the Russian liturgical texts as revised by comparison with the Greek originals, which sparked off a revolt among those whose devotion to the letter of scriptural law was so profound that they were prepared, nay eager, to sacrifice their lives in the interests of certain disputed—and false!—textual readings. Just what the mass suicides of some twenty thousand of these persecuted Old Believers, often by burning themselves in their own churches, teaches about the Russian character is difficult to specify; but a passionate dislike of the intrusion of rationality into the domain spiritual is surely a significant factor.

Despite their earlier habit of self-immolation, Russia's Old Believers have flourished and proliferated in their various forms, and are by no means extinguished to this day. But the body from which they split off, the Russian Orthodox Church, was little more than a department of state during the Empire's last two centuries. It was centrally administered from St. Petersburg by a layman, the Procurator of the Holy Synod. And its priests maintained an attitude so lacking in independence that they often seemed like another—befrocked, rather than uniformed—variety of *chinovnik,* or official. Many sank to denouncing the political misdemeanors of their flocks to the authorities. Nor, as has already been indicated, did the typical Russian village cleric inspire his parishioners with the respect which a German pastor or English rector could command. Notoriously fond of their vodka, priests were not only the butts of the equally tipsy squirearchy, but were also mocked by the not-always-sober peasantry, being traduced in dozens of homely and traditional proverbs, and tending to be valued solely for the ritual functions which they alone could perform, especially conducting services and administering the sacraments of baptism, marriage and burial.

To argue from the dependence of the Russian Church on the state, or from the lowly status of the village priest, that the Russians set little store by their religion would be misleading. At the lowest level the muzhik found his dull, hard, featureless everyday life vastly enriched by the candles, the icons, the iconostases, the antique liturgy, the vestments, the onion domes, the music of his church services—all features which might have been expressly designed to provide psychological relief from the drabness of his environment. Religion was thus, to the average pre-revolutionary villager, an element without which life was barely thinkable. It was also indissolubly fused with the idea of Russianness. A peasant would ask a stranger if he was Orthodox, meaning 'Are you a Russian?' And, as has often been remarked, there is symbolic significance in the fact that the word for 'peasant' and the word for 'Christian' are etymologically identical (*krestyanin, khristiyanin*).

Thus was the pre-revolutionary peasant's life seemingly governed at every turn, if only in externals, by his Church. He dutifully abstained from various forms of food and drink on every Wednesday and Friday, also keeping Lent and the many other extended and taxing fasts of the Orthodox calendar. He celebrated Christmas, and above all Easter, in a manner so memorable that many an unbeliever could take an enthusiastic part in such ecclesiastical ceremonies; they might mean nothing to him in a religious sense, yet remained a familiar and beloved feature of his annual routine.

That the externals of Russian religion held great significance, and for the uneducated Russian in particular, is common ground. Where observers differ is on the degree of true spirituality underlying the many religious practices of the people. One school of thought, which included the nineteenth-century Slavophiles and has since spilled over into the accounts of foreign Russia-fanciers, makes extravagant claims in this area. Dostoyevsky, whose assertions were perhaps the most extravagant of all, believed in a phenomenon termed the Russian Christ, about whom he provided no precise information beyond asserting his measureless superiority over any non-Russian Christ. A special Russian mission to pronounce a mysterious so-called New Word supposedly destined to bring about a spiritual regeneration of humanity at large—that too was a prominent feature of Dostoyevsky's teaching; and the—never spoken—New Word was apt to be linked with that other no less baffling national activity, the so-called Quest for Truth. Nor, seemingly, has humanity heard the last of such claims. For instance, the dissident author Valery Tarsis, who left the Soviet Union in 1966, has since incorporated dithyrambs to the suffering Russian soul in his book *Russia and the Russians*. Discounting Communist assertions to the contrary, he claims that his fellow-countrymen are still uniquely religious, even if they are themselves no longer aware of the intense devotion to the Orthodox Church which pulsates inside them. In the end, he grotesquely prophesies, their collective farms will be transformed into monasteries for the masses.[1]

That the average present-day Russian is more truly religious than the average non-Russian, is a thesis difficult to sustain. But what of his past? Has he ever, at any time, been the uniquely spiritual creature of Dostoyevsky's and Tarsis's harangues? Or was religion to him more a matter of superstition, mumbo-jumbo and magical incantation? These are matters so imponderable that one again marvels at the confidence with which so many observers have pronounced on them. Moreover, those who contradict the thesis ascribing a special degree of spirituality to the Russians are at least as strident in their assertions as are their opponents. It was on this point that the radical literary critic Belinsky took issue with the fiction-writing religious fanatic Gogol, writing to him in 1847 a famous open letter—one of the most remarkable of Russia's nineteenth-century cultural documents. Gogol's thesis that the Russians are the most religious people in the world was a downright lie, according to Belinsky. The Russians were, on the contrary, by nature a profoundly atheistic people. They still retained a good deal of superstition, but not a trace of true religious faith. As for Russia's priests, their distinguishing marks were their fat bellies, their barbarous ignorance and their total indifference to matters of faith.[2]

A similar argument was put forward nearly a century later by Gorky, who at least did offer evidence of a sort—a rare thing indeed among pronouncements on Russian religion. According to him, the Revolution convincingly laid bare the absence of any deep religious faith in the Russian village. The point was not so much that the peasant permitted theaters and clubs to be set up in his village church, which he did, but that he did not even protest against the desecration of such revered shrines as the Kiev-Pechersky Monastery and that of the Trinity and St. Sergius. These former objects of reverence seemed to have lost their magic overnight. But when it came to the stocks of grain which so many peasants were secretly hoarding, and which were badly needed to feed starving Moscow and St. Petersburg, the same peasants had been prepared to do what they would never do for their saints, relics and shrines: go out gun in hand and beat off assailants and requisitioners.[3]

Religious life has changed almost more than any other aspect of existence since the revolutions. Militantly atheist in its philosophy and militant in exacting affirmations of faith in the new secular creed from most of those who wish to make a career within the new structure, the new state has persecuted religion on a persistent but fluctuating basis over a period of six decades. These efforts have, despite Tarsis's claim to the contrary, reinforced a decline in religion which (since it is general in the modern world) would surely have taken place in Russia without the benefit of governmental persecution. Even at its worst, however—even with the closing of churches, the execution or incarceration of priests and believers, the infiltration of the priesthood with pseudo-priests and the recruitment of priests as police agents—the government has stopped well short of the systematic massacre of the devout. While successfully subverting or terrorizing the lukewarm into apostatizing, these efforts have only reinforced the faith of the faithful—whose numbers, though dwindling and in any case incomputable, still remain substantial. In the dissident movement of the 1970s, Russian Christians occupy a prominent place. They still have their martyrs. And church-going, though practiced most sedulously by grandmothers and their infant charges, is by no means confined to such. Among the congregations of the Orthodox, as also of the Baptists—a particularly flourishing denomination which seems to attract a higher proportion of the young and able-bodied—even an unbeliever may sense, or feel that he senses, a vibrant religious fervor such as he may never have observed before. In such a context it becomes easy to understand how the mid-nineteenth-century canon H. P. Liddon could assert, after a visit to Russia in 1867, that 'The sense of God's presence—of the supernatural—seems to me to penetrate Russian life more completely than that of any of the Western nations.' [4] And if that could be so even when the Church was protected by the state, how much the more so is it now when the faithful have, as it were, nothing but their faith to support them.

How far can the officially imposed Marxist-Leninist creed be accurately described as a new, secular religion which has supplanted the old? One can have an amusing game playing with a set of paradoxical comparisons. Like some canting priest, Stalin intoned over the newly dead Lenin's body, in 1924, a repetitive litany couched in the Old Church Slavonic which the speaker had learned as a highly unsatisfactory pupil of the Tiflis Orthodox Seminary. He then had Lenin's body embalmed and placed on show in Moscow's Red Square for the benefit of pilgrims. Himself mummified and exhibited beside Lenin from 1953, he was—in accordance with the rhythm of the *skandal*—semi-disgraced, de-mummified and interred in comparative obscurity eight years later. Meanwhile the practice of carrying Lenin's and other leaders' huge portraits in procession—like *khorugvi* (church banners)—has persisted. One may even read placards asserting the actual and coming reincarnation of Russian communism's premier messiah: LENIN LIVED, LIVES AND SHALL LIVE. And icons or graven images of the various leaders are prominently displayed in offices and public places. Like the now persecuted Orthodox Church, the new dispensation claims to be 'the executor of a species of [Marxist] scriptural revelation.' It has evolved its own devils, martyrs and angels, 'surrounding itself with a largely similar iconography, even down to the mummification of saints, and distinguished from its predecessor primarily by its concentration on the material aspects of existence here below, by its attempt to remove from the next world to this both the promise of heaven and the reality of hell.' [5]

From the Orthodox Church the Communist Party differs by exacting from its members repeated and positive affirmations of faith in the Marxist-Leninist creed, as also in the various successive and overlapping campaigns, political and economic, which are constantly and stridently promoted. It is also an élitist minority organization which subjects the applications of would-be members to the strictest examination and to probationary scrutiny. How far this is from the purely nominal allegiance required of the Orthodox Christian. Of nineteenth-century Russian Christianity it has been said that 'So long as a member refrains from openly attacking the Church and from passing over to another confession, he may entirely neglect all religious ordinances and publicly profess scientific theories logically inconsistent with any kind of religious belief, without the slightest danger of incurring ecclesiastical censure.' [6] But now, after the dethronement of religion, the new dispensation extends no comparable degree of tolerance in the opposite direction.

Despite the obligation to offer repeated affirmations of faith in the Marxist-Leninist creed and its varying ramifications, one rarely seems to detect, on personal contact with the new faithful, the presence of any profound underlying conviction. Such affirmations are among the formal, routine requirements of a man's career: to be soberly discharged without revealing the inner cynicism which one sometimes seems to sense behind them. But this is, after all, only to be expected from a political creed which has received established status, and to a far greater extent than most established religions. For more obvious signs of Communist political fervor one has to seek among the sometimes persecuted minorities in non-Com-

munist countries, just as one appears to detect the truest religious zeal among the persecuted faithful in the Communist
world.

## WORLD CITIZEN

Concern with ultimate profundities, whether religious or
political, has not prevented the Russian from taking a lively interest in mundane affairs, not least those of other countries
and peoples, and it is in his attitudes as citizen of the world
that he now comes up for scrutiny.

Remembering the care which Russian governments have
taken throughout the ages to guard their frontiers, and to seg-
regate their citizens from contact with the polluting alien, one
is amazed at the degree to which the country's evolution has
nevertheless been intimately intertwined with that of the non-
Russian world. It was largely as a by-product of the trading activities of other peoples, Viking and Greek, that the Kievan
state first came into being; and Kiev's international relations—
dynastic, diplomatic, commercial—remained fairly extensive.
In the next major phase of Russian history, that of the Tatar
yoke, a severe quarantine was imposed on foreign contacts,
except of course that the Tatar himself *was* a foreign contact,
however unwelcome, and remained one, either as a peaceable
subject of the fast-expanding Russian/Soviet Empire to the
present day, or as an external foe until the end of the eighteenth century. Meanwhile another ancient Russian center,
Novgorod—tributary to the Tatars, but never conquered by
them—had kept up lively trade with Western Europe as a

member of the Hanseatic League. When Novgorod's independence was eventually extinguished in the late fifteenth century the agent was not Tatary but Moscow, itself newly Tatar-free.

In the middle of the following century Richard Chancellor's adventurous expedition from London to Moscow, via the North Cape and the Northern Dvina, was welcomed by Ivan the Terrible. The London-based Muscovy Company was founded in consequence, after which relations between Russia and Western Europe, albeit closely monitored and sporadically hampered by Muscovite authority, were to grow ever closer in succeeding years. Many of these contacts came through fierce and prolonged wars with Western states—Sweden, Poland, Livonia—which were Muscovy's superior in technology: wars from which Muscovy eventually benefited through being forced to adopt or improve on the methods of its adversaries. Long before Peter the Great was to embark on the intensive europeanization of Russia's upper class, his predecessors had been welcoming to their service English, Scottish, French, German and other Western or Central European soldiers, traders, craftsmen and professional men. Many of them chose to resist assimilation, retaining their national identity, customs and religion; but others were transformed in a generation or two, through conversion to Orthodoxy and learning to speak the language, into Russians indistinguishable except perhaps by an outlandish surname from other Russians. Thus did the registers of the Russian nobility and gentry come to include such representatives of Western civilization as Polish noblemen and titled Germans from the Baltic lands along with Caucasian and Tatar princes. More than two-thirds of the late seventeenth-century gentry were of foreign extraction: [1] an astounding figure, eloquent indeed on the interpenetration of Russian and non-Russian on the soil of Muscovy.

As for the many non-assimilating or temporarily resident aliens, they continued to attract the deep suspicion combined with fascination which foreigners have always stimulated in the Russian. The Russians called them 'dumb ones'; for such is the original meaning of their word for foreigners, *nemtsy,* which now means 'Germans.' They might be permitted to come to Moscow and engage in a trade or profession, but were compulsorily segregated in the so-called Mutes' Ghetto (*nemets-kaya sloboda*). Then, suddenly, the bonds of old Muscovy split asunder when the young Peter the Great broke the taboo on intercourse between Muscovite Tsar and foreign devils by penetrating this alien enclave to carouse with its denizens: his German mistress Anna Mons, the Scottish General Patrick Gordon, the Swiss adventurer Franz Lefort. An even grosser breach of apartheid took place in 1699–1700 with Peter's grand tour of Western Europe in a style which might have been expressly designed to confirm the impression, common among pious Muscovites, that he was Antichrist. Returning primed with sufficient European lore to boost the technological revolution which he intended to impose on sleepy Muscovy, he savagely repressed a military mutiny which had broken out in his absence; cut off his boyars' beards; forced them out of their flowing oriental robes into a form of contemporary European dress; forbade them to marry unless they could first acquire some knowledge of mathematics; founded a new capital on his far western shores, one expressly chosen to provide him with a 'window on Europe'; set up the Table of Ranks, a new civil and military hierarchy in which were enrolled his newly europeanized Russian officers and officials who fought and administered side by side with Western Europeans attracted to his service. A particularly important reservoir of the Empire's generals and high officials was to be provided over the next two centuries by the German gentry of the Baltic lands conquered by Peter.

On the desirability or not of Peter's violent europeanizing program, Russians have been debating ever since. One unfortunate by-product was the creation of a social and cultural gap between the small minority of newly westernized officers, gentlemen and officials on the one hand, and the great gray mass of the population on the other: benighted, bearded, illiterate muzhiks together with the similarly garbed and culturally akin merchants and priests. But these members of the thronging lower orders at least were, and knew themselves to be, Russians; whereas members of the gentry as revamped by Peter were neither one thing nor the other. 'Foreigners at home and foreigners abroad; idle spectators spoilt for Russia by their Western prejudices, spoilt for the West by their Russian habits—they represented a kind of intelligent superfluity floundering in artificiality, sensual pleasures and intolerable egoism.' [2] Ironically enough, the author of these lines, Alexander Herzen, himself richly exemplified the characteristics, idleness excluded, to which he here takes exception.

Meanwhile, however numerous europeanized Russians might become, non-assimilating foreigners continued to maintain their habit of initiating Russian enterprises. The country's first factory, the Tula iron works, was built in 1632 by a Dutch concessionaire. Likewise, over two hundred years later, the coal-mining industry of the Donbass was founded by a Welshman, John Hughes. Italian and Scottish architects respectively planned the walls of the Moscow Kremlin, the St. Petersburg Winter Palace and many another notable edifice in and outside the 'two capitals.' Nineteenth-century Englishmen were to achieve the first ascent of many a mountain peak of the far-flung Russian Empire. Then again, in yet another field, a succession of distinguished Scottish doctors served as personal physicians to the eighteenth-century Russian emperors and empresses. Catherine the Great had herself innoculated against smallpox by one of these, a Dr. Dimsdale; and she is said to have kept a carriage and post-horses available so that he could flee the country in the event of some medical disaster, which, fortunately for both of them, did not occur.[3] On a humbler level, Catherine also persuaded numerous European artisans and peasants to settle in Russia, her aim being not only to populate the vast, sparsely inhabited territories of her realm, but also, with luck, to civilize some of its more boorish indigenous inhabitants.

The scale of foreigners' assimilation to Russianness admitted infinite gradations. The beginning might be to learn a little of the language, but the crucial stage was conversion to Orthodoxy. Of the country's capacity to assimilate aliens, in whatever degree, an American scholar quotes an impressive catalogue of examples. They include the Italian eighteenth-century architect Francesco Bartolomeo Rastrelli; the Scottish General Barclay de Tolly; the playwright Fonvizin and the poet Delvig, both German; the octoroon Pushkin, partly Ethiopian; the Danish lexicographer Vladimir Dal; the Swedish poetess Zinaida Gippius; and the Ukrainian-Polish author Vladimir Korolenko.[4] Gogol, who wrote in Russian, was yet a Ukrainian. And even Chekhov, coming as he did from the south, could jokingly refer to himself as a 'lazy Ukrainian,' and was once censured by a Ukrainian actress for not writing in his 'native' language.[5] Alexander Nikitenko was unambiguously Ukrainian in origin, yet became a militant Great Russian nationalist by conviction—the only unbalanced feature, perhaps, in his outlook. However, it was often such adoptive Russians who, feeling the convert's compulsion to display extra zeal, became the most rabid patriots of all. The Empire had no more zealous defenders than the Baltic German nobles who commanded so many armies and headed so many ministries. And there have arguably been few Russian patriots so extreme and persistent, if the extension of national power is an acceptable criterion, as the Georgian Stalin, though the guttural speech of that multiple slaughterer of Russians always remained alien enough to identify him at once as a foreigner.

Half German and one-quarter Kalmuck by birth, Lenin was more secure in his status as a Russian and also more apt to denigrate the Russians than his wholly foreign disciple Stalin could afford to be in pre-revolutionary days. Lenin repeatedly castigated the arrant chauvinism of the Great Russians, as revealed in their oppressions of the minority populations of their Empire—in which they formed no majority, but merely a large minority of some 43 percent at the time.[6]

However sincere Lenin's pre-revolutionary defense of Russia's non-Russian minorities may have been in intent, the consolidation of power by the Bolsheviks, under Stalin's domination and later dictatorial monopoly of power, was far indeed from conferring independence on the various nationalities, great and small, of what had now become the Soviet Union. Subjected to continuing Great Russian domination under a different name, the non-Russian nationalities now had the extra burden of being compelled to assert in public that no such domination existed, and to affirm the officially promulgated fiction that each of the Union's republics was *de facto* free—as it is and has been *de jure*—to secede from the USSR. On pain of disgrace and worse for 'bourgeois nationalism,' members of minority nationalities have been required to express gratitude to the Russian people for annexing them in the first place, and then for helping them to establish communism. That the Caucasian, the Central Asian, the Baltic and many other peoples had been wholly or partly incorporated in imperial Russia by military conquest is glossed over. Their territories, including those acquired in Tsarist times, are said to have accrued by *attachment* rather than by violent *seizure*, the term which is regularly applied to the annexationist activities of non-Russian colonial powers. Meanwhile a drive toward greater local cultural and administrative autonomy, if not toward total independence, remains a live issue among dissidents in the non-Russian Union Republics, including the most populous of all, that of the Ukraine. On the other hand, all these fourteen non-Russian republics, together with the various autonomous republics and other, smaller non-Russian national units, have produced their quota of russophiliac

Uncle Toms. Whether actuated by conviction, foolishness, fear, careerism or a desire to seem important, these are often pathetic as they regurgitate the solemn litany of gratitude to the Great Russians for having enslaved them so effectively. In such a context it is not fanciful to describe modern totalitarian Russia as the most successful colonial and imperialist power of the twentieth century. Yet the Russians by no means look down on all their colonial peoples as mere 'natives.' They have, for example, a healthy respect for Georgian commercial acumen; for Baltic skill in design and architecture; and in general for the superior *savoir-vivre,* as they are apt to feel it, of their more advanced subject nations.

Does the Russian consider himself to belong to the East or to the West?

Once again there is no lack of witness to each of two mutually exclusive propositions. Is one to believe the poet Alexander Blok when, in a famous couplet from his poem *Scythians* (1918), he truculently describes himself and his fellow-countrymen as 'Asiatics with slanted, greedy eyes'? Or does one rather accept the statement made in the opening paragraph of a recent study of *Russia and Europe* by the German scholar Reinhard Wittram, who no less roundly claims that 'It goes without saying . . . the Russians have always been a European people'? [7]

*Goes without saying?* That, with respect, it most emphatically does not. On the contrary, many billions of words have been spilled on variations of these two contrary propositions. Nor is any prize offered to readers who have discerned that the truth may lie somewhere between the two extreme statements quoted above. Neither wholly oriental nor yet wholly occidental, Russia partakes and has partaken of both elements. How little educated Russians of the last century regarded themselves as belonging exclusively to either camp is shown by certain speech conventions then common. *Yevropeytsy,* 'Europeans,' was frequently used in a sense specifically excluding

Russia: it embraced all the other, non-Russian, lands of the continent, despite the fact that Russia itself occupies a far larger area of Europe than does any other nation. On the other hand, the Russians most certainly did not think of themselves as Asians; indeed, the common, highly pejorative, use of the word *aziatchina*, 'Asian-ness,' to denote 'squalor,' suggests that they dissociated themselves in their minds even more from the East than from the West.

Opinions granting Russia intermediate status between East and West are, happily, more common than those which admit of no compromise. Pushkin evidently thought of Russia as part of Europe when he contrasted it with 'the rest' of that continent. Still, he then went on to claim, in effect, that never the twain should meet. 'Russia never had anything in common with the rest of Europe . . . her history requires ideas and formulas that are different from the ideas and formulas deduced . . . from the history of the Christian West.' Another compromise view loaded in favor of the Eastern solution was that of Custine, who claimed that Russia represented 'a terrible combination of Europe's intelligence and science with Asiatic genius'; but who also believed that Russia would always be more Asiatic than European.[8]

To the problem as to whether Russians think that they *are* more Eastern or more Western another, closely linked question is often appended. *Should* Russia be, or should it become, more Eastern or more Western? The latter view was taken by those nineteenth-century thinkers, a somewhat heterogeneous bunch, who came to be lumped together as westernists. The pioneer westernist, Chaadayev, would not commit himself on Russia's existing position: 'We are neither of the West nor of the East, and we have not the traditions of either.'[9] But when Chaadayev turned from what Russia was—a country of which, he said, both the past and present simply lacked all significance—to what it should be, he showed himself uncompromising in his westernism, claiming that the only possible future lay in adherence not only to European civilization but even to the Catholic Church.

An opposing, russocentric, view was adopted by those Russian radicals who saw their country's guarantee of political salvation in its village commune, claiming it to be a socialist-type institution unknown to the West. That Russia not only always had gone but always should go its own way was also the contention of the Slavophiles, and not least of Dostoyevsky. Hating the westernist doctrine—not that any such doctrine existed in cohesive form—and particularly exasperated by his westernizing *bête noire*, Turgenev, Dostoyevsky created a vicious caricature of that unfortunate fellow-novelist in the novel *Devils*. Here 'Karmazinov' (=Turgenev) openly proclaims a keener interest in the sewage system of his foreign city of residence, Karlsruhe, than in the entire destiny of his mother country. Yet even Dostoyevsky, Europe-hater though he might seem, could claim that the whole of Russian progress, learning, art, civic virtue and humanitarianism proceeded from Europe. And conversely the greatest westernist of all, Peter the Great, that wholesale quarrier and adapter of European technology, never regarded europeanization as an end in itself; he is reported as stating that 'We need Europe for a few decades, and then we must turn our back on it.' [10]

East-West polarization, as present in Russian minds, has been fostered in more recent times by the political split between the Communist Orient and the 'capitalist' Occident. Originally Western in basing its creed on the works of the German political thinkers Marx and Engels, the Russian Communist movement was most powerfully promoted in its early stages by revolutionaries operating in Western European emigration. Such were the two prime movers of the Bolshevik October Revolution of 1917, Lenin and Trotsky, both of whom had lived abroad for many years, as had many of their closest henchmen. This occidentalizing phase began to recede when it became increasingly clear in the early 1920s that no Western

European revolution, such as the Bolsheviks had long expected and relied upon, was in fact going to occur in the foreseeable future. The realization coincided with the acquisition of dictatorial power by a colonial, Stalin—a native, albeit a non-Russian native, of the Empire. Stalin had spent only a few weeks on foreign soil, and was far less of a European than most other influential allies of Lenin. Moreover, he pursued the avowedly insular and thus less occidental policy of socialism in one country, besides projecting in his personal style the image of an Eastern despot. Even nowadays, despite the guarded opening of East-West communications since Stalin's death, Russia is in some ways more Eastern in character than was the case in the half century preceding the revolutions. But it must also be conceded that the terms *Eastern, oriental, Western* and *occidental* are less precise than their users are often betrayed into implying.

However these concepts may be defined, the problem of the country's Western or Eastern affiliations is surely less important to an understanding of the Russian mentality than the problem of Russia's obsession with that problem.

That the West is and has been no less fascinated by Russia than Russia by the West—this emerges from much of the preceding argument, not least from the existence of so many analyses and descriptions of the country published by Western citizens from the sixteenth century onward. And yet, granted a roughly equal intensity of mutual East-West obsession, one is immediately struck by a difference in quality and attitude. Tending to regard Russia as an enigma or sphinx, the Western citizen instinctively seeks hard information about the country; he hopes to solve its riddles. But the Russian attitude to the West, in so far as it can be summed up, tends in quite a different direction. It is not so much understanding of, it is *recognition by*, the West that Russians crave. 'Though they do take some interest in what is happening in foreign parts,' wrote André Gide in 1936, 'they are far more concerned about what the foreigner thinks of them. What really interests them is to know whether we admire them enough. What they are afraid of is that we should be ill-informed as to their merits. What they want from us is not information but praise.' [11]

This desire is set in context by a more recent witness who claims that converse between present-day Russians and foreigners tends to provoke a clash between the Russians' outward self-confidence and inner uncertainty. It produces, in other words, 'a compulsion in them to elicit from the foreigner an assurance that all is well in the Soviet Union.' [12] And it is this compulsion, for example, which drives them to expressions of tedious self-congratulation—over, say, the building of apartment blocks—so exaggerated as to suggest that such achievements are unique to their civilization, which in fact has no claim whatever to preeminence in housing its citizens. To this evidence may be added the contrary urge which one encounters among those Russians who hold politically dissident views, and who express these to foreigners with the exactly contrary aim of eliciting an assurance that all is *not* well in the USSR; that all is, indeed, the worst in the worst of all possible worlds. Such denouncers of the totalitarian ambience have, in many cases, no sooner concluded their 'frank' exchanges of views with some sympathetic alien than off they run, by previous arrangement, to an agency of their political police with a detailed account of the transaction. And yet these 'spies' are so often perfectly sincere, decent people, who had spoken all along from the heart on a matter of intimate concern. Here, perhaps, is the phenomenon most difficult of all for the inquiring foreigner to accept and digest, even though he may suspect the intensity of the pressures which have been developed to produce so unnerving a manifestation.

Whether it is praise or condemnation of Russian dispensations which is elicited, the important point is that the foreigner is in either case regarded as an arbiter of ultimate reality—a status which few Russians would be accorded during their excursions on to alien soil. The average Western citizen would, one hopes, always be prepared to receive a USSR-domiciled Russian with courtesy. And if the guest should express an opinion about the 'achievements' or non-achievements, the national mentality or any other aspect of his host's country, such representations will (one again hopes) usually be received with every show of serious concern. But most Western citizens, outside the fortunately restricted Russia-fancying camp, are not sufficiently insecure to feel passionately involved in their hearts with what such a visitor may think of them—not, at least, unless and until he provides evidence of possessing a mature judgment. Such inner aloofness was once particularly prominent, perhaps too prominent, in England. The Englishman in his days of self-confidence never cared tuppence what any 'bloody foreigner' thought about him or his country. How very different from the Russian, who can seem obsessed with what foreigners think about Russia to the exclusion of everything else.

A significant gloss on this topic is provided by Valentin Kiparsky in his careful study of English and American characters in Russian fiction. Invoking the Russian practice of regularly introducing foreigners in works of fiction as a foil to the natives, he adds that 'A Russian novel without a West European or, at least, a Polish, Ukrainian, Jewish or Caucasian character, is almost as rare as a West European novel containing a Russian character.' [13] And yet, when one moves from the fictional sphere of imagination, romance and emotion to the world of factual information, the balance is in the opposite direction. Western 'books on Russia' are extremely numerous, and are usually inspired by inquisitiveness, whereas Russians' discourses on the West are relatively few, and are often preoccupied with ventilating emotional and nationalistic issues relevant to their own country rather than with conveying information or sober understanding of someone else's.

Simultaneously or by turns xenophiliac and xenophobiac,

Russians tend on the whole to react most strongly to Western nationalities in proportion to their geographical proximity to Russian territory. For example, the writings of that dedicated xenophobe Dostoyevsky maintain a fairly consistent hate-hate, rather than love-hate, relationship with Russia's immediate Western neighbors. His most virulent contempt is reserved for the Poles: topographically adjacent, Catholics, rebels against Russian rule in 1863 and damned in all three capacities. In the various *skandal* scenes of his novels a 'wretched little Pole' usually figures among the minor characters who contribute an atmosphere of absurdity to these fiascos; so too, to be fair, does the odd 'wretched little German.'

Relations with Germany probably cut deeper than those with any other major Central or Western European power. It is with Germany that Russia and later the USSR has fought the two most massive and bloody wars in history. For a century and a half preceding 1917 Russia was, as indicated above, ruled by autocrats of wholly or preponderantly German extraction. Before that a much-hated German, Biron, had in effect controlled policy as a favorite of the Empress Anne in the early eighteenth century. Another German, Count Benckendorff, headed the newly created political police organization of Nicholas I a century later, being charged with the leading role in the harassment of Pushkin. And, as Benckendorff's case illustrates, administrative or managerial positions, high and low, were commonly assigned to Germans on the by no means fanciful ground that the organizing Teuton tended to conceive more clear-cut and efficiently pursued goals than could be expected from a Slav administrator or overseer. To this belief or prejudice Russian writers commonly deferred when seeking to create 'strong men' or 'men of action': an aim often pursued, though rarely successfully brought off, in Russian literature of both the imperial and the totalitarian periods. These militantly un-Russian characters are apt to bear such names as Stolz (in Goncharov's *Oblomov*) and von

Koren (in Chekhov's *Duel*) on the apparent assumption that qualities of determination and effectiveness would never be credited by any Russian reader if attributed to someone with a name ending in -ovsky or -ishchev.

This perennial contrast between the sober, dependable German and the casual, slovenly Russian has struck many observers. Traveling to Samarkand in 1888, Lord Curzon noted the 'overwhelming antithesis between the German and Russian character, the one vigilant, uncompromising, stiff, precise; the other sleepy, nonchalant, wasteful and lax.' [14] The same contrast had impressed Nikitenko during his visit to the northern port of Archangel in 1834. The German ghetto there was distinguished by its neat, attractive cottages, whereas the Russians of the city 'live in filth and trade like swindlers.' So widespread was the national vice of drunkenness that no one would ever inquire of a stranger whether he drank but rather 'What's he like when he's tipsy?' [15]

A similar contrast might be observed between disorderly, unkempt typical Russian villages and the neat, well-organized settlements of the many German peasant communities originally attracted to Russia by the immigration policies of Catherine the Great. And yet, far from regarding German efficiency and order as a standing reproach, the muzhik remained content with his own way of life. He was not inspired to imitate these mysterious foreigners; for though Russia's gentry '. . . are singularly prone to adopt foreign manners, customs and institutions; the peasants, on the contrary, are as a rule decidedly conservative.' [16] Still, if there was little cooperation between the Orthodox and these alien infidels, there was also remarkably little friction. German peasants settled down contentedly in Russia, retaining their own language and religion while shunning avoidable contact with imperial officialdom. There were also many German traders and businessmen—so many by the mid-nineteenth century that Custine could say, albeit greatly exaggerating, that 'The manufacturers, businessmen and merchants are almost all German.'[17]

Foreigners, especially Germans, were prominent in Russian academic life. University professors, and also academicians—members of the Academy of Sciences founded in 1725—were often Germans who could not speak, and did not wish to speak, a word of Russian. But there were also many Russian citizens of German descent who might retain their German surname, but who, like Chekhov's Baron Tuzenbakh in *Three Sisters,* proclaimed themselves culturally and linguistically Russian. How thoroughly a real-life woman of German origin—Chekhov's wife Olga Knipper—could absorb a characteristic Russian tonality from her Russian education and environment, her voluminous correspondence with her husband demonstrates; it is the thoroughly Russian Chekhov who emerges as the less 'Russian,' in the vulgar sense, from their exchanges.

Not always, either in literature or in life, has the practical, efficient, punctual, businesslike German got the better of the drunken, carefree, casual Russian. Leskov's story *An Iron Will* depicts a German engineer, Hugo Pektoralis, who possesses all the national attributes in excess. But the dedicated Hugo is no match for his sloppy, vodka-swilling Russian opponent Safronych, who outwits him at every turn as if to confirm the answer implied in a rhetorical question asked on an early page of the story: 'Can anyone really hope to conquer a people capable of producing such a rogue as Chichikov [the hero of Gogol's *Dead Souls*]?'

Better known to the Western reader is a similar contrast in Tolstoy's *War and Peace,* between the efficient, determined, rational, somewhat unreal Napoleon and his lackadaisical, perhaps equally unreal military opposite number, Field Marshal Kutuzov. In his archetypal wisdom as a true Russian, Tolstoy's canny Kutuzov knows that a commander-in-chief cannot exercise any influence whatever over the course of a battle, and he therefore feels perfectly free to fall asleep during a council of war. As for the real-life Russians of the Napoleonic period, creatively casual or not, they survived the French invasion and pursued the defeated enemy back to his home territory. When Alexander I rode triumphantly into Paris on 19 March 1814, while Parisiennes asked his Cossacks to hoist them on the cruppers of their horses so that they could admire the handsome Tsar, the Russian Empire may be said to have attained its symbolic zenith. Far from interrupting French-Russian contacts, the war only strengthened them. First-hand observation of France, as of Central and Western Europe in general, helped to stimulate in the Russian army a desire for fundamental reform at home, an experience which caused many army officers to join the Decembrist conspiracy of 1825.

Meanwhile French refugees had fled to Russia and been received in a fluent, yet far from Parisian, version of their own language, at this period the common medium of communication between upper-class Russians, as Tolstoy's *War and Peace,* much of it in French, reminds one. Herzen's father was more at home in French than Russian and disdained the major Russian historico-literary monument of his age, Karamzin's *History of the Russian State,* out of high-bred distaste for the vulgarities of the subject. 'All these Izyaslaviches and Olgoviches—what a bore!' [18] Pushkin, Russia's greatest poet, was sometimes known as 'the Frenchman' because he seemed so well-versed in his second language—in which, incidentally, he habitually wrote letters to his no-less-Russian wife. As these details suggest, the Russian literary language was by no means fully formed at the beginning of the nineteenth century; and it was, indeed, Pushkin himself who played the major role in completing the process of fitting it for flexible and sophisticated utterance. To compare the evolution of such major European tongues as French and English is, therefore, to note yet another area in which Russia showed itself a strikingly late—yet in the end impressive—developer.

As time wore on, the use of French in Russian mouths

acquired different resonances. To Dostoyevsky it was a sign of not being a proper Russian, and he several times attributes a French accent or knowledge of French to such characters as the murderer Smerdyakov, ideologically disapproved of for having rejected traditional Muscovite values. To Chekhov, a generation later, the use of—sometimes inaccurate—French was an index of pseudo-genteel vulgarity. By the First World War French had sunk still further, the word *merci* being 'used by nearly all the town population (particularly so by the half-educated ones).' [19] In more recent times Russian knowledge of French has sunk to the point when the word *merci,* occurring in a printed text, must be translated in a footnote.

The British (or English, for the Russian rarely draws any distinction) have also come in for their share of Russian love and hatred, but on the lower scale which greater distance and inaccessibility dictate. After a rabidly anglomaniac phase undergone by some of the Russian gentry in the early nineteenth century and recorded, for example, in Pushkin's story *Lady into Peasant,* English tourists came to be strongly disliked. Turgenev has referred to their glassy eyes, their long, rabbitlike teeth and their droopy whiskers. They are suspicious, rude, haughty; they disdain everything foreign. Still, Englishmen made better managers than Frenchmen or Germans, even if they did exploit Russian workers. Above all the English impressed by displaying, in those far-off and very different days, the psychological security which Russians themselves so often lacked, particularly in their dealings with the West. Tolstoy once called the typical Englishman 'self-assured as being a citizen of the best-organized state in the world,' one who 'as an Englishman, always knows what he should do and knows that all he does as an Englishman is undoubtedly correct.' There are many similar tributes of grudging admiration in Dostoyevsky's *Diary of a Writer.* However, self-assurance could all too easily spill over into arrogance, as Dostoyevsky often complains: 'I am an Englishman, and you are only Russians [one of his typical Britons muses]. . . . I, as a son of Old England (at this point his heart quivers with pride), am nevertheless the first man in the world, and you are only people of the second grade.' [20]

The general view of the English in the present century has tended to concentrate on their inhibitedness, stiff upper lip, reserve, strait-lacedness. Here is the opposite of that jolly expansiveness which forms so basic an ingredient in a Russian's ideal vision of himself, so that the English may in a sense seem to him inverted Russians. An Englishman visiting Russia can find himself accused of emotional atrophy, in extreme cases by a total stranger in the first two seconds of encounter. 'Who enjoys, who really enjoys life most [as between Englishman and Russian]?' The rhetorical question is posed by Mme. Jarintzov and answered over several score pages in the Russian's favor. With the Russian, spoiled by an overflow of happiness, she contrasts the dour Englishman whose highest form of joy occurs at the moment when he can describe himself by the mundane phrase 'full of beans.' [21] This is one way of looking at things. Another is that of Mackenzie Wallace, who describes a Russian village fête as 'one of the most saddening spectacles I have ever witnessed.' Contrasting France and Italy, he laments that *all* northern nations, the Russians not least, are incapable of amusing themselves, that they 'do not know how to enjoy themselves in a harmless, rational way, and seek a refuge in intoxication.' [22] Without necessarily accepting either of these extreme statements, we may tentatively identify one typical specific in the Russian's enjoyment syndrome. He does not seem capable of absorbing satisfaction unless he is simultaneously awarding himself credit marks for doing so. He will seek out someone else and explain that he, the disadvantaged foreigner, on whom the Russian may never previously have set eyes, is by definition precluded from true happiness—another variant on the familiar 'just-watch-me-being-spontaneous' theme, and another reminder of the Russian's acute sensitivity to audience reaction.

Despite claims that the English and the Russians may be

at opposite poles owing to their respective cultivation of reserve and exuberance, the feeling has often been expressed
that the two peoples are especially close to each other.
Nicholas Khomyakov, a Russian politician of the late Empire,
once stated that 'Every Russian when he is among Englishmen
at once feels at home, though he may not be like them in character, beliefs, or education. And you will be told of corresponding feelings by every Englishman who has lived in Russia, but not by the Frenchman, the German, or the Italian.'
Endorsing this view, Wright Miller claims that, in personal
relationships and general attitude to life, 'The English have
more in common with the Russians than with many nations
nearer home.' And he specifies these common areas as 'ways
of avoiding social friction, the Russian sense of humour, the
Russian attitude to women, and that recent development, Russian sportsmanship.' [23] One senses what he means without
feeling impelled to accept his thesis. The trouble is that Russians, not necessarily uninspired by a love of *vranyo,* are so apt
to seek out representatives of a given nationality and expatiate
on the special rapport (or, depending on mood, lack of rapport) allegedly existing between Russia and the nationality in
question. It is not surprising, then, to find the fact that Russia
and Germany *had not fought on the same side in World War II*
deplored, in conversation with a German, by a Russian war
veteran who had conveniently forgotten that they had most
certainly done so: in their joint successful campaign of 1939
against Poland. 'We have a great respect for the Germans,'
continued this expert on international affairs. 'They're a . . .
people with principles, like the Russians, not a lot of sloppy
compromisers like the British and the French.' [24]

Nor is it surprising to find an American writing that the
Russians in many ways resemble the Americans more than any
other people in their eagerness to ask questions and learn new
things; in not being afraid to make mistakes: 'They have an attitude of breezy but not annoying self-confidence, born of the

knowledge that they have vast spaces and great material resources at their disposal; and they adapt themselves readily to
new and entirely untried conditions.'[25] Always impressed by
American technical and economic achievements, and often as
unstinting in praising Americans to Americans as in abusing
Americans to non-Americans, the Russian is also constantly on
the lookout for some defect which will balance American superiority. Materialism, the desire to 'make a fast buck,' an
alleged lack of intellectualism and culture—such are the common accusations.[26] As for another charge, that 'Americans
have no music in their souls'—here one recognizes a routine
item in the Russian litany of implied self-praise, that of disparaging others for lacking qualities which possess the convenient
property of being wholly unquantifiable.

As the fourth quarter of the twentieth century began,
both the British and the Americans seemed to have entered
phases of collective insecurity and self-denigration contrasting
sharply with their former self-confidence. Meanwhile the Russians continued as ever to combine, fuguelike, the melody of
self-denigration far more intense than that of the Anglo-
American with the counterpoint of bombastic nationalist
boastfulness.

## PATRIOT

In any survey of a people's mind, that people's attitude to
itself—its patriotism or lack of patriotism—must loom large,
and in Russia's case the topic is particularly obtrusive. That
Russian love of country tends to excess has been argued again

and again. Even in the bleak days of Muscovy, according to a recent authority, Tibor Szamuely, the Russian people 'regarded their national state and their social system with a feeling of pious reverence and blind faith that went beyond simple patriotism.' Listing the symptoms as ecstatic rapture, exaltation bordering on idolatry, insufferable self-righteousness, unshakable conviction of moral superiority and self-glorification carried to ridiculous lengths, he adds that 'Instead of "my country right or wrong," it was "my country —never wrong." ' [1]

Illustrations of such super-patriotism are not hard to find. One thinks of Dostoyevsky's journalistic writings, and especially of the *Diary of a Writer,* where his countrymen are credited with such virtues as 'eternal service to common human ideals.' Then there is their superior tolerance—and from Dostoyevsky, that hounder of Catholics and Jews. He claims Russia's as the most democratic social structure in the world, and that under the autocracy. He lauds its lack of territorial designs on any other country, and that hard on the annexation of central Asia and the far eastern provinces, not to mention his own cherished dream of appropriating Constantinople. The Russian was, to Dostoyevsky, an exponent of 'human universality'; was free from 'European stiffness, imperviousness, intractability'; sympathized '. . . with everything human irrespective of nationality, blood and soil'; was even—*horresco referens*—uniquely gifted in speaking foreign languages.[2]

That Dostoyevsky should pause, as he does, while projecting such national narcissism to praise the Russian's 'sober view of himself and absence of any sort of self-elevation'—this, too, is very much in the spirit of such harangues. Launched on a similar hymn to unique Russian virtues, a more recent super-patriot inserts into these splendid fanfaronades the similar claim that 'Self-advertising is not a Russian feature.' [3] But one has heard this sort of boasting from other sources, too; for example, 'We British don't go round blowing our own trumpets.'

And so, typically Russian though the practice of praising one-self for not praising oneself may seem, it is assuredly not unique.

Russian super-patriotism may not be as universal as Sza-muely pretends, but he is surely right in claiming special status for it as an emotion unconnected with the real and wearisome world of reason, evidence and fact. The Russian love of country is more akin to a religious faith, as is brought out in one famous quatrain on Russia by a Russian, Fyodor Tyut-chev. Roughly translated into dull prose, it reads, 'Russia can neither be grasped by the mind, nor measured by any com-mon yardstick. Russia's status is special: no attitude to her other than one of blind faith is admissible.' [4] Such fanatical devotion has always tended to remain unshaken by the appall-ing persecutions, including long-term imprisonment and exile, which authority has so often inflicted on the individual citizen, not uncommonly through some whim, accident or mere cleri-cal error. Hardship, poverty and other evils not wholly at-tributable to authority have made little difference either— rather the contrary. Pushkin, himself during his entire adult life a victim of petty persecution from on high, once called his fellow-citizens orangutans, even asserting that to inhabit Rus-sia was 'like living in a privy.' But though 'far from admiring all that I see around me,' he went on to swear that not for any-thing would he have consented to change his fatherland.[5] A similar attitude was expressed by Boris Pasternak, that re-nowned dissident and object of prolonged nerve warfare by the Kremlin, who, had he wished, could have left his country in 1958 at the time when he was awarded the Nobel Prize for Literature. Had he done so he would have been able to lead a dignified life abroad, well provided for by his literary earn-ings. In fact he regarded such a prospect, which he succeeded in avoiding, as an utter calamity, and told me so during a long discussion which I was privileged to have with him at the time. And yet he was living under considerable strain, as he explained, and under a system of government which, though he insisted on regarding it as comic, he also had good reason to fear. Similarly, many a humbler citizen has suffered arrest on a trumped-up, meaningless or nonexistent charge, followed by years or decades of appalling privations in Stalin's concentration camps—yet has retained his patriotism untarnished.

The Russian is accustomed to refer to his country as 'Mother' Russia, attaching much significance to the maternal symbol: 'It was remarkable how often . . . interviewees [defectors of the totalitarian period] expressed the postwar state of Russia in terms of their "starving, neglected mother." ' [6] The poorer the mother and the harsher her conditions of life, the greater the devotion of her sons.

That the Russian should sometimes adopt a truculent, challenging mien when expressing his patriotism is also characteristic, though it is also typical of nationalists everywhere. 'Already in the reign of Ivan the Terrible the incipient megalomania had reached a stage where not only the monarchs of Poland, Sweden, England and France, but even the German emperor, were, one by one, declared unfit to be treated as equals by the ruler of Muscovy.' In the end even the Turkish Sultan was deposed from the isolated peak which he had been allowed to share with the Tsar, the last remaining sovereign treated as that ruler's coequal in diplomatic traffic. This same megalomaniac Tsar once wrote to Queen Elizabeth of England accusing her of yielding power to 'clodhopping tradesmen'; and of being no true monarch, but just an 'ordinary spinster.' [7]

In the light of traditional chauvinist idiom, the Georgian Stalin was not using an un-Russian turn of phrase when he warned foreigners against 'sticking their pigs' snouts into our Soviet kitchen-garden.' [8] Nor was the undeniably Russian Khrushchev departing from accepted usage when he issued his famous warning, 'We shall bury you,' to Western diplomats at a Moscow gathering. He was also known to invoke the special nature of Russian-Soviet 'achievements' less distastefully, by citing Leskov's famous story *The Left-handed Man*. Here a cross-eyed, left-handed joiner from Tula demonstrates the superiority of Russian craftsmanship by taking an ingeniously wrought steel flea, presented to the Tsar by English metal workers, and fitting it with microscopic shoes. By this striking feat of one-upmanship is the Russian's edge over the foreigner asserted with delightful humor and irony—elements by no means uncommon in the Russian litany of self-admiration. They are, however, wholly absent from the powerful but distasteful ode *To Russia's Slanderers* in which Pushkin asserts his country's right to crush the Polish rebellion of 1830–31, promising any foreign interventionists in this domestic quarrel of Slavs that they will receive the treatment previously meted out to Napoleon. Nor has this 'our-side-your-side distinction,' as it has been well called, been confined to Tsars, statesmen and poets.[9] It can form a substantial barrier to civilized communication between the present-day Westerner and any unduly 'typical' Russian.

The replacement of the Russian Empire by the Soviet Union has made far fewer inroads on Russian patriotism than might have been expected from the adoption of a creed as avowedly global in its pretensions as Marxism. An internationalist phase did indeed follow the Bolshevik takeover of 1917—a period when the very use of the words *Russian* and *Russia* was officially discouraged or penalized, while the new regime yet drew on reserves of Russian patriotism, especially as aroused by foreign intervention during the Civil War of 1918–21. By 1934 Stalin was overtly reviving Russian nationalism, and the word *Soviet* was tending more and more to become a rough code equivalent for *Russian*. Russian nationalism was more prominent than political fervor in bringing victory over Germany in World War II, after which it was artificially nurtured by the nationalist campaign associated with the name of Zhdanov. It was the period during which all major inventions of the past, including that of radio and the steam engine, were, correctly or incorrectly, attributed to Russians. This later-modified propaganda campaign has never been entirely relaxed, and users of recent Russian encyclopedias will still find much evidence of it. In particular, wherever foreigners have played a significant role in Russian history, as did the Vikings and Greeks in the Kiev period, their importance tends to be played down, while more emphasis is given to native Russian initiatives than un-Kremlinized scholars will allow. This policy derives from a realization by the Kremlin 'that the success of its program of world expansion, and also its ability to maintain its power at home, depend upon securing the maximum possible support from the Great Russian people.' [10]

Despite this cultivation of intense Russian nationalism, recent Muscovite statesmen have not made a practice of publicly indulging in the kind of bombastic, bellicose, flamboyant utterance associated with Hitler, Mussolini and the heads of other totalitarian regimes. Khrushchev's occasional drunken lapses into abuse, as noted above, were happily exceptional.

The adoption of Russian nationalism by Marxist-Leninist revolutionaries does not mark as sharp a break with tradition as might be supposed. Though it is true that pre-1917 Russian revolutionaries often opposed the expansionist policies of their government—they did so, for example, during the Russo-Japanese War of 1904–5—they were also liable to rally to the imperial cause. Decidedly exceptional among his contemporaries was Herzen when he came out against the crushing of the Polish rebellion of 1863, for most other domestic opponents of the Russian government saw no reason why the ancestral enemy should not be put down. Even so extreme a radical as Chernyshevsky was intensely patriotic: 'Not to put too fine a point on it . . . there was a good deal of unconscious nationalism in the psychological make-up of the Russian revolutionary.' [11] And even the more internationalist Herzen could occasionally utter the language—admittedly somewhat muted by Dostoyevskian standards—of nationalist bombast. Herzen spoke, for example, of the Russians as 'that people which, by some miracle, has contrived to preserve itself under the yoke of Mongol hordes and German bureaucrats, under the corporal's stick of barrack discipline and the shameful Tatar knout; has preserved its majestic features, its lively intelligence, the broad exuberance of its rich nature under the oppression of serfdom; and which has responded to a Tsar's call to educate itself with that titanic phenomenon Pushkin. Let Europe know her neighbour. So far she only fears him. Let her find out what it is she fears.' [12]

It is a short step from some of the preoccupations mentioned above to the assumption, commonly made over the centuries by Russians in all walks of life, that they constitute a kind of Chosen People, the elect of destiny, who have performed a special role in the past and are fated to perform a still more special role in the future.

So far as the past is concerned, there is the oft-repeated claim to have 'saved Europe' from various threats. By absorbing the shock of Mongol-Tatar onslaughts in the early thirteenth century, by later active campaigning against the Tatars until their expulsion from the Crimea in 1783, Russia arguably rescued Western civilization. 'Held a shield between the two hostile races of the Mongols and of Europe' is how Blok puts it in his poem *Scythians.* In language only slightly less poetic the historian Klyuchevsky speaks of carefree Europe entranced by its dreams of colonies with their spices and recking little of the East while the infant state of Muscovy still held the pass against the barbarian, '. . . saving European culture from Tatar onslaughts. Thus we found ourselves in Europe's rearguard and defended the rear of European civilization.' [13] Without denying all force to these considerations one may yet argue that national survival played a greater role, and an altruistic mission to save European culture a lesser role, than Russian historians and poets will commonly allow.

That Russia again saved Europe or the world—from Napoleon in 1812; from the Kaiser in 1914–17; from Hitler in 1940–45—here are further claims characteristic of Russian-Soviet historians. They will not concede, on an official level, that any nation other than those ruled from Moscow contributed substantially to the defeat of Hitler and his allies, though the Anglo-American invasion of Europe in June 1944 did evoke warm praise from Stalin in the immediate aftermath. And still to this day the old boasts about medieval Russia saving Europe from the Tatars, so commonly heard from imperial Russian historians, continue to be made the basis for claiming, as it were, good conduct marks from history.[14]

As for Russia's role in the future, the prospect has alarmed Western travelers since the sixteenth century, when Richard Chancellor wrote that 'if they knew their strength, no man were able to make match with them, nor they that dwell near them should have any rest of them. . . . I may compare them to a young horse that knoweth not his strength.' Three hundred years later the Frenchman Custine received a similar impression, and concluded that Russia's destiny was world conquest. He even regarded the awesome and magnificent city of St. Petersburg as a trophy erected by the Russians to their future power. Such ideas were not only voiced by Frenchmen in the Russia of Custine's day. One native philosopher of the period, Prince Vladimir Odoyevsky, claimed that 'A Russified Europe, as a new force, will bring life to senile and decrepit Europe.' Another, Michael Pogodin, expressed similar ambitions more effusively: 'My heart trembles with joy, O Russia, O my Fatherland. . . . You, you are chosen to consummate, to crown the development of humanity, to embody all the various human achievements . . . in one great synthesis, to bring to harmony the ancient and modern civilizations, to reconcile heart with reason, to establish true justice and peace.' [15]

Nor has this sense of Russia's mission disappeared now that its people are ruled in the name of a political doctrine, Marxism-Leninism, for which universal applicability is claimed, combined with the assertion that it is destined eventually to triumph over all other creeds on a worldwide scale. Marxism is about as far as anything could be from any kind of New Word which Dostoyevsky might have had in mind when hopefully claiming that such a pronouncement would one day sound forth for the first time in Russia, thereby transforming the general human condition in some manner unspecified. Disqualified by its foreign origin, the atheist Socialist creed evolved by two German thinkers would not have suited the conservative and patriot Dostoyevsky, who believed that religion was the very stuff of life, certainly not the opium of the people.

Nevertheless the emotional force of Great Russian messianism, of which Dostoyevsky reflected one facet only, has clearly been incorporated—to a degree which cannot be determined—in the doctrines of Marxism as preached from the Kremlin. And though comparable urges may be found in the teachings of many another pre-revolutionary Russian thinker besides Dostoyevsky, the Russian government of those days lagged far behind. Compared with a Lenin, a Stalin, a Khrushchev or a Brezhnev, the last Romanov emperors were mercifully parochial in their ambitions. They might annex vast areas of the Far East and central Asia, they might hold down the Poles and bully the Finns. But they never claimed or implied that they should or would transform the entire inhabited globe in the Russian image. Nor, by contrast with certain Russian philosophers of that day and their revolutionary successors, did the imperial Russian government propagate as a dogma 'the uniqueness, superiority and universal applicability' of the Russian way of life.[16] Even in the 1890s, the period of take-off in the Russian industrial revolution, the Russian government was not in the habit of pointing to this spectacular economic growth rate, unparalleled in the contemporary world, as proof that every other country should be ruled by an autocratic absolute sprig of the House of Romanov. But comparable suggestions, allegedly proving the superior viability of the Muscovite system on the basis of—highly suspect—economic growth-rate statistics, have been not uncommon under the successor regime, particularly in the mouth of the supreme *vranyo*-monger Khrushchev.

## DOMESTIC PET

So much for Russia and the world. What of the world and Russia?

One special phenomenon associated with East-West relations within the last hundred years is that of the Russia-fancying foreign enthusiast who tends to adopt a Russian persona, and who refers to the Russians as if they were endearing but imperfectly house-trained domestic animals.

Russia-fanciers are those who, indoctrinated by Russians with the patter characteristic of the subject, return home to regurgitate it, acting in effect as unpaid public relations officers. This practice is particularly common in the political area, and has led to the phenomenon of the fellow-traveler, on which little will be said here since politics is not a direct concern of this study. The manifestation can perhaps best be invoked by a brief reference to a single, highly spectacular example of political Russia-fancying. During a visit to the far eastern Soviet concentration camp empire in 1944, the American Vice President Henry A. Wallace was induced to treat the warder-in-chief of this prison province as an 'industrial boss'; and made a speech in Irkutsk, on the very threshold of the world's largest slave empire, to the effect that 'men born in wide, free spaces will not brook injustice and tyranny. They will not even temporarily live in slavery.' [1] As this example shows, political Russia-fanciers are by no means confined to those who necessarily wish to see the Russian system adopted on a worldwide scale. They extend indeed to foreign ultra-conservatives, as also to—by definition, capitalist—businessmen: to anyone, whatever his views, who is sufficiently gullible and unobservant. Such fanciers will, while condescendingly repeating the prescribed patter, simultaneously appear to be congratulating themselves on their broadmindedness and originality in taking a viewpoint so contrary to that which, they wrongly suppose, might be expected of them. The prevalence of this habit among foreign visitors to Russia is a useful corrective to any tendency to censure as an exclusively Russian vice the practice of constantly awarding oneself implied credit marks during conversation. But it does also bear out another contention of the present study: that exposure to Russia tends to provoke Russian-type behavior in even the most stolid of aliens.

Maurice Baring's regurgitation of Dostoyevsky's views on Pushkin is a connoisseur's piece of fancying: 'There was nothing which he [Pushkin] could not understand. Dostoyevsky called him πανάνθρωπος [omnihuman], and it is this capacity for understanding everything and everybody, for being able to assimilate anything, however alien, that makes him so profoundly Russian.' [2] Seldom in the field of human communication can so much empty pretentiousness have been so expertly transferred from one cultural climate to another. A less absurd, though no less disputable, assertion is that of another witness who says that the Russian 'poetical achievement is of unique magnificence.' [3] I prefer to regard this as pardonable exaggeration rather than a sample of 'fancying'; but still wonder whether Russia's admittedly fine poetry is best praised by advancing such an extreme claim. *Unique* magnificence? But what of Greek, Latin, French, English, Italian poetry? All poetry is unique, of course, but it takes a Russian context to provoke the suggestion that one corpus is more unique than others.

Another feature of cultural Russia-fancying is the idealization of Russia's pre-1917 intelligentsia, that heterogeneous amalgam of muddle-headed and often murderous idealists, so often apostrophized by journalists and scholars of the present day as 'superb,' 'magnificent,' 'uniquely gifted,' 'noble' and the like. That the intelligentsia should be defined as a 'milieu of earnest, dedicated, passionately honest, fiercely principled scientists and thinkers, writers and philosophers'—this is not altogether misleading, especially in respect of the 'passionately' and the 'fiercely.' But is all intellectual effort to be disparaged unless conducted in this frenzied spirit? And is it really true to say that 'like a phoenix' the unique spirit of the *intelligent* (member of the pre-revolutionary Russian intelligentsia) has survived the purges and repressions of the police state? [4] And, even if it were true, would it necessarily be a subject for congratulation? These problems are complex and will be be considered in detail below.

The religious sphere is perhaps the most characteristic arena for Russia-fancying. Many are the foreign witnesses who have expounded the special spiritual significance of Russian Easter celebrations; the peculiar Russian gift for 'participating in the passion of their God'; the sense of universal *agape* and the like. It is not the assertions themselves which one wishes to contradict so much as an implied assumption which often seems to underlie them, and which seems to flourish so abundantly in the Russian context: that matters of ultimate belief, spiritual intensity and so on can be assessed at a sniff or a glance, as by a housewife buying fish. On the other hand, not all sniffers out of Russian spiritual sensibility lack professional credentials in the area. They have included, for example, the nineteenth-century canon who has been quoted above as claiming special spiritual attributes for the Russians, and who at least possessed the technical qualification of having attained field rank in the Church of England. Nor need the Russians necessarily be denied the superior degree of spirituality so often claimed for them, provided always that this superiority is not asserted with an offhand lack of sensitivity so blatant as to disqualify a given observer from claiming competence in this delicate area. Such assertions can be sadly unconvincing, especially when accompanied by reproaches against those who do not repeat this section of the patter for inability to 'see below the surface.' [5]

To induce the English, say, to join in a lamentation on their own inhibitedness, excessive reserve, hypocrisy and the like—this represents the kind of target which the Russian indoctrinator of fanciers has set himself. And yet one knows from experience that such missionaries often prefer to see their evangelizing efforts fail. Indeed, they often seem to enjoy the joke, to savor the fellow-feeling which can be promoted when the bluff of nationalist bombast is called. The Russian is no less sensitive by nature than anyone else, nor can he fail to notice that strong element of condescension which is so commonly present in the mind of a foreign fancier even as he patronizingly abases himself to what he perhaps thinks of as the Russian level. To read the embarrassingly naïve utterances of that English pioneer of Russian studies, that fancier-of-fanciers Sir Bernard Pares, is to feel that one wants to protest on the part of the vast nation which he has so complacently taken under his wing.

Extreme nationalist bombast has been evoked above as a typical Russian trait. But the suggestion has never been made that it was universal, or that it was practiced by that vast section, surely the majority, among Russians which does not necessarily qualify as typical. And even if Russians do err in boasting about their own country, it must not be forgotten that they can also show themselves, as already indicated, acutely conscious of its faults and castigate these with greater force and subtlety than any hostile foreign witness. It is also very much in their favor that even those individuals who do tend to be unacceptably boastful are rarely so in their individual capacity. The Russian will not obsessively seek to demonstrate that he is a better man than you are. Rather will he, if he is of the boastful variety, say or 'tactfully' imply: 'I belong to Category A which is superior in the following respects to Category B, that to which you have the misfortune to belong.' In this sense the 'typical' Russian does indeed manifest a collective rather than an individualist psychology.

There is also this to be said in the Russians' favor: that, though many of them can show a keen affection for foreign countries, they have not on the whole bred fanciers as the term has been qualified above. They have often felt strong emotions for and against alien cultures. And they have on occasion felt impelled to deride or to imitate the English, the Americans, the Germans, the French and other breeds. But from the fancier's prime characteristic, that of smug condescension, they have on the whole been happily immune.

## THE CLASS STRUGGLE

To what extent has Russian society fallen, to what extent does it still fall, into different social classes?

One view is that, by contrast with England of the same period, the Russian community of the eighteenth and nineteenth centuries was a simple two-tier affair.[1] By the ignorant, indeed, and by those who accept the thesis that Russians are instinctively democratic and egalitarian in the ultimate degree, they may be credited with long having achieved total classlessness. Bewailing the constant pressures on English fiction writers to respond to their own complex class system, an English novelist contrasts Dostoyevsky's advantages: 'It is all the same to him,' writes Virginia Woolf, 'whether you are noble or simple, a tramp or a great lady.' [2] That social standing was in fact one of Dostoyevsky's major concerns as a writer, particularly in his early career, escaped this witness. But though she is wrong in suggesting that Russia knew or knows no class differentiation at all, it may yet be that the Russian system, albeit permitting a yawning gap between privileged and unprivileged, is relatively simple. On the whole a given Russian has tended and still tends to belong to one of two basic categories sometimes known as 'we' and 'they.' 'We' are the vast majority of the people, the receivers and evaders of orders, passive, sporadically obedient and inwardly resentful or resigned. 'They' are the givers of orders, a relatively small group who stand toward 'us' as exploiter to exploited or officer to private soldier.

The further back one goes to the beginning of the nineteenth century, the more closely may the élite 'they' be equated with a specific social class or estate: that of the gentry, numbering about 1 percent of the total population. The élite may also be crudely equated with two other categories, those of landowners and officials, which both overlapped with the gentry in that all landowners and higher officials belonged to the gentry estate. To the peasantry, approximately eighty times as large, four-fifths of the population belonged, and this estate corresponded fairly closely with the exploited 'us.' That there were many rich peasants, that there were also many desperately poor and downtrodden gentlemen and officials— these undoubted facts still do not invalidate the general thesis. As for intermediate categories, consisting of clergy, merchants, lower townsfolk and others, these tended to remain culturally akin to the peasants, whom they resembled in speech and dress.

That every Russian citizen, up to 1917, was formally assigned to one or other of these or similar categories, which were entered in his so-called passport—an identity card required for internal travel—is a significant detail. But though the number of estates was considerable, and though the refinements of the structure brought in categories which have not been mentioned here, the essential two-tier division into élite and non-élite remained valid. Historically speaking, the élite and non-élite of the imperial period correspond respectively to the Tsar's higher and lower underlings of the Muscovite period. The former were the heirs of the administrators compulsorily shaved, educated and put into European dress by Peter the Great, while the vastly more numerous peasantry together with the associated lower townspeople, merchants and priests continued to shamble about in their beards and caftans or sheepskins. No late nineteenth-century traveler could miss the difference: 'He easily recognizes the French-speaking nobles [gentry] in West-European costume; the burly, bearded merchant in black cloth cap and long, shiny, double-breasted coat; the priest with his uncut hair and flowing robes; the peasant with his full, fair beard and unsavoury, greasy sheep-skin.'[3] Meanwhile the same visitor's Russian friends might be assuring him in all sincerity that there were no social classes at all in this supremely democratic society, and never had been—a characteristic *vranyo*-type statement.

That Russia was behindhand in certain kinds of social snobbery is nevertheless true. For instance, relatively slight importance was attached to such titles as prince, count and baron. Where all a nobleman's children, not merely the eldest son, inherited his title, princes were a fairly common phenomenon; indeed, there are said to have been about two thousand of them in 1917.[4] By the title-conscious English an *émigré* Russian prince has accordingly tended to be treated as a person of considerably more social consequence than he may in fact possess. This being so, there was little place in Russia for the obsession with pedigree which was once so noticeable a feature of Western European society. Imperial Russia also enjoyed no small degree of social mobility. Losmonosov, the eighteenth-century fisherman's son who became a leading poet, grammarian and academician, is the example most commonly quoted. To him may be added such nineteenth-century figures as Michael Pogodin, the serf's son who became a professor of history and prominent publicist; Alexander Nikitenko, born a serf, who rose to high rank in government and academic service; Anton Chekhov, the provincial grocer's son who became the world's leading short-story writer. Herzen, himself the son of a Russian gentleman, has noted and perhaps exaggerated the extraordinary ease with which a peasant of his own day could enter the gentry, or a gentleman descend to the peasantry.[5]

Another witness goes too far when he virtually discounts any ill feeling between social classes.[6] There may have been less of it than in many another country, but it was by no means totally lacking. For example, many peasants spoke with satisfaction of the hanging of the five Decembrist gentlemen-conspirators in 1826, as of the sentencing of others to Siberian hard labor, also expressing the wish that members of the élite could be given a taste of the knout;[7] for gentlemen were traditionally exempt from corporal punishment as inflicted, often with extreme brutality, on the peasantry. Another tradition of the resentful muzhik was that of 'loosing the red cock'—that is, burning down the local manor house. Nor was there anything in village traditions to prevent him shortly afterward bowing to the ground and imploring forgiveness from the squire and his family, assuming that they had survived. Other aspects of resentment from below may be freely observed in Russian folk poetry, as also in the epilogue to Dostoyevsky's *Crime and Punishment*. Here convicts from the peasantry object to the presence among them of the convicted gentleman axe-murderer Raskolnikov. They complain of his *modus operandi* as breaching class copyright. 'It's not a gent's place to bash folks with a hatchet.'

Whatever else may be urged about imperial Russia's class

structure, acute sensitivity to social gradations was certainly not lacking. Where a Frenchman or German would tend (Gogol unconvincingly asserts in his *Dead Souls*) to address a millionaire or tobacconist in much the same terms, Russia had her 'experts in sophistry.' These connoisseurs of status could grade their manner with a niceness of nuance according to whether the landowner whom they might be addressing owned one hundred, three hundred, five hundred, eight hundred or, as the case might be, a thousand souls. 'In short, you could go up to a million without running out of nuances.' [8] A coarser sample of the same phenomenon may be found in Chekhov's well-known story *Fat and Thin*, where two old schoolfriends meet accidentally after many years in a flurry of hearty and intimate effusions. But these are hurriedly cut off when it turns out that the fat one has reached the higher echelons of the Table of Ranks, while his thin friend is still skulking in the lower reaches. When this becomes evident friendly communion abruptly gives way to condescension on one side and awed sycophancy on the other.

It is against such indications, for and against, that the many claims attributing to the Russian either an exceptionally egalitarian or an exceptionally class-conscious response must be tested. And while, as usual, the assertions of Russians and their observers tend to one extreme or the other, the customary tame conclusion—that the truth tends to hover between opposed poles—will be found most helpful to those who probe these arcana in a spirit of genuine inquiry.

The elaborate formal categories of the imperial period were already falling apart, though still theoretically operative, when the whole structure was swept away by the 1917 October Revolution. That the successor society is by no means classless does not require laboring to anyone familiar with it. The country now has two classes, according to its own official doctrine: those of peasants and workers, besides which the 'toiling intelligentsia' is officially regarded as a separate category—not as a class, being termed a stratum.[9] But behind this formal structure a two-tier division into what it is tempting to call upper and lower servitors is still, broadly speaking, operative. The élite of upper servitors consists of those who have yoked their careers to making the system work. By no means can élite status be exactly equated with membership in the Communist Party, with the possession of high professional qualifications or with having undergone higher education; but it does tend to be associated with all these features. As for the non-élite—that, as ever, constitutes the majority of the population: those who are set in motion, presided over, manipulated and otherwise supervised by their betters. After a brief post-revolutionary phase during which it was thought appropriate for all, high and low, to receive or appear to receive pay and material rewards on the same scale as everyone else, this leveling policy was explicitly repudiated by Stalin. The system which he introduced, and which still operates, is one of extremely wide but deliberately camouflaged pay differentials accentuated by a tax system free of the progressive element which tends to level out net incomes in many un-Kremlinized countries. Privileged access to such amenities as housing, special shops, theater tickets and the like has also helped to create the 'new class' of Soviet bourgeois who have attracted so much attention. They figure not only in the comments of foreign observers such as the Yugoslav political dissident Milovan Djilas, who first publicized the term *new class*, but also in occasional critical works of Soviet-published Russian fiction, of which the best-known is Vladimir Dudintsev's novel *Not by Bread Alone*. These people often dispose of vast sums in roubles which they may have difficulty in spending, for it is only in the West that money, in adequate quantity, can buy practically anything.

One amusing by-product of the newly emerged totalitarian bourgeoisie is the ease with which a foreigner may be mistaken for a member of it. I was once walking absent-mindedly up Gorky Street in Moscow, swinging that hated symbol of un-

merited privilege, a leather briefcase, when an intense-looking,
strikingly handsome young woman advanced on me—like the
would-be assassin Vera Zasulich on the hated General Trepov
in 1878—and hissed the accusation 'Soviet bourgeois' at me
through her elegant teeth. (But so complicated have Russian
*mœurs* now become that I was later on the same day, without
briefcase, refused admittance to an outdoor dance floor on the
grounds that my somewhat casual rig—no tie—was considered
insufficiently 'cultured.') Not dissimilar was the experience related to me by a foreign diplomat who once chanced to be
waiting for a train in an almost deserted suburban station.
Hearing angry tones proceeding from across the rails, he observed what seemed to be, in the real rather than the symbolic
sense, an 'ordinary Soviet worker' voicing a strident reproach
from the relative safety of the other side of the track. 'How
long,' the man yelled, 'are you bastards going to go on sucking
our blood?' And it was not in my informant's capacity as capitalist lackey, but as one mistaken for a member of the native
oppressing class, that he received—or believed he received—
this incorrectly addressed but all too natural piece of abuse.

Officials, according to the popular view, have been sucking the blood of the Russian common man since time imme-
morial, and especially since the institution of the Table of
Ranks by Peter the Great in 1722 put officialdom, so to speak,
on an official basis. The official was known as a *chinovnik* until
the abolition of the Table in 1917. And *chinovnik* still remains
in use, but only as an abusive equivalent for the post-revolutionary term *sluzhashchy*, which has officially superseded it.
Under the pre-1917 regimen official rank, based on automatic
promotions in conformity with a pre-arranged timetable,
rather than on zeal or merit, secured the status of hereditary
gentleman for those who progressed as far as the eighth grade
(later raised to fifth grade); and was therefore a powerful
agent of social mobility. 'Russia was the only country except
China in which the status of noble or gentleman was con-

ferred by education. The high-school . . . passing-out examination turned the muzhik into a lord.' [10] This helps to explain nineteenth-century officials' obsessive attitude to their rank and its appurtenances, which included various medals and orders, also awarded on a more or less automatic scale. 'These people,' says Nikitenko, 'are right in wanting a cross or rank—without it, who would recognize them as people? . . . Charming female company . . . respect, popularity: all must be purchased by parading your dignities.' A contemporary of Nikitenko's, the Decembrist Nicholas Turgenev, even claimed that Russians lacking rank were 'completely outside the pale, officially and legally speaking.' [11]

This 'gigantic administrative machine which holds together all the various parts of the vast Empire' . . . seemed to penetrate every nook and cranny of Russian life.[12] Everywhere, and especially in the capital St. Petersburg, one seemed to see nothing but uniforms. These were all the more obtrusive in constituting no monopoly of the armed services, being also worn by civil servants, schoolboys, students, professors and even sometimes merchants, who did not wish to be outdone in presenting the world with outward evidence of their inner worth. The wearing of uniforms by so many categories helps to explain the common impression that officials were more numerous than was in fact the case. It also helps to show how the *chinovnik* became one of those 'typical' Russian phenomena, such as drunkenness, which caught the attention of observers to a greater extent than appears justified by a cool examination of statistics. With only a dozen civil servants, approximately, for each ten thousand of population, the Russian Empire was woefully—or happily—understaffed in the mid-nineteenth century by comparison with Western Europe, where the proportion of officials was three or four times as great.[13]

And yet, small though it was, the Russian official class somehow seemed to dominate the country and to make nineteenth-century Russia a pioneer in the development of a burgeoning bureaucracy such as has since become the curse of the civilized world. Russian officials early developed that spirit of ill-placed administrative zeal, that passion for useless formalities, that intoxication with petty power which permeated all fourteen grades of the notorious Table of Ranks; as also did a preoccupation with trivialities—a preoccupation which indeed did not, according to one masterly understatement, preclude disorder.[14] Above all it helped to generate *chinopochitaniye:* 'rank sycophancy,' as it can be punningly translated, whenever a person of junior rank such as a Titular Councillor, a mere 'Your Honor,' ran into a personage of senior rank such as a State Councillor entitled to be addressed as 'Your Excellency.'

The *chinovnik* evoked widely different reactions in the élite and non-élite. He was feared by the peasantry, but despised or mocked by the gentry and intelligentsia; being described, for example, as *'un espèce de canaille qu'on appelle chinovnik.'* The title *general,* which accrued to all officials, civilian as well as military, of the fifth grade and above, became the rough equivalent for 'pompous blockhead' to the nineteenth-century younger generation. Nor was there any lack of *chinovnik*-baiting by *chinovniki* themselves. One such civilian 'general,' himself anything but pompous, regarded his fellow officials as wretched individuals: 'the worst natural enemy of the people's welfare.'[15]

The widespread low opinion of civil servants was by no means exclusively based on the obsession with hierarchy which so many observers have noted. There was also the *chinovnik's* practice of requiring bribes from his clients, a routine dating from the Muscovite period when senior provincial administrators had received no salary, but had been expected to 'live off the country' like members of an occupying army. Paid, but on a grossly inadequate scale, in the nineteenth century, officials tended to be classified as honest if they confined the taking of bribes to an informal tariff scale. The dishonest were those whose greed exceeded this accepted norm, like the official in Gogol's *Inspector General* who was accused of accepting bribes 'above his rank.' Some of the more unscrupulous officials, and especially those stationed furthest from the capital, practiced the grossest forms of extortion. They were quite capable of accusing some rich person in their locality of an imaginary crime, and of holding him in prison until he paid over a required sum.

Russian bureaucratic methods, far from disappearing with the October Revolution of 1917 and associated abolition of the Table of Ranks, have only proliferated during the ensuing sixty years. But that need surprise no one, since proliferating bureaucracy is so common a feature of modern society in general. In totalitarian Russia the process has been accentuated through the practice of interference exercised by the state on a scale far exceeding that of any Tsar or Tsar-Emperor, and inevitably controlled by a horde of officials. To this must be added that the most successful power-seeker of modern times, Stalin, made lavish and inspired use of bureaucratic methods in a rise to power which depended not only on violence and the threat of violence, but also on card indexes, record files, dossiers and interlocking committees—all packed with the dictator's nominees and all watching over each other to an extent of which no individual member, and perhaps not even the dictator himself, could ever be quite certain. With the death of Stalin, and consequent abandonment of large-scale arbitrary arrest and imprisonment as a control technique, the essential structure yet remains, with the result that a key organization such as the Soviet Army is interpenetrated with party, police and special political controls of phenomenal intricacy. As for the bureaucratic presence, after a period under Khrushchev when this was somewhat muted by the influence conceded to specialist and technical advisers, the top structure has probably become more bureaucratized than ever since

1964.[16] And yet, while all this has been happening, the curse of bureaucracy has been vigorously condemned by modern Russia's successive rulers from Lenin onwards. Energetic attempts have been made to curb the evil; yet have been, to put it mildly, no more successful in the Kremlin's orbit than anywhere else.

As for bribery, corruption and gross inefficiency, no statistics are available on the comparative incidence of these phenomena in imperial and totalitarian Russia. That they have by no means died out the modern periodical press abundantly testifies. Here one may read of such minor idiocies as the bulk freighting of bathing costumes to the Arctic Circle, or of snow plows to the Black Sea coast, all freely admitted under the heading of 'self-criticism.' One may also read so many press denunciations of blackmailing, extortionate, venal officials that a recent, by no means hostile, foreign observer can refer to the 'bribery, corruption and knavery which are so widespread and which nowadays constitute the chief internal "enemy" of the Soviet state.' [17] The system of illicit deals and under-the-counter arrangements known as *blat* or *kombinatsiya* flourishes widely. It is frequently used, for example, by factory managers who seek to fulfill the norms imposed by the economic plans without necessarily pursuing direct personal gain; indeed, *blat* of this type—the obtaining of spare parts, for instance, on a kind of 'old boy network'—has long been an integral part of an economic structure which would surely collapse if such special arrangements were suddenly to be abandoned. Nor has excessive deference to rank by any means passed away, though its methods have changed and its incidence may have ebbed somewhat since the days of Gogol and Saltykov.

Among other social groups the peasantry has frequently been invoked above on account of its numerical importance and a special evasive attitude to authority evolved over the centuries in response to oppression. Having thus developed by the mid-nineteenth century 'a power of continued, dogged, passive resistance such as is possessed . . . by no other class of men in Europe,' [18] the peasantry was to see its numerical superiority of more than four to one slowly but inexorably eroded. Not until the year 1960 or thereabouts did the USSR cease to be a preponderantly rural country, if judged by the place of residence of the larger number of citizens. The drift to the towns had been constant throughout the nineteenth century, had accelerated with the industrial revolution of the 1890s, and had then further accelerated with Stalin's Five Year Plans from 1929 onward. But though town-dwellers have now outnumbered country-dwellers for nearly twenty years, and though urbanization still proceeds apace, the peasantry remains a numerically significant force, and to a far greater degree than any corresponding rural element in Britain or the United States. And even in the towns—in Moscow or Tula, say—a Russian crowd seems to react in a more peasantlike manner, however defined, than would be the case in Rome, Munich or Pittsburgh.

Nor is the significance of the present-day peasantry confined to the many scores of millions of those officially categorized as peasants. In his book *The Taproot of Soviet Society* (1961) an American observer, Nicholas P. Vakar, argues that Soviet leaders have modeled their politics less on the precepts of Marx and Lenin than on the parish pump mentality which they or their fathers originally absorbed in their native villages. In 1967 a consulting psychiatrist, Henry V. Dicks, could make a similar claim the basis for constructing certain helpful *Notes on the Russian National Character,* in which he writes that 'Bearers of power in the Soviet Union are largely the children of Great Russian peasants, or the urban working class, many of whom have retained a close connection with their peasant background.' [19]

Though Russians' and Russia-watchers' statements on the muzhik exhibit their usual polarity, it is rare to find a denunciation of the class as violent as that of the prime yokel-baiter

Maxim Gorky in his essay 'On the Russian Peasantry.' To peasant collective sadism, on which his views have already been quoted, may be added many other charges leveled against the muzhik, including that of exploiting his neighbors. For the lot of his fellow peasants the peasant cares nothing, according to Gorky: 'No one in Ryazan weeps over a bad harvest in Pskov.' And Gorky's peasant is equally unconcerned about famine in the towns, exploiting his position as food grower to extort the very boots and shirt off the unhappy, hungry city-dweller's feet and back.[20] Gorky's views on peasant callousness receive slight confirmation from such common rustic proverbs as 'My hut is at the end': in other words, '*I*, whose home is not endangered, am damned if I will help *you* put out the fire which is consuming *your* hut.' Once again a non-Russian equivalent ('I'm all right, Jack') indicates that certain vices are human rather than exclusively Russian. Moreover, Gorky was grossly unfair to the terrorized peasant of the early Soviet years—so often compelled to disgorge his stocks, including even seed corn, for no return whatever by armed requisitioners from the towns; and often lucky if he escaped such clashes with his life.

Such outspoken denunciations of the peasantry as that launched by Gorky, in the aftermath of the cruel Russian Civil War of 1917–21, can be balanced by innumerable hymns to the Russian peasant's alleged virtues penned and intoned by Russians of the peasant-fancying variety, who include such major figures as Leo Tolstoy and Dostoyevsky in addition to those whose love of the Russian common people (*narod*) earned for them the name of narodniks, 'populists.' Alas, persons of this type were all too commonly town-dwellers who barely knew one end of a peasant from the other. Yet they idealized the muzhik, as some have since come to idealize the—once no less oppressed—black people of America: out of a guilty conscience rather than from intimate knowledge. For centuries the Russian peasant had carried the weight of the entire country on his back, as plowman, laborer and soldier. Might he not, then, be compensated for expending so much in the way of blood, toil, tears and sweat over the ages by a little— well, rather more than a little—condescending praise; which, after all, cost nothing? Another common element in populist dithyrambs to the peasantry is the built-in self-congratulatory tone of the speaker, who is often in effect saying, 'Watch me being magnanimous toward our poor muzhik.' Here, once again, Russian hyper-consciousness of audience-reaction frequently seems to be present, and it is the audience's reaction to himself, not to the peasant, which seems to take precedence in the fancier's mind. Some of these points are made in a little-known and unjustly neglected early story of Chekhov's, *Good-for-Nothings*. Here a condescending landowner displays the laborers on his estate to his visiting brother as if they were animals in a zoo. He rhapsodizes away about the muzhik's instinctual wisdom, natural sense of justice and innate strength, as contrasted with the speaker's own class. 'We're all skin and bones . . . outsiders, rejects—how dare *we* consider ourselves *their* betters?' The muzhik-fancying squire also interrupts a peasant meal, compelling the picturesque bumpkins to sing folk songs while their buckwheat gruel congeals on the table, and eventually gives instructions for two of their lustier womenfolk to be sent up to the manor for his and his brother's after-dinner delectation; the girls are required to give a folk-dancing exhibition and, it is implied, more intimate entertainment as well.[21]

Himself for many years a country squire with an excellent record as a good neighbor to the local peasants, on whom he bestowed free medical care and three village schools, largely planned and financed by himself, Chekhov could feel fully justified in expressing his acute exasperation with the spurious element in so much contemporary intellectual peasant-fancying. Concerned to help the peasants in a practical way, and also to describe them accurately and unsentimentally in such key works as his most famous story, *Peasants* (1897), he was so repelled by the trendy folkniks of his day that he rarely uttered a generalization of his own on the Russian muzhik. And he was utterly disgusted by the cavortings of those fanciers with whom he found himself unwillingly celebrating the thirty-sixth anniversary of the Emancipation of the Serfs on 19 February 1897 at the Continental Hotel in Moscow. 'Boring and silly. To dine, to drink champagne, to make a hullabaloo, to give speeches on peasant consciousness, on the peasant conscience, freedom and so on, while all the time tail-coated slaves [the waiters] scurry about the tables, as much serfs as ever they were: and while coachmen wait out in the freezing air of the streets. This is to lie to the Holy Spirit.' [22]

Discounting the statements of many peasant-fanciers as belonging to the language of mysticism or metaphysics, one can yet collect from a host of less biased and patronizing witnesses a mass of evidence or assertions which more than counter-balances the black picture drawn by Gorky. The late nineteenth-century French journalist Victor Tissot claimed, for instance, that 'There is nothing more gentle, more humane than the Russian peasant.' And when a witness as hostile to Russian society as Custine pauses to comment on the peasants' freedom from moral degradation (in contrast to their degrading surroundings) together with their wit and their pride, he deserves to be heeded. So too does Nikitenko, who expressly dissociates himself from trendy peasant-fancying as much as any Chekhov. The man who is prepared to denounce the romanticizing of the peasant, and who does not hesitate on occasion to call the peasant a drunken savage, may be listened to when he praises the same peasant's sincerity and superiority to his educated fellow-countrymen. And Pushkin, an objective witness whom no one could tag as a peasant-fancier, has written a very paean in praise of the muzhik: of his independence, boldness, cleverness, enterprise, dexterity, honesty, industry and tolerance. These, and many other judicious witnesses, add up to a great deal.[23]

In Russian peasant communities, as they have stabilized themselves in state and collective farms from the collectivization campaign of 1929 onward, the ancestral disadvantages of the muzhik have to some extent been institutionalized. Where other citizens are issued with a 'passport' enabling them to travel inside the country, peasants have been denied this privilege, though they are now said to be on the point of receiving it. The result has been to restrict and hamper their movements, and in effect to bind them to the land, so that foreign observers have not hesitated to compare the institution of collectivization with that of serfdom. In earnings, welfare, pensions and educational activities, too, the modern peasant has lagged behind his urban brothers. Nor has he been relieved from the odious patronage of peasant-fancying non-peasants, who are just as prepared as they were a hundred years ago to dilate on his sterling qualities as unacknowledged compensation in full for the disadvantages under which he labors.

Meanwhile the peasant continues whenever possible to protect himself by traditional methods against the exactions of the state. 'The struggle between state edicts and peasant cunning is unending.' [24]

## INTIMACY

Now that the Russian's wider affiliations as a social being have been reviewed it remains to examine him as a member of his smallest unit, that of the family. This is in a sense his most important relationship of all, yet does not call for extensive treatment here, since the function and development of the Russian family has never differed strikingly from its role—if one may be permitted a particularly gross generalization—in the West as a whole. The Russian and the Western family have both tended to become progressively smaller, less cohesive, less patriarchal and less closely united by religious belief and observances.

Though the family has not played an overwhelming role in expressing or stimulating any differentiation between the Russian and the Western mind, certain significant features must be recorded. In particular, the Russian family has tended to be somewhat less united than its Western counterpart. This is partly the inevitable outcome of the greater degree of intervention in personal relationships practiced by a state so authoritarian in its various manifestations: Muscovite, imperial and totalitarian. In the days of serfdom peasant families could be split at the whim of individual landowners empowered to sell their serfs retail as well as wholesale, to draft them into the army and even to nominate them for Siberian imprisonment and exile. The most widely feared of these fates was selective drafting into the army, a function which was taken over after emancipation by the village commune. Conscription was for twenty-five years in the first half of the nineteenth century, and was mourned in the villages as an utter calamity. The recruit might never reappear in his native village, being all but permanently lost to domestic life on induction into the forces, while his abandoned wife, if he had one, tended to be considered half-widow, half-whore. Even more disruptive was sentence for a criminal offense to a prison term in Siberia, which involved the loss of civil rights and was followed by permanent exile even when the sentence had been served in full.

After reforms enacted in the middle of the nineteenth century by Alexander II to mitigate both the impact of recruitment and the severity of certain penal procedures, official assaults on the integrity of the Russian peasant family somewhat decreased. But centrifugal tendencies remained. It was still common practice for a peasant to remove himself permanently from his village, yet without severing legal ties with his commune, and to take up work in a distant town as laborer, craftsman, waiter, domestic servant and the like. Moreover, as a nineteenth-century observer has noted, 'The artisan who goes to work in a distant town never takes his wife and family with him.'[1]

Despite all such reservations family ties remained close, surviving the shattering effects of the 1917 revolutions, of the ensuing Civil War and also of the following period, up to the mid-1930s, when the newly totalitarian state actively sought to dissolve family bonds on general principle. Divorce and abortion became readily available, while free love was extensively preached and ostentatiously practiced, parental control over children being eroded and undermined. Yet the Russian family retained sufficient cohesion to be easily reinstated as an institution when Stalin decided to do so by rendering divorce and abortion difficult or impossible, and reestablishing parental control over children.

It is, then, as a result of innate domestic conservatism, fostered by official policy, that marriage and family life in present-day Russia more closely reproduce the Western pattern of these institutions than might be expected in view of the rigors of totalitarian rule and the sweeping official claims to have pioneered a new and revolutionary way of life. But a marginally smaller degree of family cohesiveness still remains a characteristic Russian feature. Since most wives and husbands work, but not necessarily in the same enterprise, and since both are at the beck and call of authority to a greater extent than their Western counterparts, one or other may suddenly receive a posting to some distant part of the country on orders not necessarily compulsory in the strictest sense, but difficult to evade in practice. For husbands and wives to take their holidays separately, and at different times of the year, seems to be almost the norm; it is certainly far more common than it is in the West. Another distinction is that, in this land of restricted privacy, the domestic hearth is more vulnerable to the intrusion of licensed or self-appointed snoopers in accordance with the assumption, so characteristic of totalitarian *mœurs,* that everybody's affairs except the state's are everybody else's business.

Another feature is the prevalence of marriages of convenience based on the desperate need to acquire living space. Whereas, in the West, an individual may be suspected of marrying for money, in Russia he or she may more probably be suspected of embracing wedlock for the sake of a half share in a room or small flat. Another motive for marriage may be that it can convey the coveted and elusive Moscow residence permit. Cases are sometimes reported of men who, for a suitable consideration, will marry and divorce in rapid succession a whole series of provincial girls thereby enabled to reside in the metropolis of which they would otherwise have seen as little as Chekhov's Three Sisters.

Less cohesive in the sense that family ties can more easily be loosed, the modern Russian family tends to be closer than that of the more advanced Western nations in the purely physical sense that, if its members live together at all, they do so in the extreme proximity imposed by dearth of space. That the people actually prefer this kind of huddling and bundling is, as indicated above, rather the contention of distant Russia-fancying witnesses than of those directly concerned.

To turn from the Russian family to the role of women, inside and outside the family, is to be struck by a significant improvement in female status after centuries of rampant male dominance. 'If the [Russian] woman be not beaten with the whip once a week she will not be good,' reports the sixteenth-century English witness Antony Jenkinson. 'And the women say if their husbands did not beat them they would not love them.' Meanwhile a contemporary manual of etiquette, the *Domostroy,* was instructing the Muscovite husband in the tech-

nique of beating his wife: this must be done courteously, lov-
ingly and in such a way as neither to blind her nor render her
permanently deaf; the possibility of a husband *not* beating his
wife does not seem to be considered. Two centuries later a
French monk, the Abbé Chappe d'Auteroche, denounces Russia's barbarous provinces, where 'men tyrannize over their
wives, whom they treat as their slaves, requiring of them the
most servile offices,' such as pulling off their boots. To skip a
further two centuries is to find a twentieth-century authority
lamenting that nowhere have women been more cruelly
beaten than in the Russian village, and instancing the typical
Russian male chauvinist peasant proverb, 'The harder you
beat a woman the tastier the cabbage soup.' Such homely anti-
feminist tags are legion, from the notorious 'Woman is long
on hair but short on brain' to such collectors' pieces as 'A mare
ain't a horse, a hen ain't a bird, a woman ain't a person';
'Seven women have only one soul between them'; 'Woman has
no soul, only a vapor.' [2]

So much for the status of the pre-revolutionary Russian
peasant woman at its lowest. Her more privileged sisters also
suffered grave disabilities in imperial times. Subjected to
legally imposed male tutelage, they were only permitted the
passport required for internal travel purposes by consent of a
father or husband, who thus almost had the right to keep a
daughter or wife under house arrest. Women could own
property. But they found access to careers difficult apart from
a few special areas such as governess-ship, prostitution and
the stage, being debarred in varying degrees from access to
higher education. For these reasons feminism became a burning issue with the radical movement, reformist or revolutionary, which first acquired significant momentum in the
1860s. So addicted was the pioneer radical Chernyshevsky to
the cause of female liberation that he went far beyond the goal
of mere equality between the sexes, maintaining that woman
had been so long under-privileged as to have fallen due at last,

like it or not, for a spell of over-privilege. Hitherto a man had
been able to run a whole string of mistresses without incurring
social censure, whereas his wife had found it impossible to
maintain a single miserable lover. Now, in all fairness, so ineq-
uitable an arrangement must be reversed. Chernyshevsky insisted on his own wife, Olga, conforming to his program; also
illustrating its implications in his atrocious but highly influential novel *What Is to Be Done?* 'My dear, hitherto I have only
loved you. Now I respect you.' Such, according to that scourge
of radicals Dostoyevsky, was the reaction prescribed for a
Chernyshevsky-indoctrinated husband at the blissful moment
when he should receive the news that his wife had at last asserted her integrity by embracing adultery.[3]

In present-day Russia the old male-dominated marriage is
no longer the norm. And though no statistics are to be had on
wife-beating through the ages, one may safely claim that this
barbarous practice has ceased to be the widespread phenomenon which so many nineteenth-century and earlier observers
have reported. In any case the modern Russian woman seems
both morally and physically equipped to stand up for herself.
She often looks well capable of husband-beating if necessary;
and, even if physically weaker than the male, is likely to
possess greater stamina and force of character. Thus has the
new Russia evolved a corps of formidable, energetic and
sometimes lamentably smug matrons. Transferring into the
low-level or middling political sphere, to which they are confined, woman's traditional role as guardian of tradition, these
now constitute a bulwark of a system which might conceivably
fall apart were it left in the exclusive custodianship of the relatively easy-going Russian male. Nor is this impressive breed of
woman exclusively a product of totalitarianism. The Russian
peasant, a pre-revolutionary authority notes, 'rather admires
vigour and strength in his mate'; [4] and has long ago invented
the term *boy-baba* as a term of praise—meaning, as near as one
may translate, a Woman Embattled.

Russian literature again and again throws up a situation particularly familiar to Turgenev's readers: that in which a beautiful, strong, well-integrated, decisive young woman becomes erotically implicated with some spineless, dithering pipsqueak of a man who invariably emerges discredited from the involvement. In fiction of the totalitarian period the clash between strong female and weak male is more than ever in vogue, and has been well analyzed in terms which appropriately recall the life-cycle of the spider. In Russian fiction, pre-revolutionary and post-revolutionary alike, a feeble, vacillating hero is indeed again and again 'contrasted with a young woman of unusual strength and integrity of character' who shows 'more purity and dedication and also more practical common sense than the man.' [5] Thus do firmness of purpose and strength of character tend, in Russian fiction through the ages, to be confined to the female sex.

And yet, for all the Russian female's undoubted strength of character and physique, and for all the undoubted progress made in establishing equality between the sexes, a considerable degree of officially unavowed male domination continues. No woman has yet attained a truly influential position in the post-revolutionary political world, which may be scanned in vain for Catherine the Greats. The most eminent, to date, has been Catherine Furtsev, who was appointed to the Party Presidium in 1956, but lost this commanding position in 1961. Nor is this kind of discrimination at the higher levels confined to Communist Party organization. Despite the prominence of women in medicine, teaching and cultural work, few indeed are appointed to the most senior posts in these or other areas.

On a humbler level, too, the modern Russian woman remains at some disadvantage when compared to her male partner. Her equality is enshrined in law; she receives equal pay for equal work. But her 'right to work' has become blurred with something far less desirable: a *de facto* obligation to work outside the home, even if she is a wife and mother, since the generally low standard of living makes it impossible for most husbands to support a full-time housewife. Women have constituted about half the total labor force for some years now.[6] But this is, again, no unmixed gain for the feminist cause owing to the common domestic arrangement, not enshrined in law, whereby—in addition to doing a full-time outside job— the Russian housewife may be faced with the appalling daily martyrdom of queuing for food and other household necessities, besides having to do housework, and to feed and clothe her family. Meanwhile her allegedly equal spouse is happily playing dominoes or drinking with his pals.

In their attitude to divorce, as to parenthood, present-day Russians once again tend to show themselves marginally less addicted than their Western counterparts to maintaining the family as a cohesive institution. Divorce is now easily obtained in Russia, and its incidence has recently been recorded as exceeding the notoriously high level found in the United States. There are even districts of Moscow where the number of divorces in a given year is in excess of the number of marriages. As for children, they tend—in view of the desperate economic strain imposed by the burden of feeding and housing extra dependants—to be regarded as a nuisance rather than a blessing. Wide use is made of abortion, legalized in 1955, to limit their numbers: a procedure all the more crucial in view of the poor quality or unavailability of contraceptives. Abortion thus seems to constitute, both inside and outside marriage, pretty well the main method of birth control—and an increasingly effective one, too, to judge from the fall in the birth rate from 2.7 percent in 1950 to 1.8 percent in 1973.[7]

Turning to the sexual activities and preoccupations of Russians, and the extent to which these may differ from Western practice, one generalizes with reluctance in an area so private. One point may, however, be made with confidence. So far as public utterance is concerned—whether in posters, in films or in the printed word—there is none of the por-

nography so extensively cultivated in the West. Rather is pru-
dishness the fault. But here, too, the usual double standard
seems to operate. For instance, the Russian visitor to a foreign
country may in his official persona high-mindedly condemn
such appalling manifestations of capitalist decadence as placards advertising strip-tease joints, or—in one bizarre instance
which I recall—certain highly unvoluptuous female dummies
standing unashamedly undraped in a dress-shop window. Yet
the same puritan scourge of capitalist immorality may, if he is
that kind of person, later be heard retailing the Russian equivalent of 'locker-room' stories, which may be extremely amusing, or which may alternatively descend to a level of obscenity
and tastelessness almost passing belief. May one perhaps relate
the observance of such a double standard to the traditional
pre-revolutionary peasant custom of veiling the holy icon with
a curtain, or removing the cross from one's neck, before en-
gaging in sexual intercourse?

On sexual morals in general it is difficult or impossible to
achieve statistically valid conclusions. That a high degree of
freedom, casualness and promiscuity is cultivated by some sections of the community is, however, beyond doubt. Having extensively investigated this problem in the field, one American
journalist even reckons that at least seven out of ten of Moscow's young women are instantly available for bedding by any
presentable male.[8] These are respectable girls looking for a
little light relief from the drabness of everyday life: enthusiastic amateurs, in fact, not the professionals who may also be
found and who ply for hire rather than kicks.

Reticent or even priggish in public utterance on sexual
matters, Russians—or at least their less cultured representatives—can be extremely free in informal contexts with their
use of equivalents for English 'four-letter words.' A Russian of
the more uninhibited brand will unhesitatingly consign someone else's mother to an incestuous form of what used to be
called a fate worse than death. Moreover, so flexionally rich is

the language, such its wealth of affixes, such its facility in forming derivatives, that the creatively inspired need not confine themselves to such crudities as the form *yob*, 'fuck.' They can, for instance, add a further dimension by uttering the compound imprecation *yob tebya pereyob*, 'Fuck you in the *n*th degree.' Or they can refer to someone as a *nedoyobysh*: for which the nearest English equivalent seems to be 'one scraped off the sheets with a spoon,' like the luckless young man of Dunoon in the limerick. Meanwhile, though pornography may be officially prohibited, just as the existence of prostitution may be officially denied, foreign visitors to the Soviet Union continue to observe both manifestations, though they are of course less openly paraded than in societies more permissive.

An unusually reliable foreign witness has told me of a visit made some time ago to the provincial city of Astrakhan, where he chanced to fall in with the town's chief pimp. This organizer of Caspian call girls willingly explained the local tariff and other technicalities of his profession in an earthy idiom which other languages might envy. He remarked, for example, that it might be necessary to pay as much as a hundred roubles for a *baba s bagazhom* (roughly translated into American English as 'a piece of prime ass'); but that a mere twenty would be quite enough for *kakoye-nibud nikudyshnoye vyyebannoye barakhlo*, 'some useless piece of clapped out junk.' He also remarked of one of his 'hotter' items that she was of late unfortunately *sovershenno syeblas*, of which the kindest rendering might be 'had been rather overdoing things.'

Bawdy verse has a tradition long antedating the revolutions. The classic, somewhat overrated tragi-comic ballad *Luka Mudishchev*, Russia's equivalent of *Eskimo Nell* and often mistakenly attributed to the minor eighteenth-century poet Barkov, has recently been published (in Russian) in the West. And Pushkin's long outlawed bawdy ballad *Tsar Nikita and his Forty Daughters* has even been found to possess sufficient literary merit to receive publication in English translation by the

American magazine *Playboy*, in December 1965.[9] Author of many such sallies, Russia's greatest poet often found himself in trouble through offending the prudish official standards of his day. A particularly acute *skandal* was created by his mock-heroic *Gabrieliad* in which Lucifer and the Archangel Gabriel are shown competing for the favors of the Virgin Mary, thereby casting doubt on the paternity of Jesus Christ.

# ❧ IV ❧

# REGIMENTATION AND
# RESISTANCE

## AUTHORITY AND SUBMISSION

The Russian techniques of imposing central authority throughout the ages are now to be reviewed, together with the responses which these have evoked in conformists.

That the Russians were 'born for slavery,' that they actively preferred enslavement to freedom, that they would happily exhibit the bumps on their foreheads raised through excess of zeal in executing the kowtow—such claims are common in Western travelers' tales of the sixteenth century.[1] Three hundred years later a Russia-domiciled Englishwoman, a Mrs. Smith, saw a serf thank his master for a beating, and concluded that such a people would certainly take centuries to appreciate the blessings of freedom. 'Perhaps they are too Asiatic ever properly to do so.' Meanwhile her French contemporary Custine was accusing the whole nation of being intoxicated with servility, and commenting on the general atmosphere of sycophancy; of which, incidentally, one seems to detect not a little in that French Marquis's own attitude to the all-powerful Nicholas I.[2]

Despite all the changes which have occurred since Cus-

tine's day, traces of what might seem a slave mentality have by
no means disappeared from Muscovite psychology: 'Their
long history of subservience makes it easy for the Russian people to slip back into the habits of servility when the occasion
demands it.' For freedom and civil liberties as understood
elsewhere the average citizen seems to have little desire, especially among the lowest social groups.[3] Should his views on
freedom be solicited, the typical Russian is liable—if in patriotic and *vranyo*-intoxicated mood—to claim that his country already has far more of it than anywhere else in the world. 'I
know of no other land where man breathes so freely,' a well-
known Russian song unconvincingly asserts. No less common,
though, is a contrary statement: a frank admission that the
country lacks freedom in any shape or form, and this combined with the vehement hope that such a curse may never
alight. 'Heaven forbid that we should have freedom here': the
sentiment may be heard again and again.

Poised, as he so often seems, to carry any idea to its logical
extreme, the Russian is apt to equate the concept of freedom
with that of anarchic license. To him freedom 'means making
mischief,' according to the nineteenth-century critic Vissarion
Belinsky. He claims that the Russian nation would not, if liberated, move toward a parliament; it would rush off to the pot-
house to drink spirits, smash glasses and hang members of the
gentry, those beard-shavers who wear frock coats instead of
homespun smocks.[4] The modern *émigré* philosopher Fedotov
reckons the following items as prominent in the national conception of liberty: 'the wild open spaces, vagabondage, the
gipsy ethos, hard liquor, orgies of debauchery, blind sen-
sualism, highway robbery, rioting, despotism.'[5] But though
some may actively revel in anarchic violence, they are certainly
not the majority. 'If we ever have freedom here I shall be
hanged from the first lamp post,' is a sentiment which one
seems to hear very frequently. Orgiastic outbursts, wild ex-
cesses are not to every individual's taste, and there still seems

to lurk in the popular consciousness a fear of the kind of license which once raged so perilously during the Time of Troubles, the revolts of Razin and Pugachov and all three twentieth-century revolutions. So starved of liberty, moreover, has the people been, especially under Stalin, that many a defector or refugee has experienced great difficulty in adjusting to American, British, French, Israeli or other foreign life; to one drilled and regimented from the cradle such alien environments can easily present the nightmare spectacle of utter chaos.

If the nation's attitude to freedom and authority exhibits these strikingly peculiar features, an explanation may be sought in the evolution of regimentation during the last half-millennium. A force overwhelming and above all arbitrarily imposed, commanding total obedience except on those fortunately frequent occasions when deceit and trickery allow loopholes for evasion, a force feared but not respected—such, by and large, has been authority to the Russian throughout the ages. There is, surely, no other feature which more sharply differentiates the generalized Russian experience from that of the West. This is partly due to the shattering impact which Russian authority has traditionally made, especially in view of its random and excessively capricious nature. Furthermore, authority has not only tended to bear down more severely on the Russian; it has also tended (as already noted) to do so progressively. In other words, it has grown ever more rigorous over the centuries, by contrast with the West, where the exactions of centralized power have tended to decline.

The onward march of authoritarianism has been no smooth, orderly progression. Bouts of intense governmental oppression have alternated with periods of relaxation. The graph of oppressiveness is, consequently, no steadily rising straight line, but rather an ascending meander.

Kievan society presents few special features indicating a penchant for regimentation outstripping that of other medieval states. It is, rather, Tatar influence from 1240 onward which seems to have given disciplinary trends their initial impetus, imparting certain despotic and traditionally 'oriental' features. Without keeping the country under permanent occupation, the Tatars instituted in effect a grandiose protection racket. They took a census of the subjugated Russian population and imposed a quota of recruits and tribute, then retreated to a distance, swooping to conduct appalling reprisals whenever their demands were not met. Before a Russian prince or princeling could ascend his throne he was compelled to journey to Tatar headquarters at Saray on the lower Volga, there to make obeisance to the Khan and to undergo various humiliations before receiving, if he found favor, a patent to rule. The system put a premium on extreme sycophancy toward the Khan, combined with extreme treachery toward competing princelings—a process of natural selection which only the most cunning, ambitious and obsequious could hope to survive. In the end it was the princes of Moscow, eventually promoted to Grand Princes, who revealed the greatest pertinacity in ingratiating themselves with their masters and betraying their fellows. The Tatars accordingly found it convenient to allow these Muscovite rulers to operate as enforcers empowered to collect tribute from lesser princelings, who thereby fell under Muscovite rule, at first within the framework of the Tatar Empire known as the Golden Horde. Then, when the Golden Horde declined, and Moscow became strong enough to withhold tribute, no change was necessary: exactions previously passed on by Moscow to Saray now stayed in Moscow, while Muscovite Grand Princes continued to rule on principles absorbed from the Tatars: arbitrary despotic violence and the total absence of concern for the welfare of the subject.

How deep an imprint did the Tatars leave? One extreme view is that of Karl Marx: 'The bloody mire of Mongol [Tatar] slavery . . . forms the cradle of Muscovy, and modern Russia is but a metamorphosis of Muscovy.' Referring to the principle, introduced by the Tatars, whereby unlimited service obligations were placed on the entire population,' the historian George Vernadsky has called the Tatar-imposed administration 'a peculiar system of state socialism.' In keeping with this suggestion Belinsky, himself an early Russian Socialist, has referred to the centuries of the Tatar yoke with approval as forging the scattered parts of the country into unity. So great a boon did he rate this contribution that it outweighed for him many less desirable legacies: the seclusion of women, a slavish mentality, the knout, corruption in justice, squalid habits, mental laziness, ignorance and self-contempt.[6] Belinsky thus roundly ascribes traditional Russian slovenliness to Tatar influence. It may be added that certain significant words—*kabala*, 'bondage'; *nagayka*, 'whip'; *kandaly*, 'fetters'—came into Russian from Tatar together with terms reflecting administrative practices: those describing the postal and customs services, and also the word for money.

Emerging from the Tatar yoke, the Grand Princes—soon to call themselves Tsars—of Moscow already seem to enjoy absolute power. He 'holds unlimited control over the lives and property of all his subjects,'[7] said Herberstein of Grand Prince Basil III in the early sixteenth century. Linking lives and property together in this way, the ambassador shows how keenly he appreciated the superlatively authoritarian nature of Muscovite rule, which went far beyond mere sovereignty. The monarch was considered literally to own, as his personal property, everything within his realm, including all his subjects' persons as well as their possessions, a principle sometimes called patrimonial. The Tsar was thus more than a mere despot who abuses and infringes the rights of his subjects; to do that, indeed, was beyond even his unlimited power, since they possessed no rights.

'In the sway which he [the Tsar] holds over his people, he surpasses all the monarchs of the whole world.' 'The state and forme of their government is plaine tyrannicall.' 'No Master hath more power over his slaves than the Great Duke [Grand Prince] hath over his subjects.' Such was the almost universal verdict on Muscovy delivered by its sixteenth- and seventeenth-century foreign visitors as represented by Herberstein, Fletcher and Olearius respectively.[8] They unite in portraying a simply structured society. First there is, alone in all his glory, the ruler himself, absolute master of all he surveys. Then come his higher slaves—princelings, boyars and other upper servitors, the predecessors of the later *dvoryanstvo,* 'gentry'— whose function it is to transmit or issue instructions. Their recipients form the third and lowest level, that of the underslaves who constitute the vast majority of the population, whether peasants or inhabitants of the sparse and not very numerous towns. 'All the classes of the nation from top to bottom . . . were bound to the service of the state,' Vernadsky has asserted. And the philosopher Berdyayev claims outright that 'the Moscow Orthodox Kingdom was a totalitarian state.' I do not agree, for reasons to be given below, but it is not hard to see how such an impression could arise. Nor is a similar thesis—that all Russian land had already been fully nationalized by the late fifteenth century—difficult to sustain if one calls to mind the sudden, forcible transplantation of large populations from one part of the country to another for reasons of administrative convenience.[9]

Yet the authority, already seemingly absolute, which Muscovy's rulers had inherited from the Tatars, appeared to possess the curious logic-defying property already noted: that of becoming progressively more absolute as the decades rolled by. Successive rulers busily extended their power and territory in all possible directions. They also exerted irresistible pressure to erode the right of free movement whereby virtually all citizens, whether lesser princes, boyars or mere peasants, had been permitted to transfer allegiance from one master to another. The process of bonding all lower servitors to higher and all higher servitors to the sovereign was long and bloody. One of its most spectacular episodes was Ivan the Terrible's onslaught on his ruling class of boyars and princes. In this sanguinary campaign he showed himself prepared to risk destroying his entire country, provided that his personal power within that shattered realm could be made to predominate ever more. He thus anticipated Stalin's seemingly wanton liquidation of *his* higher servitors—his managers, his officer corps, his senior Party officials—in the purge years 1936–38. Both these orgies of destruction, Ivan's and Stalin's, took place at times of national peril: from Poland and Livonia in the sixteenth century, from Hitler nearly four hundred years later. One is also reminded that Stalin once expressed approval of Ivan's methods in the presence of a well-known film star, only deriding that dread Tsar for wasting on his prayers time which would have been better spent killing still more boyars.[10]

Did the Russians feel some irresistible inner drive to submit to absolute rule? Their seventeenth-century evolution seems to suggest as much. The period began with that decade of chaos, starvation, civil strife, plunder, confusion and despair termed the Time of Troubles (1604–13). Muscovy was now partially and incompetently ruled, misruled and competed for by various pretenders to the throne; also suffering attack by Swedes and occupation by Poles, not to mention recurrent devastating famines and peasant revolts. Here was the first occasion on which Russian regimentation has broken down so calamitously, giving way to the no-less-extreme phenomenon of Russian anarchy. From this the election of a boy Tsar, Michael, by a kind of national assembly brought relief in 1613, instituting the new dynasty of the Romanovs which was to rule until 1917.

Michael Romanov and his two immediate successors were comparative mediocrities, even Alexis—the second and least feeble of the trio—being nicknamed the Most Gentle Tsar. But though the progressive relaxation of authoritarianism might have been expected to take place under such benign and seemingly impotent rule, in fact nothing of the sort occurred. In 1649 a new and unprecedentedly rigorous law code formally completed the total bondage of all citizens. The peasants' reaction was to stage mutinies and revolts which evoked atrocious memories of the Time of Troubles before they were put down. Was it the recollection of that decade of anarchy which chiefly reconciled the people to slavery under a single all-powerful master who, though passive, was capable of maintaining or restoring civil peace, even if it seemed like the peace of near-stagnation?

With the advent of Peter the Great at the end of the seventeenth century, authoritarianism received yet another boost—not because the ruler's notional powers, assumed to be theoretically unlimited all along, had necessarily increased, but because the new sovereign was able and willing to use those powers far more aggressively than his three limp Romanov predecessors could have contrived. A dragooner of conscripted laborers and recruits, Peter transformed Russia by sweeping and ruthless measures, all ultimately designed to improve his military effectiveness. Not least among his achievements was the invention of two discipline-enhancing institutions destined to flourish on a global scale after his death: military conscription and a political police force. But the many atrocities inflicted on his subjects differed from the still more appalling cruelties of Ivan the Terrible in being more rationally conceived. Torturings and executions were indeed part of Peter's method but were imposed on a far smaller scale and at least tended to serve the understandable purpose of maintaining and increasing his own power and that of the Russian state. Above all, Peter differed from Ivan in being less concerned to appease the demons within his own soul. And yet, paradoxical though it may seem, Ivan had retained a far stronger hold on his subjects' affections than the hated Peter could command. Russians like a touch of magic or even madness in their rulers. To be forced to obey another in the name of logic and expediency is, in the last resort, a deadly insult—what self-respecting man can, in his heart, feel it reasonable for another to be his master? But to be forced to obey in defiance of all sense and reason by the black magic of an Ivan—this was a more tolerable alternative than the bleakness of Peter's authority purportedly based on rationality. No wonder the muzhiks were so convinced that he was Antichrist. Similarly, to invoke a parallel from modern times, Stalin—a fearsomely cruel ruler who had the happy instinct of investing his person with an aura of myth, cult and absurdity—was probably less unpopular than Khrushchev, who was far more concerned to explain his frequently grotesque maneuvers to the public in terms of rational motivation.

In the middle and late eighteenth century the character of Russian authoritarianism was modified through a major social change: the gentry acquired its freedom from all service obligations. Once liberated, Russian gentlemen exploited their new opportunities to bring about several palace revolutions resulting on more than one occasion in the slaughter of an ousted sovereign. Yet the gentry's new freedoms remained precarious; just how precarious the mentally unbalanced Emperor Paul abundantly demonstrated, during his brief reign of 1796–1801, by a series of eccentric oppressions. That these provoked his own assassination by a gang of intoxicated officers and gentlemen shows how careful both sides had to be in the unofficial alliance between sovereign and gentry created in the late eighteenth century.

Between 1801 and 1855 two successive Tsars fought a powerful rear-guard action in defense of Russian absolutism, now menaced by libertarian urges. The first of these, Alexander I, was prepared to pay lip service to liberty and equality, but only provided that there was no question of implementing such notions associated with the French Revolution. French political thinkers, German philosophers—ideas emanating from these Western sources already seemed to threaten, as they still do, Russian authoritarian government. Alexander's successor, Nicholas I, certainly thought so, and sponsored steps to check the influx of alien concepts. So rigorously, indeed, did he assert the autocratic principle that he has been accused of inventing the police state. Yet even Nicholas was far from muzzling the press, that vehicle for Russian literature at the beginning of its greatest age: a literature remarkable both for artistic originality and for a surprisingly prominent element of political protest.

The years 1855 to 1917 see Russian authoritarianism on the defensive. Alexander II made a determined, by no means unsuccessful, attempt to reform the country's institutions and democratize society. After his assassination in 1881 his successor Alexander III took fright and enacted much reactionary legislation, yet by no means destroyed the new-found atmosphere of relative freedom. The last Tsar, Nicholas II, made the same attempt with even less success; and felt compelled, in 1906, to grant an embryonic parliament, the State Duma. Though its powers were minuscule, the concession marks the abandonment, in however small a degree, of the principle of absolute rule.

The establishment of Bolshevik rule in 1917 sees a dramatic upsurge in Russian state authoritarianism. The increase in rigor derived partly from the adoption of a political program with claims to universal applicability such as no Romanov emperor had ever dreamed of putting forward. To this must be added the benefits of modern technology permitting the establishment of a totalitarian terrorist bureaucracy such as could not be created even by a Peter the Great before the days of radio, telegraph, typewriter, general literacy—and, finally, computers. Yet the graph of Russian authoritarianism has failed to proceed in a smooth and orderly line after 1917, just as it had in the previous period. Governmental violence reached its peak during the quarter century of Stalin's supreme power, from 1929 to 1953. Compared with that period the preceding years, those of Lenin and the struggle for Lenin's succession, have been marked by greater restraint, as have the following eras, those of Khrushchev and Brezhnev. But the totalitarian apparatus—the rigorous censorship, the travel restrictions, the thought control, the general conscription and browbeating of the citizenry—all remains intact. One new feature distinguishing the totalitarian from the imperial period has been the obligation to pretend that no such controls exist, and even that the modern Russian citizen is considerably freer than his Western counterpart. With this one may contrast the blunt admission of the bluff soldier-Tsar Nicholas I that the Russian system was an outright despotism and that such a system accorded with the genius of his people.[11]

Seen from below, Russian state power has always worn an awesome, crushing aspect. From the ruler's angle, however, things tend to look different. It is the precariousness, the vulnerability, of his position which is apt to strike him as its dominant feature. Never in Russian history has there been any accepted procedure for transferring power from one ruler to another. Indeed, Khrushchev's removal by the Party Central Committee in October 1964 has been called the first occasion 'in the entire history of Russia since Riurik [in the ninth century] that the established leader of the country was removed by the rules of representative procedure.' [12] And though a sitting ruler might be thought to gain additional security through the lack of any means providing for his removal, in fact the opposite was often the case, since he could in practice be ousted by one device only: a *coup d'état* usually accompanied by assassination. Hence Mme. de Staël's well-known quip, that Russia was a despotism mitigated by strangulation.

It is from his own immediate entourage, not from the masses of his humbler subjects, that the Russian ruler has usually had most to fear. In such an atmosphere despotic urges at the summit begin to seem, if not excusable, at least more human, natural and intelligible than they might otherwise appear. Then again, it is not merely fear for his personal safety which has bred in the Russian ruler the instinct to quell his subjects before they seize a chance to quell him. If, like an Ivan the Terrible, a Peter the Great or a Stalin, he has conceived the ambition not merely of staying alive, but also of strengthening his fief economically, militarily and culturally— a by no means eccentric or insane ambition—he is apt to become frustrated by certain mental habits of the Russian people, that instrument through which he is obliged to operate. Seen from outside, they may indeed wear an exceedingly docile air. But why has it so often been necessary to discipline them into docility so extreme? Surely because many of them are the very reverse of regimentation-prone in their souls? Their charmingly evasive tactics, their disarming unreliability, their delightful unpunctuality—all these qualities may well enchant the casual observer as much or more than the Russia-fancier. But what of the man in charge with a practical job to be done? To him these same endearing features can assume a different aspect.

Many years ago in London I chanced to set up and head a sizable teaching institution which employed about a score of Russians over a period of years. That they cheerfully cooperated and efficiently discharged their duties I can happily testify, while adding, however, that this satisfactory consummation was preceded by a difficult phase in which they virtually compelled me (by persistent unpunctuality and so on) to adopt the methods of an Ivan, a Peter or a Stalin writ exceeding small. Either the institution was to dissolve in hopeless *bezalabershchina,* or the boss had to develop the instincts of a petty tyrant. Once the second of these options had been firmly grasped—which was what my colleagues evidently wished, though I did not—no further serious difficulties occurred. The experience did not reconcile me to the methods of an

Ivan the Terrible, a Peter the Great or a Stalin. But it did make it possible, as nothing else could, to understand that neither elemental perversity nor an evil-be-thou-my-good philosophy need necessarily be invoked to explain the proceedings of the Russians' many despotic masters. Perhaps there was just no other way of achieving results: of bringing about, in other words, that happy transition from the imperfective to the perfective aspect which, as the strict compartmentalization of these two Russian verbal categories suggests, can be extremely hard to accomplish in the land where they hold sway.

The mailed fist or total anarchy: here is the choice with which subordinate Russians tend to face anyone who may find himself responsible for their collective efforts. Must one then conclude that it was the Russian mind which molded the authoritarian state? Or is the Russian mind rather the outcome of that authoritarian state? All one can assert with confidence is that the two phenomena have interacted as intimately as any chicken and egg.

## TSARISM AND ANTI-TSARISM

Having considered submission to authority, the argument now turns to the no-less-productive theme of resistance to authority.

That the Russian people is not genetically precluded from grasping the concept of freedom under the law; that it can enjoy and intelligently use liberty when available; that it can hanker after freedom in a sober and dignified spirit when it is not available—of these propositions abundant evidence can be adduced. It is also true that many Russians neither accept nor respect in their hearts the all-powerful authority which so often compels their obedience. Even under the special rigors of totalitarian regimentation they are careful to distinguish between those ordinances, usually with political implications, which it is prudent to obey, and other regulations which may safely be flouted. Traffic codes, injunctions against poaching, the requirement to show one's ticket to a train conductor, whistles blown by official beach-masters to command holiday-making sunbathers to turn over and thus avoid undue exposure—all these things can be and are blatantly ignored. Obliged, as part of his university course, to take interminable instruction in the liturgy of dialectical materialism, a student will chatter loudly to his neighbor during lectures on the subject, and in a manner which few Western citizens would think legitimate when absorbing divine revelation in church, their nearest equivalent to such a devotional context. But then the Russian Orthodox always did gossip away uninhibitedly during church services, even in the days when their now dethroned Church represented authority, just as they have long tended to ignore No Smoking notices in public places. Such was firmly established practice in the universities of the nineteenth century, when indeed 'no law was firmly enforced.' An exaggeration, certainly, then as it would be now, but an understandable one. It is precisely for punctilio in obeying such regulations that the Russian tends to despise the Germans, whom he thinks of as regimented in their souls. And not only Germans. 'We [Russians] never see English people lying on the grass for hours, and missing their meals for the pure pleasure of it. . . . *We* do not give up our afternoons to enjoy Nature in a decent, organized way by means of out-door games.' Such a contrast has also been drawn (by an American) with Americans, who allegedly conform with society's taboos because they wish to conform; how much more slavish an attitude, it might seem, than that of the Russian conformist who conforms because he has to.[1]

Here, then, is yet another paradox: that of members of a

strictly regimented society despising others for being over-regimented. And here, once again, the familiar concept of polarization seems relevant. At any given moment the Russian tends to be highly conscious either of being or of not being in a hierarchic situation. And if he is in such a situation he is apt to wallow in it, playing to the limit one or the other of two contrary roles: that of giving or that of receiving orders. Outside that context, though, he has a keen sense of human equality. 'In all relations which are not defined as leader and led, superordinate and subordinate . . . Russians demand the most absolute equality in their personal relationships. It would appear that Russians do not conceive of any intermediate positions: there is either complete equality, or complete superordination and subordination.' [2] They are thus apt to seem doubly polarized: first, between wholly authority-free and wholly authority-dominated situations; secondly, within the latter only, between total domination and total submissiveness.

With this twin, double-pronged attitude to freedom and authority is intimately linked—whether as cause or effect or both—one particularly striking feature of Russia throughout the ages: the absence of any institutionalized means for registering political opposition. There is nothing which more sharply distinguishes the country's evolution from that of the major Western European countries. Lacking until the last years of the Empire even the semblance of a parliament, of political parties and of effective corporate pressure groups, the Russians long ago developed their own techniques of resistance based on flight, peasant revolt, pretenders to the throne and palace revolutions.

Flight from the service of an oppressive central or local overlord has already been mentioned as a traditional right of peasants and princelings in the centuries preceding the consolidation of autocratic power by Moscow's Grand Princes, later Tsars. And the abolition of this right, through enserfment and the binding of the gentry to lifelong service, has been noted as one of the means whereby Muscovy rose to absolute dominion over other principalities. But flight from the oppressive center did not end just because it had become illegal and hazardous. On the contrary, it became the main process whereby the peasant masses expressed their opposition to authority. 'Opposition to the state did exist among the lower orders, but owing to the super-abundance of physical space it expressed itself in running away, in removing oneself from the burdens which the state placed on the people, and not in active resistance or struggle.' [3]

There thus arose on the southern and southeastern periphery of Russia, and also in Siberia, communities of unruly, rough frontiersmen known as Cossacks. These jolly professional hooligans fought against each other and various neighbors—Poles, Tatars, Turks, Caucasian tribesmen—siding now with, now against the centrally controlled Russian state in which most of them had originated. The situation has been compared to that of the American Wild West, with the Tatar as Red Indian, the Russian army as the US cavalry and the Cossack as pioneering frontiersman vaguely owing allegiance to his ataman or sheriff. Nor was there any lack of hard liquor, cattle rustling, lynching, punch-ups, posses chasing badmen and so on. The claim has even been made that the Cossack—with his high spirits, comic humor, boozing, brigandage and brawling—was 'in many ways closer to the popular idea of the cowboy than was the cowboy himself.' [4] Meanwhile the constantly expanding central state was progressively reembracing its prodigal Cossack sons until the drilled and militarized descendants of swaggering frontiersmen had eventually been so firmly incorporated in the Empire that they became the government's most reliable riot police, and could be depended upon literally to whip protesting students into a semblance of submission.

On three major occasions earlier Cossacks had allied themselves with disaffected peasantry—the distinction between a Cossack and a disaffected peasant not being always easy to draw—and had promoted great upheavals which overthrew or severely threatened the central power. In the early seventeenth century they had helped to set a pretender, False Dmitry, on the throne of Moscow, thus sparking off the Time of Troubles. They were also prominent in the many other peasant revolts of that period. These affairs established the new Russian tradition of a devastating but fortunately rare class war in which rampaging peasants and Cossacks massacred the rich and shared out their wives and property. This same simple ideology also helped to inspire the terrible Cossack-peasant revolts of Stenka Razin in 1670–71, and of Pugachov over a century later. In these conflicts Russian anarchy, a phenomenon no less extreme than Russian regimentation, ran riot; but with one curious reservation. In all such upheavals, and in many a minor revolt, a pretender or false Tsar—either the rebel leader himself, as with Pugachov, or a puppet figure—remained an indispensable item in the equipment of the mutineers. They thus clearly signified, while attempting to unseat an individual monarch, their loyalty to the monarchy as an institution. In other words, even the most violently disaffected Russians were not yet trying to overthrow their system of government.

The same claim can be made for rebellions at the other end of the social scale: the palace revolutions carried out, mainly in the eighteenth century, by guards officers of St. Petersburg. These guardee conspirators were gallantly prone to install ladies on the throne: the Empresses Catherine I, Elizabeth and Catherine the Great. The fourth and last notable palace revolution occurred with the strangling of the eccentric Emperor Paul by a posse of drunken officers and achieved the accession of his son Alexander I, in some degree an accomplice, on 12 March 1801. And far removed though these intimate high-level conspiracies were from the peasant and Cossack risings invoked above, they too were similarly concerned to replace an uncongenial with a congenial absolute monarch—not to replace absolute monarchy with some other kind of government.

On these primitive forms of opposition the Decembrist Revolt of 1825 represented a considerable advance. It was at once repressed, but the aspirations behind it were not so easily quelled. On this occasion at last a change of system, not simply a change of rulers, had been the goal. Thus, though the Decembrists had no common program—some aiming at a constitutional monarchy while others hankered after a republic—their motives were more broadly political, and hence more modern, than the dynastic urges which had fired Russia's previous peasant and palace revolutionaries. The Decembrist movement also brought in the common people as rank-and-file mutineers, if only because they were ordered to take part by their revolutionary officers.

The accession of Alexander II in 1855 heralded a significant new chapter in the saga of Russian political dissent. Hitherto the political resistance movement had worn as primitive an air as had the autocratic power. Still, to the extent that the political *coup,* particularly if mounted by serving officers, has become so prominent a global institution in the late twentieth century, even eighteenth-century Russia now seems to have marched in the very van of modernity and progress. Of developments from 1855 onward this claim may be made more confidently.

After beginning his reign by relaxing the harsher measures of his predecessor, Alexander II soon discovered that to dismantle a tyranny may be to invite reprisals which might with greater justice have been undertaken against the earlier dispensation. Finding it safe to express oppositionist views long banned as seditious, disaffected Russians leapt in to denounce and attack the new administration. Thus the adoption of liberal measures, including the emancipation of the serfs, came to coincide with the development of Russia's first serious revolutionary movement. So far, however, the number of active conspirators was small: a few score, perhaps, in the 1860s, and a few hundred in the 1870s. Nor did they subscribe to any common doctrine or program. Their impact derived rather from the scandalous nature of their methods, especially political assassination. A political police chief, General Mezentsov, was fatally stabbed on a main street in St. Petersburg; Prince Dmitry Kropotkin, a provincial governor-general, was shot dead in his carriage. Eventually, on 1 March 1881, the emperor himself was slaughtered by a home-made hand grenade on a St. Petersburg quayside.

Other oppositionist practices were the distribution of blood-curdling manifestos and the attempted manipulation of the downtrodden peasantry which should have been, but so infuriatingly was not, ripe for revolt. Efforts to educate, agitate or otherwise activate the muzhik by peaceful persuasion took on a widespread character in 1873–74, when hundreds of young intellectuals went out into the villages, seeking contact with the 'dark masses,' but seeking it with conspicuous lack of success. Still loyal to the Tsar, still infuriatingly non-militant despite his appalling poverty, the Russian yokel was more likely to denounce these touring student agitators to the police than to turn revolutionary himself. On the one notable occasion when urban revolutionaries did manage to stir up a genuine village revolt, at Chigirin in southern Russia in 1877, they could do so only by issuing a forged manifesto—*and that in the name of the Tsar*—calling on the peasants to rise against the landlords and officials. That the rising was cruelly suppressed, that the peasants were flogged, that the intellectual instigators were not flogged but briefly imprisoned, and then staged a daring escape—all was, once again, very much in the spirit of this boisterous epoch.

Throughout Alexander II's reign the conflict between government and revolutionaries had remained a small-scale duel which intrigued the population at large while failing to enlist broadly based sympathies on either the governmental or the revolutionary side. While the general attitude thus remained that of apathetic political voyeurism, the imperial administration proved incompetent to quell the handful of terrorists who threatened the throne and virtually imprisoned the monarch in his palace during his last years. It took the Tsar's assassination, followed by the accession of the tough-minded Alexander III, to drive the terrorists onto the defensive. And on the defensive they remained until the accession of Nicholas II, in 1894, at about which time the resistance movement began to acquire new strength and confidence. Political parties—illegal, legal and semi-legal—were founded: those of the (Marxist) Social Democrats, later to split into Bolsheviks and Mensheviks; of the peasant-fancying Socialist Revolutionaries; of the liberal Kadets.

The 1905 Revolution was the first mass explosion of popular discontent since the Pugachov revolt of 1773–74 had menaced the throne of Catherine the Great. Once again, in the later rising as in those earlier affairs, masses of the common people suddenly threw off restraint with a gusto corresponding to the degree of regimentation under which they had labored, slumbered and occasionally smoldered so long. Here was no coordinated upheaval—rather a series of widespread sporadic strikes and rural riots coinciding with mutinies among uniformed peasant conscripts returning from recent defeat in the Russo-Japanese war, which had begun in the previous year. The revolution was sparked off by the massacre, in St. Petersburg on 9 January 1905, of peacefully demonstrating workers by imperial troops. That 9 January came to be known as Bloody Sunday, as the result of these events, is less significant than that the emperor had begun to acquire, among the common people, the by no means merited nickname Bloody Nicholas. Here was the writing on the wall for the Romanov dynasty, so long protected by the almost mystical reverence in which Russian peasants had held their Tsar.

Moreover, however closely the appalling riots, assassinations and lynchings of the revolutionary year might echo earlier peasant upheavals, the significant fact is that the days of pretenders to the throne were long gone.

Now that the throne itself was beginning to incur disrepute, the common people could at last begin to contemplate the possibility of a Tsarless Russia. Moreover, some sort of alliance now seemed at last to be operating between the disaffected popular masses and the disaffected professional classes. Teachers and even ballet dancers came out on strike in 1905 along with railwaymen and factory workers; they marched in the streets carrying red flags; they attended inflammatory political meetings. Stressing that all earlier Russian revolutionary movements had been confined to members of the educated and privileged classes, the influential liberal thinker Peter Struve emphasizes the novelty of the 1905 affair, in which 'the ideas of the intelligentsia made contact with the ideas of the common people—for the first time in Russian history in this sense and form.' [5] There is also the point that violence had now much increased by comparison with that of Alexander II's reign, during which a mere half-dozen assassinations had been enough to panic the administration. Now political murders were numbered by hundreds or thousands. So too were the executions of the period.

The 1905 Revolution was suppressed by armed force; but, as noted, the emperor bowed to the call for democratic reform sufficiently to institute the elective assembly, called the State Duma, which continued to meet in four successively elected incarnations from its establishment in 1906 until it was overthrown in 1917. Meanwhile Nicholas II still retained, and exercised with alarming frequency, the right to dismiss and appoint prime and other ministers obliged to execute his policy of pious but vacillating conservatism. The Duma continued to deliberate away during the years of the First World War—

that calamity which far more drastically undermined popular confidence in the imperial regime than any Bloody Sunday.

## *PSYCHOPATHOLITICS*

To turn from oppositionist activities of 1855–1917 to the mentality of the individuals concerned is to enter an area of confused terminology. In the 1860s there 'arose,' as is commonly said, Russians of a hitherto unfamiliar brand. Some of them called themselves 'new men'; and also, being little troubled by doubts about their own moral probity, 'honest' or 'decent' people. They figure additionally as men of the sixties, as progressives and as radicals, besides being further described on occasion as dissidents, revolutionaries, Socialists, Communists, Jacobins, liberals, terrorists, anarchists, Reds—not to mention Nihilists, narodniks and members of that mysterious category, the intelligentsia. Too easily does one receive from the literature of the subject the impression that these hazy terms possessed a more precise connotation than they had or could have. Too easily, also, may it seem that these same terms are mutually exclusive, whereas they very considerably overlap. Few indeed were the Russian oppositionists of the nineteenth century who could not be described by several of them at the same time.

As this plethora of categories suggests, the spectrum of political opposition in the late Empire admitted infinite gradations between infra-red and pale pink. At the extreme end of the band, resistance to the Tsars was sometimes embraced by persons who, outside the political context which seems to excuse everything, might have been more appropriately located in a ward for the criminally insane than among harbingers of rationally based social justice. Even in Russia, however, the tally of political psychopaths was smaller than that of those who tended toward the central bands of the spectrum. They were oppositionists of a very different, milder tint—those whose gradual, considered approach did not exclude such considerations as compromise and practical common sense: the country's moderate liberals.

As is no secret, Russian oppositionists of the more restrained type lost the day ultimately, and were swept away by the events of 1917. But the liberals' signal failure to achieve the peaceful transformation of their country was arguably due to historical accident rather than to any lack of persistence or intelligence. The fact that they eventually failed so catastrophically by no means necessarily proves that they were foredoomed.

Yet Russian liberalism of the milder variety has received comparatively little attention from Western historians. This neglect derives partly from a natural human tendency to ignore political losers, and partly from the failure of the tamer brand of oppositionist to project those exotic and arresting qualities which the outside world has come to expect from a Russian. What, compared to the gibbering anarchist Bakunin and the murderous fanatic Nechayev, were such humdrum figures as a Shipov, a Chicherin, a Maklakov, a Milyukov—or hundreds of others who have failed to attract posterity's attention outside specialist ranks owing to their incompatibility with the stereotype of the wild, arm-flailing, inspired, bomb-throwing Russian? But though such figures have been comparatively neglected in the West, they have not been passed over in silence. For example, one modern authority, George Fischer, has treated the phenomenon extensively in his *Russian Liberalism,* while another recent historian, Richard Pipes, has embarked on a full-scale biography of that outstanding representative of the type, Peter Struve. The former study stresses the prolonged and patient work carried on by Russian liberals in their main areas of endeavor. These included the universities and various influential professional associations as well as the periodical press—censored by the government, as has been seen, but very far from censored out of existence. Then there were the elective organs of local government instituted by the very central government from 1864 onward. In them all social classes were represented, albeit on a franchise weighted in favor of gentlemen and property owners. Though these bodies were indeed subject to restrictive governmental interference, they yet offered considerable scope for those very numerous altruistic Russians who found their vocation in practical service to their fellows. Many of these modest persons preferred to practice medicine, to build roads, to teach and to administer on a local level, rather than to throw bombs or redefine for the $n$th time the term *intelligentsia*.

In the light of such considerations one may understand Michael Karpovich's contention that the feebleness of the Russian liberal movement has 'too often . . . been asserted as something self-evident, and thus not in need of further investigation.' The same point is made in a different way by Pipes when he claims that, during the fifty years preceding the downfall of the old regime 'liberalism was the dominating philosophy of Russia's educated classes . . . the force behind all the major constructive changes carried out by the imperial government.' [1]

Turning from moderate to extremist oppositionists, one is once more reminded of the pioneering function performed by Russian society of the late imperial period. To notable progress, as indicated above, in the field of assassination and assault by high explosive, must now be added the triumphant breaching of any tendency toward male monopoly in these crucial areas. Delicately nurtured bomb-throwing girls with nerves of steel—Russia pioneered the evolution of this type, which has since become a commonplace throughout the world.

Among the female pioneers of Russian terrorism was Vera Zasulich, would-be assassin of the hated St. Petersburg City Prefect, General Trepov, on 24 January 1878. Obtaining audience with him, she drew a revolver and fired, but succeeded only in wounding the monster, to the great regret of his many ill-wishers, before standing trial and effecting her escape to foreign parts. In the following generation another woman terrorist, a high official's daughter called Tatyana Leontyev, kept a secret dynamite store in her family home, also planning to shoot the Emperor Nicholas II through a bouquet of flowers. When this failed she went abroad and assassinated, at Interlaken, an unfortunate Frenchman whom she had mistaken for the unpopular Russian Home Secretary, P. N. Durnovo—a reminder that no less than three Russian home secretaries were assassinated in the brief period 1902–11. But the most illustrious of Russia's lady killers was Sophia Perovsky, that former schoolmistress and provincial governor's daughter who led the victorious bomb squad into action against Alexander II on the Catherine Quay on 1 March 1881. The tenacity of the *skandal* as an institution may be illustrated by the lamentable circumstances of her public execution, together with that of her four accomplices. The affair was outrageously bungled, though eventually brought off successfully, by an incompetent hangman who drowned the protests of the attendant medical officer with drunken abuse. One is reminded of a comment made many years earlier, during the execution of the five Decembrist leaders in 1826, an affair managed with an even greater degree of *bezalabershchina*. 'My God, they can't even hang a man decently in Russia,' one of the temporarily reprieved victims was moved to remark.[2]

Male assassins and would-be assassins were also legion,

and included such psychotic personalities as Dmitry Karakozov, that twice-expelled university student who attempted to
shoot Alexander II in 1866. His frequent suicide attempts, a
pilgrimage which he made to the Monastery of the Trinity
and St. Sergius shortly before the attempt, the manifesto
which he circulated announcing his intentions in advance to
authorities too sunk in complacent incompetence to take the
appropriate steps—all these features mark Karakozov as a
representative of the resistance movement's lunatic fringe.
Another assassin writ larger than life was Sergey Kravchinsky,
author of Chief of Gendarmes Mezentsov's death by stabbing
on a St. Petersburg street in 1878, but only after being with
difficulty dissuaded from attempting literally to decapitate
that inoffensive high functionary with a single swish of a
heavy saber.

The most grotesque figure of the political resistance
movement was, by common consent, Sergey Nechayev: apostle
of wholesale destruction for its own sake, dedicated extor-
tioner, blackmailer, confidence trickster and murderer.
Nechayev was also an enthusiastic recruiter to political secret
societies dominated by himself, units which he contrived to
represent to their few members as part of a nonexistent
world-wide conspiratorial network. One of his many feats was
the slaughter of a backsliding comrade, the absurdly named
student Ivan Ivanovich Ivanov. This murder, accomplished
collectively by a group of political dupes under Nechayev's
supervision, was designed to assert his personal authority
while binding his associates together in common guilt. But the
episode was sufficiently unusual, despite the Russian context,
to cause considerable public scandal when the facts emerged.
Not least through its very sordidness, it seemed so symbolic of
extremist political opposition as to obsess Dostoyevsky, stimulating him to write the novel Devils. Here Nechayev himself,
his dupes and his victim all figure under other names. Devils is
surely the greatest political novel ever written—perhaps the

greatest novel ever written. It analyzes with superb insight the phenomenon of political psychopathology, here termed *psychopatholitics,* of which Nechayev was so outstanding an exemplar. Even as a prisoner in the St. Petersburg Peter and Paul Fortress this demoniac revolutionary contrived, long after *Devils* had been published, to suborn his warders and smuggle out of his dungeon with their aid a correspondence course in assassination for the edification of fellow-terrorists who were then plotting the death of Alexander II.

Another oppositionist activity, the dissemination of blood-curdling revolutionary manifestos, received particularly exuberant expression on the occasion when a daring horseman careered down St. Petersburg's Nevsky Prospekt on a galloping charger, scattering subversive literature in all directions. And a further, even more notorious, example of oppositionist publishing enterprise occurred when another terrorist composed a particularly bloodthirsty revolutionary proclamation in a cell in a Moscow jail and smuggled it out with the aid of a complaisant or bribed warder. As many similar episodes also illustrate, the imperial government's security measures were remarkably lax; they fell spectacularly short of the 'Tsarist reign of terror' as which the successor regime has contrived to present them to posterity.

If the Russian revolutionary movement still arouses confusion, the cause may be sought in its remarkably muddled development. As the Empire drew toward its close, oppositionists increasingly tended to mix up their roles, and even to interchange them with those of police agents. A revolutionary infiltrates the police, who—not necessarily unaware of his original affiliations—then instruct him to infiltrate the revolutionary organization to which he already belongs even as he pretends to betray it, or genuinely betrays it? He thus becomes a double agent, only a preliminary to further refinements whereby his oscillating and simultaneously dwindling loyalties turn him into a treble, quadruple and so on agent. In the end the poor man confronts both himself and his historian with the impossibility of deciding just what, at any stage of his career, he may have thought he was at. The prince of these multiple agents was Yevno Azef, who headed the most dangerous group of political assassins of the early 1900s while simultaneously working or pretending to work in close collusion with, and in violent opposition to, the general in charge of political security. Then there was Dmitry Bogrov, the secret police agent who assassinated his ultimate employer, Prime Minister and Home Secretary Stolypin, in the Kiev opera theater in 1911, and whose motives—never elucidated—were again very possibly unclear even to the man himself. There was also Roman Malinovsky, the police agent who infiltrated the Bolsheviks so successfully that he became their leader in the State Duma; he was later executed by Lenin for being too effective a policeman—or too embarrassing a Bolshevik?

Among many similarly ambivalent role-players of the period was Sergey Zubatov, a schoolboy revolutionary who later rose high in the political police. In his capacity as police officer he established special trade unions designed to wean disaffected workers from revolutionary leadership by securing tangible economic benefits calculated to reduce their interest in causing merely political unrest. With this in view Zubatov organized widespread strikes aimed at extorting extensive concessions from employers. But so successful were these stoppages as to threaten public order and eventually cause Zubatov's dismissal, either for excess of zeal or because, in this treacherous and ambivalent context, no one could be quite sure where such a person stood. Though Zubatov was presumably no oppositionist, but rather a bulwark of authority, 'The suspicion inevitably arose that he was a crypto-revolutionary exploiting police techniques to further the cause of subversion.'[3] A still more ambiguous trade-union boss of the period was Father George Gapon, leader of the massacred demonstrating workers of Bloody Sunday, 9 January 1905.

Gapon too combined leadership of organized labor with other functions: that of police collaborator and those, more surprisingly, of minister of religion and international playboy. It was in the first of these three capacities that Father George was eventually assassinated by an ex-comrade who had, incidentally, saved his life on Bloody Sunday.

Nothing, perhaps, will ever fully explain this weird form of policeman-revolutionary symbiosis which so effectively sapped the morale of the late Russian Empire. Moreover, even among revolutionaries who were not also police spies, many actively supported the less liberal policies of those very authorities whom they were trying to overthrow, by directly advocating extreme reactionary measures. An astonishing posture? And yet they could claim logic on their side. Wishing to demolish the political system entirely, they were above all reluctant to see it introduce reforms which might prolong its life by rendering it more acceptable to the population. This is why Chernyshevsky, for example, would have liked to see Russia's serfs emancipated *without land,* and hence without any means of livelihood: this harsh provision would have satisfactorily inflamed their grievances, thus increasing the chance of transforming them into a revolutionary force.[4] Similarly, a high official who considered himself a moderate progressive could incur rebukes from progressives of more militant hue for his fight against extreme conservative trends in the Tsar's administration. He was being reproached, he wrote, for delaying a crisis by opposing the kind of reactionary measure which he should have been wholeheartedly supporting as likely to expose the absurdity of a doomed regime more effectively than any arguments.[5] The more tyrannically the Russian government could be induced to behave, the greater the likelihood of it being eventually overthrown by bloody revolution. For this reason the assassination of Alexander II, though a tactical failure—since it led to the effective suppression of opposition for over a decade and a half—was yet a strategic success since it diverted the government from the path of reform, thus making its violent overthrow more likely in the end. That bloody revolution was a self-justifying activity; that it could in some mysterious sense be equated with the true interests of humanity, irrespective of any context in which it might occur; even that the more people killed the greater the benefit to the human race—such were the calculations of a section of the Russian political opposition by no means restricted to those who had most violently inflamed within themselves the sadistic-masochistic elements portrayed so effectively in Dostoyevsky's *Devils*.

However seriously one may attempt to do justice to Russia's moderate oppositionists, who may well have outnumbered the wilder specimens of the tribe, the latter will always exercise a greater spell over posterity, if only because they pioneered a more distinctive national style. Liberals such as Turgenev or Nikitenko could be found almost anywhere in the civilized world, but one had to go to St. Petersburg or points east to be sure of meeting a Nechayev or a Sophia Perovsky. Not that all extremists were assassins or psychopaths, for many a less violent dissenter was to be found among those who, too far to the left in their views to be termed liberals, were for a time categorized by their critics as Nihilists. That there were also extremists of the right, for example in the ranks of the nationalist and anti-Semitic Black Hundreds, is also true. But here, least of all, can Russia claim any monopoly. It was its leftist, not rightist, fanatics who typified the broader streak in the national mentality.

The term *Nihilist*, as applied to politically disaffected Russians, was introduced by Turgenev in his novel *Fathers and Children* (1862) to denote one who 'does not bow down before any authority, and accepts no principles on trust, however much respect they may enjoy.' The Nihilist was or pretended to be a stern, matter-of-fact individual judging objects in terms of their practical utility and assessing art from an anti-aesthetic angle: 'A decent chemist is twenty times more useful than any poet.' Nor, according to another saying of the period, were the entire works of Pushkin worth a single well-made pair of boots. Atheism; egalitarianism; feminism; a general contempt for property, as for the state and all its works—these too were features of Nihilist belief. But it was less Nihilist philosophy which caught the attention of non-Nihilists than certain externals foreshadowing the 'hippie' or 'beatnik' of the mid-twentieth century. Loud voices, loutish manners, aggressively untidy clothing, dirty chewed fingernails, an unwashed appearance—such was the uniform of the tribe. Straggly beards and long hair were cultivated by the male, as was bobbed hair by the female of the species—who was equally prominent in the movement. Blue-tinted spectacles, high boots, walking sticks, a rug flung over the shoulder were also part of the style, as was chain-smoking and the renunciation of such frivolities as combs, soap, crinolines and the practice of men kissing women's hands by way of greeting. Above all, extreme youth was characteristic of the Nihilist, who naturally added contempt for parental authority to contempt for every other form of authority—yet while simultaneously accepting the sanction of his own elaborate taboos, among which the simulation of non-conformism was the most rigorously conformist feature of all.

Most Nihilists had been touched or lightly brushed at some stage by higher education. Indeed, the classic Nihilist had been expelled from at least one university, preferably for hounding some 'reactionary' professor. No less typical, though, was having attended—and again, preferably, having been expelled from—one of the many theological seminaries designed for the training of future clerics, but now informally doubling as breeding grounds for future revolutionaries. The nation's high schools were hotbeds of nihilism, too.

Nihilism could never have flourished without the connivance of older people, and this took two diametrically opposed forms. There were, on the one hand, those members of the older generation who greeted these juvenile aberrations with gratifying and undignified displays of indignation, spluttering and the like, an encouragement to the young to intensify their provocations and grow their hair even longer. Equally characteristic, though, were those senior citizens who pandered to the young through feebleness of spirit or a no-less-craven desire to court popularity. The novelist Turgenev was himself given to these postures—one of the many points made against him by his ideological enemy Dostoyevsky in the novel *Devils*. Here the 'great writer' Karmazinov is pilloried as, Turgenev-like, pathologically scared of modern revolutionary youth: 'Imagining from ignorance that they held in their hands the keys of Russia's future, [he] ingratiated himself with them in a humiliating way, mainly because they paid no attention to him whatsoever.' [6]

Still, however witty the folk-fancier Dostoyevsky might be at the expense of Turgenev the Nihilist-fancier, it was neither Dostoyevsky nor Turgenev to whom Nihilist youth turned for lessons in the art of living. That function was chiefly performed by Nicholas Chernyshevsky, whose novel *What Is to Be Done?* (1863) has been described again and again as the worst work of fiction ever written. Aesthetic values had, however, been explicitly renounced by those who accepted this document as their Bible and guide to etiquette. From Chernyshevsky's book young people could learn how to regulate their relations with the opposite sex; but not on the basis of equality, for the author had gone far beyond that—asserting, as has been noted above, the need to grant women superior privileges sufficient to compensate them for centuries of male domination. More important as a guide to conduct was the dynamic and dedicated asceticism of the novel's main hero, the herculean revolutionary saint Rakhmetov. Not that Chernyshevsky could directly describe this weird superman as a revolutionary, for censorship made it impossible to spell this out in so many words. But Rakhmetov's contempt for money, his cult of physical hardship, his sexual and alcoholic abstinence, his habit of eating raw beef, combined with an occasional excursion into outright masochism (such as a night spent on a bed of nails)—all combined to suggest a very monster of militancy who might, through witchcraft if not through sheer will power, succeed in toppling even the massive and formidable battlements of the Tsarist state.

## THE INTELLIGENTSIA

To turn from Russian nihilism to the Russian *intelligentsia*—another term which gained currency in the 1860s—is, in a sense, not to change the subject, since many an individual Nihilist could equally well be classed as an *intelligent*, 'member of the intelligentsia.' *Intelligent, intelligentsia*—the terms lacked the pejorative implications of nihilism. They suggested neither extreme youth nor dirty fingernails, and have continued in use long after nihilism began to seem dated. The main trouble with the new concept was its vagueness. Everyone could recognize a Nihilist when he saw one. But how on earth did one detect an *intelligent*? The notion of intelligentsia did indeed more or less embrace nihilism, but it also seemed capable of more or less embracing many other schools of thought as well. And the concept could also be invoked disparagingly, by use of the contemptuous derivative *intelligentik*, 'egghead.'

In its broadest sense intelligentsia is still used in the USSR as a rough equivalent for white-collar workers. Officially the

Soviet intelligentsia has been defined more portentously: as a 'social stratum consisting of persons professionally employed in mental labor. Included in it are scientists and artists, engineers, technicians, agronomists, doctors, lawyers, teachers, and the great majority of office workers.' In this sense the word has an admirable clarity, and has been further refined to cover all persons who have received or engaged in higher education, together with any others who occupy posts normally requiring a higher educational qualification. One advantage of this definition is its precision: the individuals concerned can be counted, and there were in fact 10,676,000 of them in 1967, according to a recent historian.[1]

In the last six decades of the monarchy, too, the term could carry exactly the same sense: for example, when a nineteenth-century novelist writes of a ball in a provincial capital being attended by 'all the local intelligentsia.' The trouble was, though, that the word also possessed an infinite range of narrower meanings, as has been well expressed by the literary historian D. S. Mirsky. First equating the intelligentsia with the educated and professional classes as a whole, he goes on to attribute to the term a second, more restricted sense, confining it to that section of the educated and professional classes which was intensely and actively interested in political and social issues. He then notes a third, still narrower usage, whereby the word was applied only to 'those groups which were more or less radically inclined.'[2]

As Mirsky's explanation suggests, other historians of pre-1917 Russian culture have been apt to locate the intelligentsia at some purportedly specific point between its narrowest and broadest poles, as specified above, with the unspoken implication that those who place it anywhere else have failed to perceive the true nature of the phenomenon as apprehended by the speaker. Hence the innumerable definitions of the intelligentsia, of which a whole anthology could be collected. It is not enough to say, as one authority does, that 'Each generation of the intelligentsia has defined itself in its own way, re-nouncing its ancestors and beginning—for a decade—a new era.' Rather does it begin to seem as if every individual poten-tial *intelligent* was principally or even exclusively engaged in the narcissistic process of defining and redefining the category. 'One of the favourite occupations of the Russian intelligentsia had always been the absorbed study of itself.' [3]

As emerges from the above, the chief criterion distin-guishing one man's conception of the intelligentsia from an in-finitude of others is the degree—ranging from nil to infinity—of political radicalism which is regarded as mandatory. Ac-cording to the early twentieth-century thinker Sergey Bulga-kov, the 1905 Revolution was 'the spiritual offspring of the intelligentsia.' The same claim has been made for the 1917 revolutions, of which the intelligentsia has been described as constituting the general staff. Yet the claim is explicitly denied by a post-revolutionary Russian *émigré* authority, Fedotov, as emanating from the intelligentsia's enemies: 'Quite apart from the fact that a very significant section of the intelligentsia—the liberals—never thought of revolution, there are names in the pantheon of the movement's saints which have nothing in common with political struggle.' [4] Fedotov instances the Slavo-philes—a category explicitly excluded by Mirsky from the in-telligentsia in one of his narrower senses.

Unfortunately this and many other such disquisitions on the intelligentsia serve only to demonstrate yet again the folly of attributing to so impalpable and elusive an assortment of phenomena a degree of cohesiveness which has simply never been there.

However defined and classified, a significant and ob-trusive section of educated or semi-educated Russians con-tinued, long after nihilism had become obsolete, to hold ideas commonly associated with that movement: opposition to state, church and property; positivism, utilitarianism, feminism, egal-itarianism, an obsession with the importance of science. So tenacious, too, was the cult of youth in Russia that Bulgakov, writing in 1909, could call spiritual paedocracy (toddler power) the greatest evil of Russian society. It was also 'a symptomatic feature of the heroic style cultivated by the intelligentsia, of its basic traits, but in . . . exaggerated form. This grotesque interrelationship, whereby the assessments and views of school-children and students function as guide-lines for their elders—it inverts the natural state of affairs and is equally detrimental to both parties.'[5] A desire among older people to stand high, at whatever cost, in the estimation of the young—a desire which the sneering contempt of the young only inflamed and reinforced—also remained a prominent feature of Russian intellectual society.

Another legacy of the 1860s was a tendency to embrace the cause of social and political betterment with wholeheartedness bordering on total abandon. The crusading spirit, a marked degree of altruism and idealism on the credit side; dogmatism, intolerance, rancor, censoriousness, masochism, a compulsion toward self-martyrdom in the debit column—all these features tend to recur in the evolution of Russian intellectuals in the last decades of the Empire. They help to explain certain well-known descriptions of the intelligentsia: 'a sect, almost an order of knighthood'; 'something like medieval knights'; 'a monastic order or sect, with its own very intolerant ethics, its obligatory outlook on life, with its own manners and customs and even its own particular physical appearance.'[6]

Such comparisons are helpful in emphasizing the missionary spirit as a key element in the mentality under review. But they are also misleading in suggesting so extreme a degree of cohesiveness. Monasticism and knighthood have this in common, that an individual either joins or does not join these orders, and that the exact tally of their adherents could, at least in principle, be produced at any given moment by reference to the relevant authorities. But the Russian intelligentsia, however defined, had no register of members, no formal oath of allegiance, no records, no files, no offices, and thus no clear distinction between members and non-members. Potential adherents therefore found it impossible to compute their own numbers, much as they wished to do so. One hit-or-miss method—counting the signatures collected, at the turn of the century, to honor a jubilee of the radical journalist N. K. Mikhaylovsky—gave a total of 20,000.[7] And this figure, however vague, does at least underline the vast numerical difference between the multiply redefined nineteenth-century intelligentsia and the very differently, far more explicitly defined Soviet intelligentsia of the 1960s with its ten million-odd members, as noted above.

Since the pre-1914 intelligentsia, however categorized, was nothing as precise as a club, political party, religious sect or order of knighthood, but rather a fluid and amorphous concept, individuals might seem to enter and leave the category with considerable ease. Chekhov, in no sense a member of the group as commonly conceived, once wrote that he distrusted 'our hypocritical, bogus, hysterical, uneducated, lazy intelligentsia' because it regularly bred its own oppressors: former young rebels or liberals who, in later life, had joined the conservative establishment as reactionary officials, editors and the like.[8] Even to abuse the intelligentsia effectively seemed to require some sort of intelligentsia apprenticeship. Among many witty and scathing Russian denunciations of the Russian intelligentsia, the most devastating of all—the symposium *Landmarks* (1909)—is the work of members of, or certainly former members of, the category, however conceived. These were all intellectuals whose argumentative methodology, vocabulary and general style of thought still remain very much that of those whom they so wholeheartedly denounce. Might they not have denounced still more effectively had they wielded a less cumbrous tool than the language of the intelligentsia? Similarly—to compare small things with great while invoking a parallel from a remote discipline—the poet

Homer probably wished, in Book 9 of the *Iliad,* to cause Achilles to express disillusionment with the heroic ethos of the Greek epic tradition, but found himself in a linguistic quandary. 'Homer in fact, has no language, no terms, in which to express this kind of basic disillusionment with society and the external world.' [9] And where Homer nods, what can be expected from a Berdyayev, a Bulgakov or any other Russian *intelligentik?*

A further demonstration of the fluidity of intelligentsia as a concept is the frequency with which philosophers of the subject parade outstanding exemplars of Russian culture in order to decide whether they do—or, more usually, do not—'belong.' Peter Struve excludes Pushkin, Lermontov, Gogol, Turgenev, Chekhov, Vladimir Solovyov, Saltykov. He is doubtful even about Belinsky and Herzen; and seems wholeheartedly to embrace only Bakunin and Chernyshevsky. A similar review by Fedotov excludes such leading minds as Samarin, Ostrovsky, Pisemsky, Leskov, Klyuchevsky—and, of course, Tolstoy and Dostoyevsky.[10] Here, then, is the remarkable picture of a Russian intelligentsia from which virtually all the most prominent Russian intellectuals have been rigorously banished!

One striking feature often associated, rightly or wrongly, with the intelligentsia was a failure to register solid intellectual achievement in any field. Intellectual work, in the sense of the systematic accumulation of knowledge, of writing and completing a competent novel, of painting an adequate picture, composing a technically competent symphony, compiling a reputable dictionary, grammar or edition—work in that sense, if representing achievement spread over several years and carried to a successful conclusion, tended to seem incompatible with membership in the intelligentsia. An individual *intelligent* might be a very powerhouse of cerebral activity; his collected writings might even total many volumes. But the activity must be essentially narcissistic or masturbatory, confined to the sterile world of political and social theorizing, to the juggling, rehashing and general jactitation of 'ideas,' and those often ill-digested second-hand concepts borrowed from abroad.

That Dostoyevsky and Tolstoy, for example, could not rate as members of the intelligentsia was chiefly due to the monumental size of their achievement, and only secondarily to the unsuitability of their ideas. An idle, ungifted Tolstoy would have been a fully acceptable representative of the type; to which a Chernyshevsky, for instance, could gain entrance partly through his status as a prophet and pioneer of certain notions, but even more so (one suspects) through his proven incompetence in the area of creative craftsmanship, as revealed in his atrocious fiction. Competence of any kind could not easily be reconciled with adherence to the intelligentsia. Indeed, even to have assembled a systematic stamp collection would have been to dissociate oneself from that elusive grouping as commonly conceived. 'We snatch up any old ideas and bits of knowledge, any old convictions without the solid and profound foundation of stout-hearted, sober labour.' And ignorance also tended to accompany this lack of industry, 'a lack of serious knowledge and historical experience.' [11]

Together with an incapacity for serious intellectual labor went a contempt for the labors of others and for their fruits, whether intellectual or material. This approach, which so destructively tends to unite the idle rich with the idle poor—both categories being well represented among Russian intellectuals—was partly the outcome of a rigid egalitarianism, of an obsession with the fair redistribution of wealth so extreme that the question of creating wealth in the first place was pushed completely into the background. The attitude helps to explain the militant lack of creativity so easily associated with the Russian intelligentsia. 'The interests of distribution and egalitarianism always preponderated over those of production and creativity in the mind and emotions of the Russian intelligentsia.' [12]

Uncreative and incapable of sustained labor, the typical representative of the intelligentsia was by no means intellectually lazy. On the contrary: his mental cogwheels, not being engaged in driving anything, could idly revolve with truly awesome celerity. Never wearing out his brain in any sustained and serious inquiry, he was free to talk, talk, talk. Garrulity is thus a characteristic of the type. Such was the heated atmosphere of Golushkin's dining room as described in Turgenev's novel *Virgin Soil*. 'Words of all sorts—progress, government, literature; the taxation question, the church question, the woman question, the law-court question; classicism, realism, nihilism, communism; international, clerical, liberal, capital; administration, organization, association, and even crystallization: this was what really seemed to rouse Golushkin's enthusiasm, this hubbub. It seemed to be the very essence of everything.' [13]

Another hallmark of the intelligentsia was an extreme degree of intolerance combined with the practice of imposing its taboos by bullying and intimidation. On the methods whereby a senior *intelligent* might seek to whip a deviant juvenile into line, Chekhov's early career provides an instructive example. No sooner had the young man emerged into prominence with his first important story, *The Steppe* (1888), than he found himself sharply called to order by N. K. Mikhaylovsky, the movement's Grand Inquisitor. Hitherto Chekhov had 'sinned,' Mikhaylovsky told him, by contributing to the wrong kind of periodical, especially the conservative or reactionary newspaper *Novoye vremya*. And should he dare continue writing for such journals after producing *The Steppe,* that sin would become irredeemable. Chekhov must abandon Evil and espouse Good. 'God has given you much, Anton Pavlovich, and of you much shall be required.' Strong-minded behind his courteous exterior, Chekhov coolly rejected this and further impertinent attempts to instruct him in his professional duties and groom him for *intelligentik* status.[14] But others, less strong-minded, succumbed and fell dutifully into line. In many cases their adherence to the intelligentsia was merely a form of inverted, anti-establishmentarian conformism, revealing as little originality as that of their opposites—those despised contemporaries who had 'sold out' to the imperial state by seeking careers in the civil service or other branches of the establishment.

That Mikhaylovsky, a professed agnostic, should have addressed the young Chekhov like an archbishop haranguing some delinquent candidate for holy orders—here is a feature typical indeed of the educated Russian mentality, which has always seemed prone to religious, especially godlessly religious, postures. 'The religion of revolution, of a great social transformation—that is the only religion which I bequeath to you'—such was Herzen's legacy to his son as expressed in his famous treatise of 1850, *From the Other Shore.* 'Scientific positivism, and everything else Western, was accepted in its most extreme form and converted not only into a primitive metaphysic, but even into a special religion supplanting all previous religions.' Thus the early twentieth-century philosopher Nicholas Berdyayev in *Landmarks,* and the same point is put more vehemently by another contributor to the same symposium, Semyon Frank: 'If one understands the essence of religion as *fanaticism,* as fervent, almost obsessive devotion to a pet idea, devotion which inspires man not only to self-sacrifice and heroic deeds but also to the grotesque distortion of all his perspectives in life, to the intolerant destruction of everything inconsistent with the idea in question—then, of course, the Russian intelligentsia is religious in the highest degree.' [15]

Of the Russian tendency to embrace ideas, including those militantly and exclusively secular, with religious fervor, Dostoyevsky has much to say. The Russian is, according to him, always liable to be bowled over in his tracks by an idea which falls on him 'like an enormous rock and half squashes him—and there he is writhing underneath it and unable to extricate himself.' [16] Chekhov was as immune from this tendency as Dostoyevsky was prone to it, but he recognized its existence all the same. 'If a Russian does not believe in God it means that he believes in something else, and this he does not inactively, not like a German doctor of philosophy, but so that every one of his beliefs bends him into a hoop.' [17] The urge may be related to a general tendency noted above. 'This Slavonic capacity of yielding oneself wholly to one's ideas and emotions,' is how Mme. Jarintzov puts it, predictably proceeding to contrast the stolid Englishman who could never be swept off his feet by an idea or by anything else. Unlike the despised German or Englishman, the typical Russian 'cannot go on doubting for very long; his inclination is to make a dogma for himself quickly, and to surrender himself to it wholeheartedly and entirely.' [18] Thus the nineteenth-century Russian tended to be intellectually out of tune with the skeptical West, seeming simultaneously a throwback to the days of the medieval Church and a pioneer of the conformism-imposing totalitarian, terrorist bureaucracies of a later age. As has been well, though depressingly, said, 'The pre-Revolutionary Russian *intelligent* was in many ways a precursor of that phenomenon of our time known to the social scientist as *twentieth-century mass man.*' [19]

Dedicated, totally committed, many Russian oppositionist intellectuals courted martyrdom by challenging the cumbrous embattled might of the imperial state. A few suffered capital punishment in the nineteenth century, but only for complicity in terrorist acts, and not for their beliefs as such. A far larger number underwent imprisonment and exile. Chernyshevsky's long Siberian ordeal was one of the most severe on record. For these reasons such renegades or partial renegades from the intelligentsia as the authors of *Landmarks* can allude to the self-victimization of the group's 'martyrs.' Sergey Bulgakov, for instance, praises the 'unwavering readiness for all sacrifices of the intelligentsia's best representatives. . . . The Russian intelligentsia has evolved and developed in an atmosphere of constant martyrdom. It is impossible not to bow down before the shrine of the Russian intelligentsia's sufferings.' [20] Oh? Is it? On the last point one may beg to differ on two counts. First, the degree of persecution mobilized by the imperial authorities, though by no means negligible, seems almost insignificant if compared with the oppressions of a Hitler and a Stalin, operating long after Bulgakov wrote. As a Russian gentleman, the imprisoned intellectual received from his jailers and from interrogating gendarmes a degree of courtesy and consideration which somewhat mitigated the admitted hardships of imprisonment and exile. He was, to put it mildly, more likely to be offered a Havana cigar than to be kicked in the crotch. The Russian *intelligent* was, as has been noted, generally immune from the floggings not uncommonly meted out to those peasants whom he had managed to maneuver into mutiny. A second consideration is that a readiness to sacrifice one's life, freedom and comfort for a cause need not, surely, always and under every circumstance be admired without reference to the motives inspiring these sacrifices or the results to which they have contributed.

In analyzing the self-sacrificing activities of the Russian oppositionist intellectual—activities which so easily spilled over into sacrificing non-intellectuals—one could of course stop short at their own professions: that they sought 'the good of the people,' 'the common weal,' 'freedom,' and a revolution sanctified by the struggle against a wicked and doomed regime. But behind all this there often seems to pulsate a more primitive urge toward destructiveness for its own sake, a destructiveness all the more dangerous for the mask of pseudo-creativity with which it tended to be concealed. Such, at least, is the view of many competent witnesses. One of them speaks of destruction being recognized 'not only as *one* of the techniques of creativity, but as broadly equated with creativity—or rather as entirely taking the place of creativity.' The Russian 1905 Revolution, another critic of the intelligentsia has admitted, 'developed vast destructive energy, like a gigantic earthquake, but the creative elements in it turned out much weaker than the destructive.' This recalls the slogan coined by that spokesman of nihilism, Dmitry Pisarev, in the year of emancipation, 1861: 'What can be smashed must *be* smashed.' But even Pisarev added that 'whatever will stand the blow is fit to survive'; it took a Nechayev to concentrate exclusively on the first of these propositions, without in the least bothering his head about the second.[21]

To consider the intelligentsia's evolution is, according to one school of thought, to contemplate an unending chain of noble self-sacrifices in a great cause. But is it legitimate to ignore what more cynical observers might describe as the corrupting force of its constant frenzied verbalizing, its mindless espousal of revolution for revolution's sake? Then again, those same revolutions—fostered, planned, endlessly discussed and blessed in advance by the pre-1917 intelligentsia—eventually culminated in the mass liquidation of the survivors of that 'order of knighthood' by a cunning, determined and strikingly unchivalrous non-intellectual, Joseph Stalin. To consider these things is to understand how an acute observer can speak of the intelligentsia as 'impelled by some strange kind of collective death-wish,' and as perhaps unconsciously feeling 'that the sole reason for their existence was their self-destruction.'[22]

Nowhere is the Russian tendency to combine irreconcilable opposites more evident than in the political context, as was recognized by Dostoyevsky when he created Shigalyov, the Nihilist theoretician of *Devils*. 'Proceeding from unlimited freedom, I end with unlimited slavery': such, in a much-quoted phrase, is the essence of Shigalyov's contribution to political theory. He reflects the mentality of many another politically conscious visionary who has consecrated his life to creating a notional heaven on earth, while simultaneously driven by his own ineluctable inner logic toward creating the reality of hell. Fired by 'pure' love for the common people, representatives of this section of the intelligentsia were inspired yet more by even purer hatred for those whom they could conceive as enemies of the common people—including, not least of course, the common people itself on the many occasions when it failed to behave as hoped or predicted. Enemies, enemies, enemies—the *intelligent* seemed to see them everywhere. They included all those who, however diverse their views, did not share the particular collection of dogmas espoused by himself, and were hence hindering the onward march of progress. 'Thus, out of a great love for mankind in the future is born a great hatred for human beings; thus the passion for creating a heaven on earth becomes a drive toward destruction.' [23]

In this paranoid context another feature of the world at large pioneered by Russia—the link between politics and criminality or gangsterism—becomes intelligible. 'The Nihilistic element in the intelligentsia's faith somehow sanctions criminality and hooliganism, giving them the opportunity to clothe themselves in the mantle of idealism and progressiveness.' [24]

Attached though he nominally was to egalitarian beliefs, the typical *intelligent* found it difficult to react to others except as inferiors or superiors—a trait nowhere more fully exemplified than in his relations with the common people designated as the main victim of his self-sacrificing benefactions. On the one hand the *intelligent* acknowledged his debt to the suffering masses, his duty to help them and often enough his moral inferiority to them. At the same time he always tended to look down on the peasant masses with aristocratic disdain. This attitude may be detected in Belinsky, and above all in Chernyshevsky, who sacrificed everything for 'the people' while yet believing that it had no interest outside its own material advantages: 'The mass is simply the raw material for diplomatic and political experiments.' [25]

The intellectual peasant-fancying narodnik loved the peasantry, certainly; especially as he was rarely obliged to come into contact with actual peasants. But they were, to him, an object for vaguely conceived favors bestowed by their betters rather than individuals who might possibly possess some notion of their own about the kind of help which they would prefer to receive. 'Devotion to an idealized concept of "the people" was blended with an almost aristocratic contempt for the actual down-to-earth, prosaic propensities of the real people.' [26] It was the peasant-fancying intelligentsia, never the people itself, which was to decide where the people's true needs lay. And in general the peasantry was a confounded nuisance—all these ill-treated, poverty-stricken, miserable robots who should have been ready to arise from their slumbers and rally to the revolution at the word of command; but who stolidly refused for decade after decade to see where their duty lay until at long last they began to behave in 1905 as it had been their duty to behave back in the 1870s, and to start dutifully murdering landlords, officials and other representatives of the oppressing state on an adequate scale.

While, at the turn of the century, the more peasant-fancying section of the intelligentsia was founding its own political party, that of the Socialist Revolutionaries, another section—that of the revolutionary Marxists—was founding the Social Democratic Party. This soon split into two factions, Bolshevik and Menshevik, of which the former has eventually evolved into the present-day Communist Party of the Soviet Union. Far from expecting revolution to sprout in the countryside, the Social Democrats proclaimed the peasantry a repository of stagnation and reaction, placing their hopes in the political mobilization of the industrial workers. For a long time these proletariat-fanciers seemed less dangerous to the imperial regime than the peasant-fanciers: first, because Russia's workers were so overwhelmingly outnumbered by its peasants; and secondly because the Socialist Revolutionaries were addicted to assassination as a power-seizing tactic, whereas the Social Democrats were not. It was, however, the proletariat-fanciers who eventually triumphed in October 1917—partly because factory workers could be effectively mobilized under arms in the capital city and other centers of power; they thus constituted a suitable vehicle for a *coup d'état* such as the ill-organized peasantry, despite its greater numbers, could less effectively be provoked into staging.

Another reason for eventual Bolshevik success in 1917 was the leadership of Lenin, whose acute sense of timing enabled him to launch the October Revolution at the very moment when Russia's provisional government, that temporary heir to the Tsars, was at its most defenseless. To a feel for timing Lenin added inflexible determination to seize and then hold power, as also the ability to infuse his more hesitant henchmen with similar resolution. His other talents included a gift for never being bemused by the intricate ideological signals, couched in relatively abstract terms, with which he enlisted support and paralyzed resistance without losing sight of the realities of power. This, for him, always grew out of the barrel of a gun and only secondarily out of the collected works of Marx and Engels. The master, not the slave, of ideology, Lenin was to that extent no typical Russian *intelligent*. His chief value as a reflection of the Russian mentality thus derives less from any tendency to typify it than from his skill in exploiting its more vulnerable aspects; these include both the political fanaticism and the sheer silliness which significant numbers of *intelligenty* seemed to generate so abundantly. As for his personal attitude to the tribe, he again and again voiced his contempt for the Russian *intelligentik*.

Untypical though Lenin may be of the intelligentsia, his authoritarian temper nevertheless reflects a long-standing Russian intellectual tradition. He was far indeed, as has been seen above, from being the first Russian radical to believe that social progress can only be imposed by force, and through a dictatorship exercised by a person such as himself. This authoritarian drive was truly Russian in tending to submerge the individual in the collective, and also because it mirrored (in opposition) the authoritarian elements of the very state which was to be supplanted. Long before Lenin had been heard of there had come into being, alongside the controls somewhat laxly imposed by the Russian state, a contrary set of rigorous taboos imposed by intellectuals opposed to the state. Of the 1860s, for example, Mackenzie Wallace writes that 'The Press was able for some time to exercise a "Liberal" tyranny scarcely less severe than the "Conservative" tyranny of the censors in the preceding reign.' And it was the same phenomenon which caused Nikitenko to report, in his diary for October 1857, that 'In their intolerance they [the new opposition] are becoming representatives of a new and almost greater despotism than the previous one.' Herzen went further still. Writing as early as 1851, he claimed that 'An opposition which leads a frontal attack on a government always has itself, in an inverted sense, something of the character of the government attacked. I believe that there is some justification for the fear of Communism which the Russian government begins to feel: Communism is the Russian autocracy turned upside down.' [27]

Nearly forty years later the situation had grown even more acute. Chekhov, for example, reckoned that the political despotism of the imperial Ministry of Internal Affairs was at least equaled by that exercised by the editorial offices of *Russkaya mysl*, a Muscovite oppositionist journal.[28] Indeed, the former tyranny may have been the easier to bear, since it was at least imposed, however half-heartedly, by the police-backed power of the state, whereas the other discipline was a matter of social pressure to conform with certain taboos. Even a nonconformist may bow with dignity to superior power; there is something far more slavish, surely, in the conformism of one who can be made to toe the line solely by fear of not being considered a liberal. Mikhaylovsky's unsuccessful attempt to bully Chekhov in this way has already been recorded. And it was the mentality of such as Mikhaylovsky which, on a later occasion, induced Chekhov to utter the prophecy, 'Under the banner of learning, art and persecuted freedom of thought Russia will one day be ruled by such toads and crocodiles as were unknown even in Spain under the Inquisition. Yes, you just wait. Narrow-mindedness, enormous pretensions, excessive self-importance, a total absence of any literary or social conscience: these things will do their work . . . will spawn an atmosphere so stifling that every healthy person will be bloody well nauseated.' In the same spirit are the denunciations of the intelligentsia's 'credulity without faith, struggle without creativity, fanaticism without enthusiasm,' of the dogmatism, censoriousness, woolly-mindedness, ignorance and general dottiness so eloquently expressed in *Landmarks* some twenty years later.[29]

Nikitenko, Mackenzie Wallace, Dostoyevsky, Chekhov, the authors of *Landmarks*—are these opponents of the intelligentsia to have the last word? Or should one think of the pre-revolutionary *intelligent* as one who 'took up the noble responsibility of fighting for [his] fellow-Russians against tyranny and reaction'? Is the intelligentsia more properly regarded as 'this milieu of earnest, dedicated, passionately honest, fiercely principled scientists and thinkers'? 'Dedicated souls, many endowed with wide cultural and personal charm . . . in their intellectual earnestness they present an attractive and even exciting picture.' 'Heroism . . . disinterestedness . . . personal nobility.' From the studies of modern *intelligent*-fancying observers one may multiply such quotations *ad infinitum*.[30] They show, at least, that no unanimous verdict of guilty has been uttered against the pre-revolutionary intelligentsia as a whole. Rather is the opposite the case, and the difference of opinion derives less from the nature of the intelligentsia, however defined, than from the premises with which the problem is approached. 'Intellectual earnestness,' as is evident from one of the quotations given above, can be an attractive quality to some, and it is among them that the pre-revolutionary Russian intelligentsia's most fervent posthumous admirers are likely to be found. But if the impression is left that all Russia's intellectuals, as opposed to her *intelligentiki,* were blessed or cursed with the quality of humorless earnestness, the present study has indeed been written in vain.

## *TOTALITARIANISM AND ANTI-TOTALITARIANISM*

To those who see a characteristic Russian rhythm in the alternation of anarchy and regimentation, the two revolutions of 1917 must seem a striking confirmation of a traditional pattern, now developing on a scale unprecedented in the country's earlier history and carrying new threats or hopes for the future of the world at large.

In the first revolution of that fateful year the anarchic principle was predominant, as also in the ten-month period of 'provisional government' which followed. When, at the end of February, the monarchy suddenly disappeared it was not pushed, but rather fell—even though immediate causes can be traced in a general breakdown of confidence, and especially in conditions in the capital city, then called Petrograd. They included the disaffection of certain key military units, including Cossacks; local food shortages; and, to an extent difficult to determine, the operations of agents paid by the Berlin government with which Russia was still at war. But there was no concerted *coup d'état,* no organized conspiracy to unseat the government and imperial system at this particular time. Events seemed rather to take place by accident, surprising not least the very revolutionaries and assorted *intelligentiki* who had for decades been predicting revolution, discussing the form which it would take and considering the most effective ways in which it could be channeled.

Between March and September 1917 Russia—though still at war—enjoyed the longest period of emancipation from authority in her modern history. But this proved to be the reign of lawlessness, not of freedom under the law. Lack of experience in operating representative institutions, an ineradicable craving for regimentation or anarchy or both, a spirit hostile to the principle of compromise, sheer bad luck—for whatever combination of reasons the provisional government of 1917 was permitted neither to govern nor to complete arrangements for electing a permanent successor under a new constitution. When it disappeared in October it did not simply collapse, as rule by the Romanov dynasty had collapsed earlier in the year, but was violently ousted. The instrument was a *coup d'état* plotted by the leaders of the small, highly disciplined Bolshevik movement, which combined libertarian professions with an increasing vocation for imposing rigid controls.

Though far indeed from enjoying majority support in the country as a whole, the Bolsheviks were, as already noted, heavily backed by workers and troops in key areas in or near the capital. They derived much of their appeal from their apparent ability to behave decisively in an age of indecision, as also from their skill in harnessing idealistic patter to techniques of conspiracy, intimidation and trickery which, outside the all-sanctioning political context, would have been dismissed as downright criminal.

To seek features characteristic of the Russian mind among the chaotic events of 1917 and their sequel is to enter a particularly speculative area. But it may not be fanciful to discern certain already familiar qualities. In launching themselves on the unknown with such ferocious enthusiasm the

Russians brought to bear the quality of *razmakh*, 'gusto,' which they have already been observed displaying in so many other areas. This revolutionary dynamism, together with its corollary—the ease with which these same masses, so violently aroused from their slumbers, were so quickly put to sleep again—reflects the age-old Russian tendency either to embrace or to eschew action with a totality of commitment alien to other breeds. However, it must also be remembered that the revolutions were not the work of Russians alone, but that the minority nations of the Empire also played a part, both as leaders and as led.

Another outstanding Russian trait is vulnerability to Revolution as an abstract notion conceived—like History—in personified guise as an independent agency capable of taking sweeping and inevitably beneficent initiatives in human affairs. On the hypnotic effect of this all-too-pregnant word the memoirist and poet's widow Nadezhda Mandelstam makes the point that it played a greater part than terror and bribery ('though, God knows, there was enough of both') in breaking the resistance of the post-revolutionary intelligentsia. Revolution was a word 'which none of them could bear to give up . . . and its force was such that one wonders why our rulers still needed prisons and capital punishment.' However, as she also sagely notes, revolution is 'a word to which whole nations have succumbed.' [1] That intellectuals in countries other than Russia can be manipulated through the threat of being considered inadequately liberal, revolutionary or left-wing in their views is too widely observed a phenomenon to require illustration. Here again, the Russian claim to preeminence can only be that of early initiators, not of continuing monopolizers.

On Revolution as a logic-defying concept manifested in Petrograd in early 1917, the historian George Katkov makes an acute comment. Quoting a contemporary observation ascribing the sudden death of a counter-revolutionary major to 'a well-aimed stray bullet,' he continues, 'A well-aimed *stray* bullet! When these words were written the dreamlike logic of revolutionary rhetoric had already replaced common sense in Russia.' [2]

After their tactical victory and seizure of power in Petrograd in October 1917 the Bolsheviks remained vulnerable owing to their lack of support in the country at large, where the Socialist Revolutionaries were known to command considerably more votes. And since these votes were likely to prove decisive in overthrowing Bolshevism at the elections (to which the Bolsheviks were nominally committed) for a constituent assembly, the new rulers were faced with the alternative of immediately suppressing opposition by force or being unseated by the inevitable course of events. Lenin, who saw this dilemma with admirable clarity, persuaded wavering colleagues to support the destruction of their political opponents. The campaign of suppression began with right-wing movements, soon moving on to fellow Socialists and then to fellow Marxists of non-Leninist persuasion. The publications of these rival movements were banned; their spokesmen were imprisoned or executed—a policy to which extra momentum was imparted by a civil war of increasing ferocity. The process of totalitarianization had not been completed by Lenin's death in 1924, and during the whole of the 1920s considerable freedom of speech still remained. Literary censorship was largely negative at the time, in the sense that writers were forbidden to attack the assumptions of the new state; but were not, as later, required to make positive affirmations in its favor. However, Nadezhda Mandelstam has rightly warned against a common tendency to regard the Soviet 1920s as a kind of golden age. She points out that it too was an age of terror, however effectively the even severer persecutions of the 1930s may blind observers to the realities of the earlier decade. The same point is also made by other present-day observers, figuring prominently for example in Solzhenitsyn's monumental study of Stalinist horrors, *The Gulag Archipelago*. In any case full totalitarianism had been established by the time of Stalin's fiftieth birthday in December 1929, after which he ruled as unchallenged dictator for nearly a quarter of a century.

With the virtual end of the Civil War in 1921, Lenin and his government had found themselves committed to establishing a heaven on earth in a territory which, by no means exclusively through their own operations, had become a fairly near approximation to hell. Such were the devastations, human and material, inflicted by seven years of war, first against Germany and then against the forces of White Russia. No power on earth could have restored so shattered a realm for many years or even decades, and it was therefore necessary to mobilize the weapon of pretense lest the miracle-working claims of the newly triumphant political creed, its assertion that it could create a utopia, be exposed. In a sense, therefore, the whole of Russia together with its surviving Empire, soon named the USSR, was converted into a giant simulated prestige project. Or, rather, certain isolated areas were picked out for minor, genuine prestige projects, such as the great Dneprostroy Dam, while a continuing propaganda campaign proclaimed by suggestion that these spectacular enterprises were typical, if not of the country's progress as a whole, at least of achievements so imminent that they could be claimed as actual.

Perhaps the most striking example of such an enterprise has been the impressive Exhibition of the Achievements (i.e., non-achievements) of the National Economy in Moscow. Around this foreign tourists are traditionally freighted, and can observe a few spectacularly fecund cows, sheaves of super-corn and gleaming combine-harvesters, the hope being that they will regard these as typical, not as the glaring exceptions which they regrettably constitute. It was a lucky accident for the post-revolutionary government that traditional Russian *vranyo*, together with the age-old training in hieratic speech forms, could be harnessed to such operations.

The government has also exploited the traditional Russian genius for blurring the concept of time. On the one hand both citizenry and foreign visitors are deluged with endless, *vranyo*-infused, self-pitying tirades about the iniquities of the inglorious past: those of the Tsarist regime, of foreign intervention in the Civil War, of the Teuton occupant in 1941–45. And on the other hand they are also bemused by ecstatic visions of the glorious future when, in *x* years, America will be overtaken and such problems as providing abundant food, transport, living space and other amenities will have been triumphantly solved in a manner destined to shame every other society on earth. Thus is every attempt made to divert attention from present actualities which, though not necessarily sordid or discreditable in all their aspects, most emphatically do not bear out the utopistic, wonder-working claims of official doctrine. To pretend, at one and the same time, that a paradise has been (well, is just about to be) triumphantly established on earth, while simultaneously explaining that the total failure to realize such a goal is due to the machinations of various enemies (Tsars, Whites, Hitlerites, Americans, capitalists)—here is one of those splendidly self-contradictory operations which so baffle observers who have not been initiated into the mysteries of *vranyo*. And one notes that this sensation of being surrounded by 'enemies,' now sedulously inculcated into the Russian masses, has been lifted directly from the paranoid fantasies of the pre-revolutionary Russian *intelligentik*.

So much for the psychology of post-revolutionary official policy. But what of opposition to the new authority? To what extent does that reflect traditional elements in Russian mentality or mark the evolution of new traits? The investigation is hampered by the difficulty of disentangling the Russian mind from its near or not-so-near relative, the Soviet mind.

Since the earliest years of Soviet rule there has been considerably less scope for political opposition than was to be observed even during the severest period of nineteenth-century oppression, that of the later reign of Nicholas I (1848–55). The newly established Bolsheviks had, during the decades preceding their assumption of power, already learned through personal experience how easily an authoritarian state could be undermined and brought to collapse by political disaffection. Knowing full well that a more ruthless or intelligent exercise of power by the imperial government might have led to the effective suppression of their own movement, they had been put on the alert in advance. Never were they likely to forget how thoroughly they themselves had been able to exploit the inefficiency and corruption of the imperial police. They had written inflammatory anti-Tsarist propaganda in jail, they had spirited it out through bribed or duped warders. They had smuggled weapons, explosives and illicit pamphlets into the country. Their spies had infiltrated the imperial political police. They had even benefited in the end, in terms of the corruption of the imperial apparatus, through the infiltration of their own ranks by police spies. And they were damned if they were going to have this sort of thing going on in reverse now that they themselves were in charge. Hence the immediate establishment of a new, Bolshevik political security police (the Cheka) and the appointment, as its head, of a revolutionary with a long record of arrests and escapes under the previous dispensation: Felix Dzerzhinsky. Hence too the vastly more rigorous penal conditions progressively imposed in the prisons and newly instituted concentration camps of the Soviet period, from which escape was rendered infinitely more hazardous than it had been under the Empire. Before 1917 an imprisoned or exiled Bakunin, Kropotkin, Trotsky or Stalin could and did flee from Siberian confinement with what seems ridiculous ease; he could travel about the Empire despite the extensive passport controls notionally in force; he could slip illicitly abroad for a conference with other revolutionaries and return equally easily, equally illicitly. This type of activity could not be halted entirely, but it was restricted with far greater success than the nineteenth-century Romanovs had ever achieved.

Under these grim conditions post-revolutionary political opposition has rarely attained the panache so often exhibited in imperial times. There were no more dissident broadsheets scattered by galloping riders, no more stabbings of chiefs of police in daylight on the capital's main streets. By such citizens as wished to oppose the new government established in Moscow, duller and less exuberant methods had to be adopted; and to this extent the mentality of the Russian in opposition has undergone considerable modification.

So severe was Stalinist oppression from the 1930s onward that opposition virtually disappeared within a few years. Much of the fundamental resistance had come from the peasants, compelled to enter collective farms *en masse* and driven to such despair that they self-destructively slaughtered their own livestock rather than yield it to the robber-state. Their opposition was crushed by armed force, mass arrest and wholesale consignment to concentration camps, combined with Stalin's no-less-cruel policy of contumaciously failing to relieve, and even of fostering, the great peasant famine of 1931–32. What of resistance to authority at a higher level? Such an episode as the clandestinely circulated Ryutin manifesto of 1932, in which Stalin's removal for incompetence was demanded by a moderately important Party official—this was highly exceptional. By now the dictator had destroyed all serious potential opposition. Wishing to consolidate his rule in the ultimate degree, he adopted from 1934 onward a policy of preemptive overkill directed against all those who, though in practice not pursuing policies disloyal to him, might conceivably have joined a notional opposition under hypothetical circumstances. The dictator thus invented and proceeded to liquidate an impotent or non-existent conspiracy of wreckers, saboteurs, rightists, Trotskyites and the like. It was on faked charges that the victims of Stalin's great show trials perished, as did the myriads of those anonymously liquidated in the concentration camps for political deviation of various imaginary brands.

During the Second World War popular opposition to Stalin was expressed by those sizable sections of the population which initially welcomed the German invader, only to be repelled later by the infliction of Hitlerite atrocities on a scale greater even than that of those previously inflicted by Stalin. On the whole it was the non-Russian peoples of the USSR, and notably the Ukrainians, who initially welcomed the enemy. But many disaffected Russians joined the ill-fated army of General Vlasov, which fought on the German side during the war. These forms of resistance to Russian authority are without parallel in the imperial period, confirming the thesis that opposition is an area in which the traditional Russian mentality has maintained itself less durably than elsewhere.

The same is true of the post-Stalin period. Since the dictator's death in 1953 the political resistance movement has undergone a highly complex evolution which cannot be described in detail here. As every reader of the Western press knows, dissent has flourished, if that is not too strong a word, in the climate of 'thaw' or comparative relaxation introduced by Stalin's death. Unfortunately the nature and importance of this movement have been distorted in the minds of many Western observers, including not a few specialists as well as those non-specialists who are informed on these matters largely through the 'media.' First, the degree of relaxation permitted since 1953 has tended to be grossly exaggerated. And secondly, the assumption has often been made that the post-Stalin relaxations are progressive: that they have, in other words, gradually increased and are somehow bound to go on increasing until, one day, Russia will turn out to have been transformed into a liberal and democratic society in the Western sense. As one who has sought to expose this popular misconception for at least twenty years, I note with melancholy satisfaction that the realities of the situation seem at last, in the late 1970s, to be becoming clearer to the Western folk brain. In the minds of Western politicians, on the other hand, the old heresy of automatic Kremlinite self-liberalization seems to have been supplanted by a new and no less dangerous illusion: that the Kremlin can be bribed or mollified by concessionary shipments of grain, machinery and other tangible inducements to behave itself.

That these misunderstandings should have been fostered by 'capitalist' journalists is probably inevitable in an atmosphere which encourages both editors and readers to demand two features above all in newspaper reports and comments on Russia: novelty and comfort. In reality, alas, the country has rarely justified either requirement. To this atmosphere of unjustified hopes must be added the spectacular but in some ways regrettable newsworthiness of Soviet dissidents. In them the sensation-craving Western newspaper reader can contemplate from a safe distance brave men defying an all-powerful state, which—it has all too easily been inferred—will one day succumb like a blundering Goliath to a very army of Davids, eagerly mend its naughty ways and tamely join the community of free nations.

Despite such comforting illusions, it is now at last dawning on the Western mind that the Brezhnev period is more, not less, oppressive than the preceding Khrushchev era. Nor can it now seem surprising to find the year 1962—in which Alexander Solzhenitsyn's *One Day in the Life of Ivan Denisovich* erupted into a Moscow-published journal—rated as the highwater mark of post-Stalinist liberalization. A well-qualified British observer of the mid-1970s has described the general intellectual climate in the USSR as 'undoubtedly harsher and less promising than ten to fifteen years ago.'[3] As the example of Solzhenitsyn's story indicates, imaginative literature has continued in the totalitarian period to perform a function analogous to its traditional role in the imperial period: that of a vehicle in which material critical of authority can appear more readily than anywhere else, and of a barometer indicating the atmospheric pressure on society at large. But, as the example of Solzhenitsyn also shows, this function has been in decline since 1962.

Aware as they are of Western urges to exaggerate Soviet liberalization, and realizing that it is in their interests to foster the erroneous impression that Russia is moving toward the 'Western way of life' (and therefore constitutes far less of a menace than might otherwise be supposed), the Moscow authorities have been known to make use of their own licensed liberals. These are sanctioned to tour foreign countries demonstrating that the Russians, too, are human beings possessing the usual complement of eyes, ears and limbs, and that they are capable of baring their teeth in the rictus of simulated benevolence: all of which purportedly proves that their 'system,' contrary to the claims of ill-wishers, does tolerate political opposition. Even in Stalin's day this role could be, and was, performed with no little skill by an Ilya Ehrenburg. Since his time the main liberal, in this rather special sense, seems to have been the poet Yevgeny Yevtushenko. To say this is not at all to suggest that such licensed liberals are insincere when they express their views, merely that the authorities appear to tolerate or approve their activities as a device for further bemusing the Western brain already so pathetically ill-adapted to assess the non-Western brain. Licensed liberals in the above sense are a relatively new phenomenon, for such refinements in public relations were beyond the range of the imperial Russian government.

Though an Ehrenburg or a Yevtushenko may indeed have been operating under informal license, as indicated here, this is certainly not true of the literary dissidents as a whole. Two of them in particular have captured the imagination of the world at large through prolonged defiance clearly unwelcome to officialdom: Pasternak and Solzhenitsyn.

Pasternak was the post-Stalinist pioneer of what, for want of a better word, has been called 'smuggled' Soviet literature: smuggled in the sense that works which have either been rejected for publication in Russia, or would be unlikely ever to achieve such publication, have somehow been spirited abroad and issued in foreign translation. Here again a tradition of imperial Russia has been revived, for censorship-menaced works of that period were often first published abroad: some of Pushkin's political and blasphemous verse, for instance, and certain writings of Tolstoy. In the 1920s, too, it was by no means unknown for USSR-dominated Russian writers to publish—at first without official disapproval—in Berlin or other foreign centers.

Pasternak's novel *Doctor Zhivago* (1957) revived such memories by becoming the first notable post-Stalin work to be spirited abroad for publication. Though denounced by Kremlinized critics as heretical, it is a measured, cool and objectively presented tale: in no way a rabid anti-Kremlinist tirade or Cold War pamphlet. And yet, by assuming the private life of any private individual to be inevitably more important than his function as a collectivized cog, Pasternak struck at the roots of official dogma. He also did so by implying in private conversation that the premises of his society were too absurd even to be worth refuting, though no decent man could long refrain from laughing at them. Here Pasternak was rejecting not merely a Soviet but also a common Russian train of thought. In *Doctor Zhivago* he chides Gogol, Tolstoy and Dostoyevsky for excess of portentousness: for 'preparing for death, worrying, looking for meanings, drawing up balance-sheets.' With these philosophically uptight figures he contrasts Pushkin and Chekhov, praising their 'childlike Russian quality . . . their modest unconcern with such pompous themes as mankind's ultimate destiny and their own salvation. . . . They lived out their lives unobtrusively in an individual manner personal to themselves.' [4]

In making that distinction, and in inferentially ranging himself with Chekhov and Pushkin, the author of *Doctor Zhivago* was underlining a point which I have hoped to make here in a different way. Not every Russian is a great howling prophet sounding off about ultimate profundities. The quieter, the less theatrical approach is not necessarily less common on Russian soil than the flamboyancy which has somehow become registered as typical. And, as the names invoked by Pasternak show, it would be a grave error to suppose that there was any monopoly in genius on either side of the register.

Pasternak died in 1960, and his place as premier literary dissident was taken by Alexander Solzhenitsyn. The documentary-type story *One Day in the Life of Ivan Denisovich,* with which he first attracted attention, was the first unvarnished account of Stalinist concentration-camp life to appear in any Kremlin-sanctioned publication. This work remains one of the most powerful evocations of the theme on record, and I well recall the satisfaction of discovering it for myself in the Moscow literary journal *Novy mir* and of being the first translator to publish an extensive extract from it in English. Its taut, austere, restrained manner gave no indication that its author was or was about to become one of the most prolific and undisciplined scribes on record. He now has to his credit many items of fiction, long and short, together with numerous other works: autobiographical, historical and publicistic. Virtually all his writings, whether nominally fictional or not, bear a documentary character, and all combine to present a panoramic view of twentieth-century Russia. In these wide-ranging works, as in his personal style, Solzhenitsyn does not project himself as one of those modest, self-effacing Russian geniuses praised by Pasternak. Here is a figure larger than even Russian life, whose personal history—as camp victim, sufferer from grave illness and target for official persecution—has demanded resources of courage and perseverance far exceeding the normal human limit. Solzhenitsyn has also become, since his expulsion from the Soviet Union in early 1974, a notable figure on the world stage. His thunderous manner, his wide range, his moral earnestness, his tendency majestically to ignore or neglect the subtler and more elusive virtues of literary creativity—these traits, all of them traditionally Russian, contrast vividly with the frivolity and facile optimism of much political thinking and literary criticism in the West. It is therefore perhaps inevitable that his version of the facts of life in the global power-contending area should have met with a response far from universally sympathetic.

Solzhenitsyn has been said to speak for Russia with as much authority as the very Soviet government.[5] But he is also a major figure in an older Russian tradition. While still resident in his native country he acquired a status similar to that of the later Tolstoy—the Tolstoy who long defied the might of the imperial Russian government, protected only by his international reputation. Now, in exile, Solzhenitsyn has veered more toward the position of Alexander Herzen, who emigrated in 1847, and whose denunciations of Russian tyranny helped to make him the country's leading nineteenth-century political *émigré*.

Among dissidents still resident in the USSR at the time of writing, an outstanding figure is Andrew Sakharov. No author of belles-lettres, he is a leading atomic physicist and has been called 'the father of the Soviet H-bomb,' a title which he himself disavows. Once again the dissident movement has thrown up, as it has in the case of others too numerous to mention, a man of remarkable independence and courage. To tag Sakharov as an heir to the pre-revolutionary Russian intelligentsia, as one dissident-fancier has done,[6] is surely to misread his character and achievements. A man of great intellectual distinction in his specialized field, Sakharov has shown in his writings on global politics a degree of sober common sense, personal modesty and lack of narcissism about as far removed as possible from the style of the nineteenth-century intelligentsia. He has been involved in controversy with Solzhenitsyn, whose lapses into old-fashioned narodnik sentimentality about the 'ordinary' Russian (as in his novel *August 1914*) the more fastidious scientist does not share. Sakharov has preached a phased democratization of the Soviet Union, whereas Solzhenitsyn seems to believe that a period of continuing, albeit dwindling, authoritarianism must be an essential prelude to progress there. However, there is more in common between the two men than has sometimes been allowed. Both have taken issue with Western politicians and Western public opinion for ignoring the menace of the USSR as an aggressive terroristic bureaucracy, and for being willing to play the 'peaceful coexistence' game by Russian rules. In particular the policy of *détente*—that whereby Western states make tangible concessions to Moscow in return for soothing but meaningless and unenforceable assurances—has incurred the criticism of both.

In personal style Sakharov differs from the flamboyant Solzhenitsyn, belonging rather to the modest and unobtrusive Russian type of which Chekhov, Pasternak, Nikitenko and others have been cited above as exemplars. As this reminds one, the ranks of Soviet dissidents have naturally included figures at all points of the spectrum from exuberance to restraint. Of the former, Valery Tarsis seems an outstanding representative, while a more disciplined approach—in his writings as well as in his personal style—has been cultivated by Victor Nekrasov.

As for the rank-and-file of Soviet-domiciled dissenters, they have inclined rather to the sober and solid approach of the 'untypical' Russian, if only because official controls render any other posture extremely difficult. They have not, taken as a group, advocated the overthrow of the Soviet system either by force or peaceful means. Rather have they urged by all possible means that the system should live up to its own by-no-means-illiberal pretensions. It is the flouting—through traditional official *proizvol* or arbitrariness—of laws guaranteeing extensive civil rights which the dissidents attack, particularly in their remarkable periodical publication, the *Chronicle of Current Events*. Anonymously published and circulated in typescript, this is a notable example of *samizdat* or 'do-it-yourself' publishing. The practice has flourished since the death of Stalin, again reviving a long-standing tradition. Much of Pushkin's work, for instance, was first read by his fellow-countrymen in privily circulated manuscript copies.

The *Chronicle of Current Events* has been appearing since 1968, with a break of two years in 1972–74 when the authorities contrived to suppress it. It is a sober, restrained publication which details in objective, equable style the various abuses to which Soviet citizens are exposed by authority—very often, as noted above, in defiance of its own regulations. This impressive publication presents a further demonstration of the abiding truth that to be a Russian is not necessarily to err on the side of over-exuberance. Recent dissidence, as charted in the *Chronicle* and elsewhere, has tended to focus on three issues: on the rights of non-Russian minorities, which are no direct concern of the present study; on the situation of religious believers, a topic discussed above; and, finally, on political freedom in general—a transcending theme which comprehends all the others.

Why does a state as repressive as the USSR—and one, moreover, equipped with a vast under-employed political police authority—tolerate these heresies? First, despite all controls, the authorities may be simply unable to suppress a movement as broadly based as Soviet political dissent. Secondly, they may not wish to do so. It is, after all, normal police practice in civil as well as political areas to allow the 'criminal' to continue his activities under surveillance rather than to drive him and his associates underground by immediately proceeding to arrest all and sundry. The Okhrana (imperial political police) followed this procedure before 1917 and the KGB does so now. Furthermore, the Soviet authorities derive considerable propaganda advantages from permitting dissidence to continue, inasmuch as the befogged Western folk brain has long insisted on interpreting the phenomenon as proof of that blessed progressive 'liberalization' of the USSR which, it is wishfully expected, will one day deliver the world from all its problems. In a sense, then, the West has tended to feel that it can lie back and relax so long as Russia maintains these dissidents whose 'movement' will one day peacefully transform the Kremlin into a source of international sweetness and light.

In any case by no means all dissenters are left unmolested. Many have been treated with great severity. They have been sentenced to imprisonment for anti-Soviet activity, incarcerated in mental hospitals, harassed in many other ways. A dissenter can never know where he stands. The authorities may allow a given individual his head for a while. Or they will bully and intimidate him and his associates as a prelude to arrest, compulsory psychiatric 'treatment' or expulsion from the USSR. Solzhenitsyn, Tarsis and Nekrasov are only a few of the many troublemakers, as the Kremlin sees them, who have been unceremoniously dumped on the world at large either by expulsion or by the withdrawal of a passport after foreign travel has been sanctioned and embarked upon.

Opinions naturally differ as to the future of Soviet dissidence. Some of its foremost representatives are also among the most pessimistic: 'If a man does not keep silent it does not mean that he hopes necessarily to achieve something,' Sakharov once stated.[7] And he would probably agree in finding Western public opinion tragically mistaken to the extent that Russian or Soviet dissidents are still conceived as capable of miraculously halting Kremlinite expansionism unaided. This is all the less likely to happen in that Soviet dissent remains, as for a long time the nineteenth-century narodnik movement remained, chiefly a purview of the educated classes. A large percentage of its representatives are academics, and it has few links with the masses of workers and peasants. They, too, have occasionally mounted their riots or strikes, which have been suppressed with considerable severity and of which news has often filtered out only after considerable delay. Meanwhile the divorce between educated and less educated dissent is more remarkable for recalling the dilemmas and exasperations of the 1870s than for offering any hope of political change in the immediate future.

In attempting to measure the degree of disaffection, actual and potential, in present-day Russia as a whole, this investigation will maintain a modest reticence. Even in Western societies, where sophisticated opinion-polling techniques are freely and openly operated, the assessment of group political attitudes is a notoriously tricky and unreliable affair. How much the more so in the closed society of totalitarian Russia, where even the most innocent and casual question by an unofficial inquirer can be interpreted as an attempt to subvert the entire structure of the state. As for the confidence with which Russia-watchers will pronounce on the population's loyalty to the regime, on the attitudes of 'Soviet youth' and so on, I can only marvel once more from the sidelines at the readiness with which, in a Russian context, even level-headed observers will commit themselves to dogmatic assertions about the unknowable. Yet this is, after all, a vital matter on which even an uninspired guess may have some slight significance. That the general underlying political attitude is one of profound apathy, despite the various nominally enthusiastic ritual affirmations periodically extorted from sections of the community—this at least it seems safe to suggest. The passionate believers and the passionate disbelievers in the totalitarian system are, one may also confidently conjecture, far less numerous than are the internal neutrals. This neutral or apathetic mass would, however, probably rally to the national cause in the event of war, according to a fairly general assumption from which I see no reason to dissent. Nor do I feel that one may build many hopes for constructive change on the undoubted fascination exercised on Russians, especially the young, by almost any manifestation of Western culture, including such books, films and even 'pop groups' as illicitly seep out or are officially permitted to filter through to the Russian consumer.

# V

# CONTINUITY AND CHANGE

To what extent has post-1917 Russia retained and even institutionalized traditional pre-revolutionary features of the national outlook? Conversely, to what extent is one notable Kremlinite claim—that of having evolved, in Soviet Man, a new and superior brand of human being—to be taken seriously?

To the skeptical this last assertion may seem absurd enough to send him to the opposite extreme, inducing him to exaggerate the many elements of permanence in the Russian psyche. From the pages of this book alone much evidence could be adduced to suggest that the Russian, far from being change-prone or revolutionary-minded, is supremely immutable in his mentality and in the various institutions, taboos and customs which that mentality has evolved as appropriate to itself.

Among these is numbered the lavish use of arbitrary government-sponsored terror against wide sections of the citizenry. Governmental terror—whether Muscovite, imperial or totalitarian—has embraced such typically though not exclusively Russian features as mass deportation by ukase from on high; arrest and imprisonment administratively ordained through officials uncontrolled by the judiciary or any *habeas corpus* act; the periodical sacrifice of the country's very terror-purveying high officials as scapegoats for official policy; the victimization of disgraced persons' relatives and associates; the mass conscription of labor for prestige projects; the preemptive punishment of those deemed liable to commit offenses which they may in practice not have committed even in imagination; the persecution of those considered guilty of facecrime (failure to simulate adequate political subservience); laws providing harsh penalties for those seeking to change the system of government; laws, no less severe, directed against failure to denounce such persons.

Such are some among many considerations suggesting that, while systems may come and systems may go, perennial Russia rolls on forever.

In comparatively minor detail, too, one may trace much continuity between pre-1917 and post-1917 punitive practice. There is, for instance, the tendency to sentence those involved in vehicular accidents, no matter whether traction by Tsarist quadruped or post-Tsarist internal combustion engine is involved, to harsh terms of imprisonment with total disregard to any degree of culpability.[1] And what is there about the Russian climate which has led two leading despots separated by a century—Nicholas I and Stalin—to decree independently of each other that certain political prisoners should be incarcerated in *windowless cells*? The imposition of compulsory psychiatric or other medical 'treatment' on political offenders is also sometimes invoked as a parallel between Russia old and new. However, the only well-known nineteenth-century victim—Chaadayev—was treated with far less severity than the unfortunate modern dissident objects of this macabre persecution. And Nicholas I, in strong contrast to Stalin, was prevailed upon to restore window privileges to the sentenced political miscreants, the Decembrists, whom he had sought to mew in eyeless dungeons: a reminder that Russian imperial penal procedures, certainly from the early nineteenth century onward, have been far milder than those of the succeeding period.

In the area of official propaganda and political myth the wide gulf between appearance and reality has also been stressed as an abiding feature of Muscovite, imperial and post-imperial Russia. Here too a general proposition seems convincingly reinforced by relatively trivial details. For instance, it was a nineteenth-century custom to make a special point of publishing in Russian translation such foreign books as seemed to reveal particularly discreditable features in other European countries. This policy has, again, been followed in the totalitarian period. It has also taken in films such as the Italian *La Dolce Vita:* sanctioned (one surmises) for distribution less on artistic grounds than because they seem to portray 'capitalist' civilization as reeling, doomed, into anarchy and chaos. Then again, there is the traditional Russian governmental practice of representing as *concessions to popular demand* measures and policies which have in fact sprung from the whim or individual decision of a single autocrat. The rewriting of history to suit official myth is another procedure common to Tsarist and post-Tsarist Russia alike. To this may be added persisting official secretiveness as expressed in the imposition of unperson status; in the unavailability of such basic reference material as guides, street plans and—later—telephone directories; in the suppression or non-publication of statistics about suicides, criminal prosecutions and accidents.

Then there is the special place occupied in Russian tradition by imaginative literature as a medium through which opposition to official policies may, despite severe censorship controls, be more effectively expressed than elsewhere. The circulation of banned works in manuscript or typescript (now called *samizdat*), the practice of smuggling these works abroad for publication banned at home (now called *tamizdat*)—here are features common to the evolution of a Pushkin and a Solzhenitsyn. No less common to the nineteenth and twentieth centuries is the practice of disciplining imaginative authors through literary bureaucrats: themselves, in many instances, mediocre or failed writers. 'Official optimism'—the obligation placed upon authors of belles-lettres to present Russian conditions in an unreal and cheerful light—had influenced the processing of a Pushkin and a Chekhov long before it was enshrined in the government-imposed literary method evolved in the 1930s and known as Socialist Realism. 'Russia's past has been admirable. Her present is more than magnificent. As to the future, it is beyond the power of the most daring imagination to portray it.' This homily to historians was formulated by that early nineteenth-century chief of political police General Count Benckendorff. But his words transcend both the historical discipline and the speaker's era. Then again, peasant-fancying by imaginative writers, that marked feature of late nineteenth-century Russian literature, has resurfaced in astonishingly similar form in neo-populist stories and novels treating the collective farm of the 1960s and 1970s.

Many other miscellaneous features might be quoted to reinforce the aspect of immutability presented by the Russian mentality throughout the ages. They include the love-hate neurosis about the West; the suppression of a Hungarian revolution by both Nicholas I (in 1849) and Nikita Khrushchev (in 1956); the close parallels in peasant life between nineteenth-century enserfment and twentieth-century collectivization; the tendency for Russians to harangue the world on their country's mission to liberate humanity—a tendency which seems to flourish most in eras of acutest domestic self-enslavement and aggressiveness toward other peoples. There is also the tendency for Russian society to resemble some enormous, badly organized school which never has an end of term, or a comically inefficient military formation from which there is no discharge. In the British army troops have notoriously been required, in the not-so-distant past, to whitewash lumps of coal in preparation for a general's inspection. But in Russia civilians, too, seem subject to such grotesque manifestations of martial law. When the Crown Prince (the future Alexander II) descended to inspect the provincial town of Vyatka in 1837, all the fences had to be hurriedly painted, the muzhiks were put into special festive caftans and one destitute widow of the locality was even compelled to pull up the floorboards in her house as material for refurbishing the wooden pavement in front of it.[2] A similar position is that of Moscow apartment-dwellers doomed to weeks of near-darkness during World Youth Festivals and similar fatuous junketings of the 1970s because their windows are compulsorily blocked out by red bunting as part of the city's decoration plan for the occasion.

Yet I am suspicious of attempts to press too hard on the undoubtedly striking parallels between the pre-1917 and post-1917 Russian collective mind. The latter has certainly responded to political developments by becoming more cautious, calculating and apprehensive—less volatile and reckless—than its Tsarist counterpart. Now less likely to perish in infancy from cholera, smallpox or famine, the Russian is far more exposed to bureaucrats and other human vermin than previously, and his life is accordingly safer (but only since Stalin's departure) and duller. He carries a watch. He has learned to tell the time and be punctual. He can also read and write, which renders him still more controllable by officials, but also gives him access to his country's great storehouse of imaginative literature, previously unavailable, on grounds of illiteracy, to a majority of the population. Then again, the age-old pastime of wife-beating has surely become less common even in the backwoods, though no statistics are available on the incidence of this evil. Furthermore, in the key area of penal procedure, the traditional privileges extended to political prisoners under the Tsars have been abolished. Under Stalin, indeed, ordinary non-political criminals were granted a franchise to murder, terrorize and bully their 'political' cell-mates. Now relieved from such gross abuses, the latter still suffer the indignity of living under laws specially worded so as to delude simpletons into believing that incarceration for political reasons is no longer practiced.

For these and other reasons—some creditable, some dis-creditable to the new dispensation—many reputable observers have claimed change as a factor more significant than continu-ity in post-1917 Russia. Mehnert states outright that 'Soviet man is not the Russian our fathers knew and often saw in a romantic light.' He speaks of a decline in spontaneity and an increase in personal discipline together with 'a firm determi-nation to succeed and a strong faith in technological prog-ress.' [3] Another highly qualified Russia-watcher, anything but a 'fancier'—Frederick C. Barghoorn—takes issue with two no-table Russian *émigré* philosophers, Berdyayev and Fedotov, for over-emphasizing the continuity between pre-1917 and post-1917 traits. 'There is certainly,' Barghoorn claims, 'no such cultural gulf between élite and masses in Soviet Russia as ex-isted in pre-revolutionary Russia, divided, as Lenin put it, into "two nations." ' Discussing the Kremlin's assertion that social-ism has produced a new and superior type of human being, the same observer well adds that 'The Russian and Soviet ele-ments in this pattern stand in an uneasy relationship to one another.' [4]

With this creatively blurred formula one may perhaps leave the last word on the vexed problem of Russian-Soviet continuity, for here if anywhere is an aspect of national psy-chology where a craving for precise outlines risks becoming unhelpful and counter-productive.

So much for the Russian as traditionalist and innovator in his domestic context. But what of changes in the outlook of the world at large as influenced by the Russian psyche? Here too the special achievements of Russian authoritarianism spring to mind. Two worldwide institutions—military conscription and political policing—were, as stated above, introduced by Peter the Great long before countries deemed more civilized had even dreamed of evolving these crucial adjuncts to modern life. More significant still was the creation, for the Russians by Stalin, of the control system known as totalitarianism—another notable innovation which has since been extensively imitated by nations less administratively adventurous.

Ingenious in evolving official controls, the Russian mind has proved no less successful in evolving techniques of subverting those controls. From the 1860s onward some uncanny process of anticipation was inspiring the country's oppositionists to develop a special style and *modus operandi* which, though it might well have seemed bizarre and even primitive at that time to peoples reputedly more sophisticated, has since been adopted throughout the world by many who are blissfully unconscious, in the 1970s, of retreading a path beaten out so long ago by Chernyshevsky and his Tsarist Russian contemporaries. Militantly trumpeted sexual egalitarianism and permissiveness; the deference complacently paid by spineless, popularity-craving middle-aged men to noisy, rude, hirsute, ignorant, slogan-mumbling adolescents; contempt for money, property and professional competence high-mindedly voiced by the idle, pampered, professionally unqualified sons and daughters of the rich; campus revolutions and the hounding of prefessors derided as fuddy-duddies because they seek to maintain academic standards; the advocacy of destructiveness and revolutionary violence for their own sake; political idealism and utopistic utterance mindlessly babbled forth by bomb-throwing juvenile gangsters; the thesis that more mundane forms of crime are the fault of 'society' for which responsibility must be taken by a mysterious body defined as 'all of us'; supreme contempt, pompously preached by a harshly intolerant semi-educated 'intelligentsia,' for the rights of individuals; the whole dismal apparatus, in other words, of twentieth-century psychopatholitics—before the second half of the present century such phenomena could have been dismissed as the transitory, quaint and barbarous eccentricities of a backward nineteenth-century people. Since then, however, these and allied notions have moved into the very forefront of modernity. They have become remarkably fashionable and respected everywhere: everywhere, that is, with the spectacular exception of their country of origin. The new Russia may be envied or despised, according to individual taste, for its effectiveness in suppressing many of the above features—not least that of juvenile political delinquency—which the old Russia invented, or at least extensively pioneered, in the first place.

For such reasons history-conscious Russian visitors to the West can easily receive the impression of seeing their own past reenacted before their eyes. The point has been well made by Solzhenitsyn, who instances 'adults deferring to the opinion of their children . . . professors scared of being unfashionable; journalists refusing to take responsibility for the words they squander so profusely; universal sympathy for revolutionary extremists; people with serious objections unable or unwilling to voice them.' To these phenomena the Russian sage appends the general Western sense of doom; feeble government; societies whose defensive reactions have become atrophied and 'spiritual confusion leading to political upheaval.' [5]

Can it be then that 'we' are all Russians, albeit nineteenth-century Russians, now? If so, it is a pity that this collective psyche—a formidable and fascinating but also, like most other national mentalities, partly regrettable phenomenon—should be advancing internationally even as it may be receding in its country of origin. But how fortunate it is too that, whatever sweeping statements may be made about a generalized 'Russian mind,' there are still so many individual Russians with minds of their own.

*ACKNOWLEDGMENTS AND CONVENTIONS*

*REFERENCE NOTES*

*INDEX TO REFERENCE NOTES*

*INDEX*

# ACKNOWLEDGMENTS AND CONVENTIONS

I am most grateful to the editors of *Soviet Analyst* (London) for kind permission to use, in Chapter 2, certain (considerably modified) material from my article *Kremlinological Inexactitudes,* as published in their vol. 1, 12–14, on 3, 17 and 31 August 1972. That publication was in turn by kind permission of *Problems of Communism* (Washington, D.C.), which had brought out the article in its original form in vol. 11, no. 2 (March–April 1962) under a title which is not the author's: *That's no Lie, Comrade.*

For much useful help and advice I am also grateful to my colleagues Paul Foote, Jane Grayson, Max Hayward, David Howells, Valerie Jensen, Mary Kendall, Harvey Pitcher and Harry Willetts; to Geoffrey Henny, and to my sons Martin and Andrew; as also for particularly close and skilled editorial help to Jeremy Newton and to my wife.

Transliteration, dating and certain other conventions adopted in the text are as laid down in my *A New Life of Anton Chekhov* (London and New York, 1976), pp. xvii–xix. Consequently authors' names may appear in a different form in the Index to Reference Notes (where the title page must be paramount) from that which they have in the text. Hence, for example, 'Tourguéneff' (Index to Reference Notes) but 'Turgenev' (text).

# REFERENCE NOTES

There are so many references in this book that it has often been necessary to consolidate them in groups at or near the end of the paragraph to
which they apply in order to avoid disfiguring the body of the text with an
excess of figures. References are by authors' or editors' names, or by book
titles, as listed in alphabetical order in the Index to Reference Notes, pp.
282–87.

## CHAPTER 1. FOREGROUND AND BACKGROUND

### Life-Enhancers or Life-Deniers? (pp. 3–18)

**1.** Klyuchevsky, 2:190; Karamzin, 9:156–57. **2.** Waliszewski, 153. **3.** Westwood, 30. **4.** Private information. **5.** Orlov, 350. **6.** Tupper, 200. **7.** Hingley,
*The Tsars*, 157. **8.** Solovyov, 11:140. **9.** Hingley, *The Russian Secret Police*,
45–46. **10.** Conquest, *The Great Terror*, 95. **11.** Olearius, 192. **12.** Herling, 59.
**13.** Conquest, *The Nation Killers*, 102. **14.** Khokhlov, 240. **15.** F. Dostoyevsky,
cited in Hingley, *The Undiscovered Dostoyevsky*, 149 ff. **16.** A. de Staël, cited in
Wilson, 187; A. de Custine, cited ibid., 224; Mackenzie Wallace, 1:252–54;
Chekhov, 15:67. **17.** Paléologue, 431–32. **18.** Leacock, 155–61. **19.** Herzen,
*Byloye i dumy*, 1:170. **20.** Woolf, 174. **21.** G. Gould, cited in Brewster, 175.

### Problems of Perspective (pp. 18–33)

**1.** Baena, 5, 16. **2.** K. Aksakov, in Raeff, *Russian Intellectual History*, 231.
**3.** Jarintzov, 25–26. **4.** Pipes, *Russia under the Old Regime*, 83. **5.** Fedotov, 22.

### Thesis or Antithesis? (pp. 34–56)

**1.** Mehnert, 207; Nikitenko, 1:12. **2.** F. Barghoorn, in Simmons, 535; Stalin,
6:186. **3.** Nikitenko, 1:13. **4.** Klyuchevsky, 1:313–14. **5.** Mackenzie Wallace,
1:356. **6.** Nikitenko, 1:13. **7.** Hingley, *The Tsars*, 16. **8.** Gorer, 93 ff. **9.** Pares,
16. **10.** Pitcher, *Understanding the Russians*, 97. **11.** Hingley, *The Undiscovered
Dostoyevsky*, 20. **12.** Hingley, *The Tsars*, 167–68. **13.** Ibid., 245; Custine, 109,

114. **14.** Shaw, 4; Hitler, 661. **15.** Mackenzie Wallace, 2:229. **16.** Gorer, 141. **17.** Nikitenko, 1:49; 2:270, 548. **18.** Solzhenitsyn, 89–90. **19.** Paléologue, 447. **20.** Miliukov, 1:46. **21.** K. Mehnert, in Black, 509; Mehnert, 31–32; Woolf, 179. **22.** Pipes, *Russia under the Old Regime,* 157–58; Mehnert, 182; Custine, 343. **23.** Gorky, 17, 19, 40. **24.** Gorer, 145. **25.** Mead, 27. **26.** A. Brumberg, in Strong, 2. **27.** F. Dostoyevsky, cited in Hingley, *The Undiscovered Dostoyevsky,* 203–4. **28.** Szamuely, 172–73. **29.** Pitcher, op. cit., 92. **30.** Pipes, op. cit., 187. **31.** Mackenzie Wallace, 1:368; Custine, 230. **32.** Hingley, *Under Soviet Skins,* 188–89. **33.** Aristophanes, *Ach.,* 77–79. **34.** Mehnert, 179. **35.** Turbervile, in Herberstein, cxlix; Fletcher, 124; Olearius, 179–80. **36.** Herberstein, cxxvii. **37.** Olearius, 183. **38.** *Trud* (Moscow), 21 Sept. 1973. **39.** Schlesinger, 14; Bruford, 46–47. **40.** Mackenzie Wallace, 1:379. **41.** Lermontov, 4:28–29. **42.** Dostoyevsky, 11:455–71. **43.** Wilson, 208; J. Kohl, cited ibid., 240. **44.** Pitcher, op. cit., 99; Miller, W., 184; Mackenzie Wallace, 2:231.

## CHAPTER 2. COMMUNICATION SYSTEMS

### *Signaling Devices* (pp. 57–69)

**1.** R. Hingley, in *Problems of Communism* (Washington, D.C.), Nov.–Dec. 1972. **2.** Tolstoy, 13:12. **3.** Jarintzov, 46–47. **4.** Ibid., 51–52. **5.** Mehnert, 68. **6.** Forbes, 56–57. **7.** Walshe, 26–27. **8.** Harrison, 3, 11. **9.** Ibid., 11–13; Josselson, 20. **10.** *The New Statesman* (London), 11 Dec. 1915. **11.** Fedotov, 28. **12.** F. Barghoorn, in Simmons, 548. **13.** Jarintzov, 4–8. **14.** V. Nabokov, cited in 'Profferings,' *The Times Literary Supplement* (London), 10 Oct. 1968.

### *Display Postures* (pp. 70–90)

**1.** Jarintzov, 148; Pitcher, *Understanding the Russians,* 189; Pares, 11; Woolf, 176; Belfrage, 185; Mehnert, 133. **2.** Jarintzov, 11, 100–101, 204. **3.** Josselson, 50; Brewster, 170; Woolf, 177, 179; Jarintzov, 138–39. **4.** Ibid., 59, 94. **5.** Coulson, vii. **6.** Custine, 351. **7.** *Oxford Chekhov,* 3:x. **8.** Knipper, 1:432; Chekhov, 19:122. **9.** Ibid., 16:32. **10.** *Oxford Chekhov,* 6:12–13. **11.** E. Garnett, cited in Brewster, 145. **12.** I. Bunin, in Golubov, 520. **13.** Nabokov, *Speak Memory,* 285–86. **14.** Nikitenko, 1:116, 2:453. **15.** Jarintzov, 60. **16.** Ibid., 12–14. **17.** Miller, W., 85; Woolf, 174. Emphasis added. **18.** Hingley, *Chekhov* (1950), 232. Emphasis added. **19.** R. Lyall, cited in Wilson, 194. **20.** Pares, 11. **21.** Mehnert, 180. **22.** Tr. by C. Garnett, cited in *Oxford Chekhov,* 8:xii. **23.** Pitcher, op. cit., 106. Emphasis added. **24.** F. Dostoyevsky, cited in Hingley, *The Undiscovered Dostoyevsky*, 56. Emphasis added. **25.** Hingley, *Under Soviet Skins*, 203. **26.** Custine, 152; Nikitenko, 2:299; idem, cited in Szamuely, 155; A. de Custine, cited in Kennan, George F., 81. **27.** Hingley, *Under Soviet Skins*, 160. **28.** Pitcher, op. cit., 22; Davidson-Houston, 41–42. **29.** Pitcher, op. cit., 61. **30.** Miller, W., 85. **31.** Chekhov, 14:184. **32.** Custine, 197.

*Camouflage Drill* (pp. 90–104)

**1.** Andreyev, L., 6:225–26. **2.** Turgenev, 4:95–96. **3.** Andreyev, L., loc. cit., 226. **4.** Ibid. Emphasis added. **5.** O. Wormser-Migot, in Gaxotte, 204. **6.** M. Speransky, cited in Szamuely, 131. **7.** Custine, 197. **8.** Dostoyevsky, 9:321. **9.** Ibid. Emphasis added. **10.** Idem, 9:322. **11.** R. Tucker, in Black, 604.

*Deception Tactics* (pp. 104–10)

**1.** A. Jenkinson, cited in Wilson, 38. **2.** G. Fletcher, cited in Wilson, 59; Fletcher, 129. **3.** Mackenzie Wallace, 2:72–73; Olearius, 172; Dostoyevsky, 9:320. **4.** Custine, 192; Mackenzie Wallace, 1:275; Belfrage, 185–86. **5.** Jarintzov, 148; Woolf, 173. **6.** Gorer, 185. **7.** Nikitenko, 3:329. **8.** Herzen, *Polnoye sobraniye sochineniy*, 6:445. **9.** Mackenzie Wallace, 2:33–34. **10.** Kennan, George F., 80. **11.** Redlikh, 67–101; Hingley, *Joseph Stalin*, 435–36.

*Sealed Lips* (pp. 110–20)

**1.** Herberstein, cvii–cviii. **2.** Miliukov, 1:31–32. Emphasis added. **3.** W. Richardson, cited in Wilson, 146; A. de Staël, cited ibid., 189. **4.** Wilson, 215. **5.** Custine, 201. **6.** *Soviet Analyst* (London), 2:19. **7.** Hingley, *Joseph Stalin*, 311. **8.** Pipes, *Russia under the Old Regime*, 95; Custine, 119. **9.** Szamuely, 185; Conquest, *The Nation Killers*, 48–49. **10.** A. de Custine, cited in Szamuely, 4. **11.** Pipes, op. cit., 289. **12.** Keenan, passim; V. Avtokratov, cited in Andreyev, N., 592–98. **13.** Khrushchev (1971 and 1974), passim; Rigby. **14.** Raeff, *Michael Speransky*, 190–91. **15.** Nikitenko, 1:336. **16.** L. Vladimirov, cited in *Soviet Analyst* (London), 2:19. **17.** R. Hingley, 'Emergency Encyclopaedia,' *Punch* (London), 2 June 1954. **18.** Rush, 21–22. **19.** R. Littledale, cited in Brewster, 139. **20.** Nove, 12–13. **21.** Gardiner, 61. **22.** Hingley, *A Concise History of Russia*, 9.

## CHAPTER 3. GROUP CONSCIOUSNESS

### Togetherness (pp. 121–27)

**1.** Yu. Samarin, cited in Pipes, *Struve*, 36. **2.** Mehnert, 183. **3.** Miller, W., 67, 106, 112–13. **4.** Gorer, 135. **5.** Gorky, 18. **6.** Miller, W., 110. **7.** F. Dostoyevsky, cited in Szamuely, 72. **8.** A. Solzhenitsyn, cited in *Soviet Analyst* (London), 3:7. **9.** Pitcher, *Understanding the Russians*, 129. **10.** Miller, W., 67–68. **11.** Nikitenko, 1:408. **12.** Pipes, *Russia under the Old Regime*, 180. **13.** Churchward, 63. **14.** Pitcher, *The Chekhov Play*, 10.

### Supranationalist (pp. 128–36)

**1.** V. Tarsis, cited by R. Hingley, *Spectator* (London), 28 Feb. 1970. **2.** V. Belinsky, cited in Pipes, *Russia under the Old Regime*, 160–61. **3.** Gorky, 28–29. **4.** H. Liddon, cited in Wilson, 157. **5.** Kennan, George F., 127–28. **6.** Mackenzie Wallace, 2:193.

### World Citizen (pp. 136–55)

**1.** Pipes, *Russia under the Old Regime*, 182. **2.** Herzen, *Byloye i dumy*, 1:59. **3.** Szamuely, 53; Seton-Watson, 407; Wilson, 161, 197. **4.** J. Reshetar, in Black, 572. **5.** M. Zankovetskaya, in *Literaturnoye nasledstvo: Chekhov*, 593. **6.** V. Lenin, cited in Black, 568. **7.** Wittram, 7. **8.** A. Pushkin, cited in Szamuely, 81; Custine, 148, 176. **9.** P. Chaadayev, in Raeff, *Russian Intellectual History*, 162. **10.** F. Dostoyevsky, cited in Hingley, *The Undiscovered Dostoyevsky*, 63; Peter I, cited in Pipes, op. cit., 113. **11.** Gide, 49. **12.** Mehnert, 206. **13.** Kiparsky, 11. **14.** G. Curzon, cited in Wilson, 214. **15.** Nikitenko, 1:153. **16.** Mackenzie Wallace, 2:98. **17.** Custine, 132. **18.** Herzen, *Byloye i dumy*, 1:60. **19.** Jarintzov, 29. **20.** Kiparsky, 18, 23, 35; F. Dostoyevsky, cited in Hingley, *The Undiscovered Dostoyevsky*, 177. **21.** Jarintzov, 13 ff. **22.** Mackenzie Wallace, 1:149. **23.** Miller, W., 97. **24.** Mehnert, 193. **25.** V. Dean, cited in Pares, 21. **26.** Kiparsky, 107 ff.

### Patriot (pp. 155–64)

**1.** Szamuely, 59–60. **2.** F. Dostoyevsky, cited in Hingley, *The Undiscovered Dostoyevsky*, 182; and by J. Reshetar, in Black, 564–65. **3.** Idem, cited in Hingley, op. cit., 62; Jarintzov, 74. **4.** Tyutchev, 195. **5.** Pushkin, 10:598. **6.** H. Dicks, in Black, 643. **7.** Ivan IV, 142. **8.** Stalin, 13:305. **9.** J. Reshetar, in Black, 561–63; Pushkin, 3:222–23; Pitcher, *Understanding the Russians*, 56. **10.** Pipes, *Russia under the Old Regime*, 33; F. Barghoorn, in Simmons, 532.

# REFERENCE NOTES

**11.** Szamuely, 332. **12.** Herzen, *Polnoye sobraniye sochineniy,* 5:391. **13.** Blok, 1:453; Klyuchevsky, 2:398. **14.** Stalin, 15:150; F. Barghoorn, in Simmons, 541. **15.** R. Chancellor, cited in Wilson, 33; A. de Custine, cited in Kennan, George F., 87; V. Odoyevsky, cited in Kohn, 16; M. Pogodin, cited ibid., 67–68. **16.** F. Barghoorn, in Simmons, 531.

## Domestic Pet (pp. 164–68)

**1.** Dallin, xiii. **2.** Baring, xxv. **3.** I. Berlin, in Raeff, *Russian Intellectual History,* 6. **4.** H. Salisbury, in Sakharov, 8. **5.** Wilson, 30, 59, 157, 261.

## The Class Struggle (pp. 168–83)

**1.** Kiparksy, 97. **2.** Woolf, 179. **3.** Mackenzie Wallace, 1:437. **4.** Brown, 23. **5.** Herzen, *Polnoye sobraniye sochineniy,* 6:454. **6.** Mackenzie Wallace, 1:442. **7.** Nechkina, 2:419. **8.** Gogol, 5:51. **9.** Churchward, 3–4. **10.** Fedotov, 157. **11.** Nikitenko, 1:126; Tourguéneff, 2:17. **12.** Mackenzie Wallace, 1:297. **13.** Starr, 48–49. **14.** Custine, 100–101; idem, cited in Kennan, George F., 55. **15.** Jarintzov, 88; Mackenzie Wallace, 2:227; Nikitenko, 2:204. **16.** Churchward, 112. **17.** Miller, W., 167. **18.** Mackenzie Wallace, 2:264. **19.** H. Dicks, in Black, 636. **20.** Gorky, 34, 37. **21.** A. Chekhov, cited in Hingley, *A New Life of Anton Chekhov,* 59–60. **22.** Chekhov, 12:335. **23.** V. Tissot, cited in Wilson, 279; Custine, 129; Nikitenko, 3:329; Pushkin, 7:291. **24.** Mehnert, 81.

## Intimacy (pp. 183–93)

**1.** Mackenzie Wallace, 1:154. **2.** A. Jenkinson, cited in Wilson, 39; C. d'Auteroche, cited ibid., 139; Gorky, 19–20; Dal, 369–70; Mackenzie Wallace, 1:197. **3.** F. Dostoyevsky, cited in Hingley, *The Undiscovered Dostoyevsky,* 139–40. **4.** Jarintzov, 127. **5.** V. Dunham, in Black, 459 ff.; Kohn, 14. **6.** Churchward, 27–28. **7.** Miller, J., 139; private information; A. Belyavsky, cited in *The Daily Telegraph* (London), 21 March 1976. **8.** Feifer, 167–68. **9.** Cross, 225.

## CHAPTER 4. REGIMENTATION AND RESISTANCE

### Authority and Submission (pp. 194–206)

**1.** Olearius, 184; Herberstein, 95; A. Jenkinson, cited in Wilson, 60. **2.** M. Smith, cited in Wilson, 260; Custine, 114, 172 ff. **3.** Mehnert, 111; Bauer,

122. **4.** Belinsky, 621. **5.** Fedotov, 152. **6.** K. Marx, cited in Szamuely, 19; Vernadsky, *A History of Russia,* 56; V. Belinsky, in Kohn, 126. **7.** Herberstein, 32. **8.** S. von Herberstein, G. Fletcher and A. Olearius, cited in Szamuely, 7. **9.** Vernadsky, *The Mongols and Russia,* 367; Berdyaev, 10. **10.** N. Cherkasov, cited in Conquest, *The Great Terror,* 75–76. **11.** Custine, 170. **12.** R. Daniels, in Strong, 22.

## Tsarism and Anti-Tsarism (pp. 206–15)

**1.** Nikitenko, 2:376; Jarintzov, 12; Belfrage, 186. **2.** Gorer, 177. **3.** N. Kostomarov, cited in Gorky, 7. **4.** Longworth, 4. **5.** P. Struve, in *Vekhi,* 164–65.

## Psychopatholitics (pp. 215–26)

**1.** M. Karpovich, in Simmons, 129; Pipes, *Struve,* 283. **2.** Gernet, 2:156. **3.** Hingley, *The Russian Secret Police,* 90. **4.** Steklov, 2:85. **5.** Nikitenko, 2:80. **6.** F. Dostoyevsky, cited in Hingley, *The Undiscovered Dostoyevsky,* 144.

## The Intelligentsia (pp. 226–43)

**1.** Churchward, 3–7. **2.** Mirsky, 321–22. **3.** Fedotov, 11; Szamuely, 144. **4.** Fedotov, 13. **5.** S. Bulgakov, in *Vekhi,* 43. **6.** Mirsky, 322; Fedotov, 13; Berdyayev, 19. **7.** Gorer, 118. **8.** Chekhov, 18:88–89. **9.** A. Parry, in Kirk, 53. **10.** P. Struve, in *Vekhi,* 163–64; Fedotov, 16. **11.** Nikitenko, 1:432; S. Bulgakov, in *Vekhi,* 37. **12.** N. Berdyayev, in *Vekhi,* 3. **13.** Turgenev, 4:325. **14.** Feyder, 97–101. **15.** Herzen, *Polnoye sobraniye sochineniy,* 5:383; N. Berdyayev, in *Vekhi,* 11; S. Frank, ibid., 180. **16.** Dostoyevsky, 10:197. **17.** A. Chekhov, cited in Jarintzov, 97. **18.** Jarintzov, 124. **19.** Szamuely, 178. **20.** S. Bulgakov, in *Vekhi,* 30, 37–38. **21.** S. Frank, in *Vekhi,* 194; S. Bulgakov, ibid., 24; D. Pisarev, cited in Kohn, 140. **22.** Szamuely, 161. **23.** S. Frank, in *Vekhi,* 193. **27.** Ibid., 207. **25.** Szamuely, 194; Chernyshevsky, 6:491. **26.** Szamuely, 156. **27.** Mackenzie Wallace, 2:226; Nikitenko, 1:462; Herzen, in Kohn, 163. **28.** I. Leontyev (Shcheglov), in Feyder, 121. **29.** Chekhov, 14:154; P. Struve, in *Vekhi,* 167. **30.** Miller, W., 123; H. Salisbury, in Sakharov, 8; Kohn, 13; I. Berlin, in Venturi, xxvii.

## Totalitarianism and Anti-Totalitarianism (pp. 243–61)

**1.** Mandelstam, 126. **2.** Katkov, 273. **3.** M. Dewhirst, in *Soviet Analyst* (London), 3:2. **4.** Pasternak, 294. **5.** R. Conquest, in *Soviet Analyst* (London), 4:4. **6.** H. Salisbury, in Sakharov, 7–8. **7.** Sakharov, 173.

# REFERENCE NOTES

## CHAPTER 5. CONTINUITY AND CHANGE

**1.** J. Kohn, cited in Wilson, 233; Hingley, *Under Soviet Skins,* 156–57.
**2.** Herzen, *Byloye i dumy,* 1:204. **3.** Mehnert, 284. **4.** F. Barghoorn, in Simmons, 534, 539. **5.** A. Solzhenitsyn, cited in *The Daily Telegraph* (London), 24 March 1976.

# INDEX TO REFERENCE NOTES

The following list of works is not offered as a systematic bibliography of the Russian mind, but consists exclusively of titles invoked in the Reference Notes because they are cited in the text or otherwise used as evidence.

Andreyev, Leonid, 'Vserossiyskoye vranyo,' in *Polnoye sobraniye sochineniy*, 8 vols (St. Petersburg, 1913).

Andreyev, Nikolay, 'The Authenticity of the Correspondence between Ivan IV and Prince Andrey Kurbsky,' *Slavonic and East European Review* (London), vol. liii, no. 133, Oct. 1975.

Baena, Duke de, *The Dutch Puzzle* (The Hague, 1975).

Baring, Maurice, Introduction to *The Oxford Book of Russian Verse* (Oxford, 1948).

Bauer, Raymond A., *How the Soviet System Works* (Cambridge, Mass., 1957).

Belfrage, Sally, *A Room in Moscow* (London, 1958).

Belinsky, V. G., *Izbrannyye sochineniya*, ed. F. M. Golovenchenko (Moscow, 1947).

Berdyaev, Nicolas, *The Origin of Russian Communism*, tr. by R. M. French (London, 1948).

Black, Cyril E., ed., *The Transformation of Russian Society: Aspects of Social Change Since 1861* (Cambridge, Mass., 1967).

Blok, Aleksandr, *Sochineniya*, 2 vols. (Moscow, 1955).

Brewster, Dorothy, *East-West Passage: A Study in Literary Relationships* (London, 1954).

Brown, Douglas, *Doomsday 1917: The Destruction of Russia's Ruling Class* (London, 1975).

Bruford, W. H., *Chekhov and His Russia: A Sociological Study* (London, 1947).

Chekhov, Anton, *Polnoye sobraniye sochineniy i pisem*, 20 vols. (Moscow, 1944–51).

Chernyshevsky, N. G., *Polnoye sobraniye sochineniy*, 10 vols. (St. Petersburg, 1906).

Churchward, L. G., *The Soviet Intelligentsia: An Essay on the Social Structure and Roles of Soviet Intellectuals During the 1960s* (London, 1973).

Conquest, Robert, *The Great Terror: Stalin's Purge of the Thirties* (London, 1968).

———, *The Nation Killers: The Soviet Deportation of Nationalities* (London, 1970).

Coulson, Jessie, ed. and tr., *Anton Chekhov: Selected Stories* (London, 1963).

Cross, Anthony, 'Pushkin's Bawdy; or, Notes from the Literary Underground,' *Russian Literary Triquarterly* (Ann Arbor, Michigan) no. 10, Fall 1974.

Custine, Marquis A. de, *Lettres de Russie* (Paris, 1951).

Dal, V., *Poslovitsy russkago naroda* (Moscow, 1862).

Dallin, David J., and Nicolaevsky, Boris I., *Forced Labor in Soviet Russia* (London, 1947).

Davidson-Houston, J. V., *Armed Diplomat: A Military Attaché in Russia* (London, 1959).

Dostoyevsky, F. M., *Polnoye sobraniye sochineniy,* 12 vols. (St. Petersburg, 1895).

Fedotov, G. P., *Novy grad: sbornik statey* (New York, 1952).

Feifer, George, *Moscow Farewell* (New York, 1976).

Feyder, V., ed., *A. P. Chekhov: literaturny byt i tvorchestvo po memuarnym materialam* (Leningrad, 1928).

Fischer, George, *Russian Liberalism: From Gentry to Intelligentsia* (Cambridge, Mass., 1958).

Fletcher, Giles, *O gosudarstve russkom,* tr. from English, 3rd ed. (St. Petersburg, 1906).

Forbes, Nevill, *Russian Grammar,* 2nd ed. (Oxford, 1916).

Gardiner, Alan, *Egypt of the Pharaohs: An Introduction* (London, 1961).

Gaxotte, Pierre, and others, *Catherine de Russie* (Paris, 1966).

Gernet, M. N., *Istoriya tsarskoy tyurmy,* 3rd ed., 5 vols. (Moscow, 1960–63).

Gide, André, *Back from the USSR* (London, 1937).

Gogol, N. V., *Sobraniye sochineniy,* 6 vols. (Moscow, 1952–53).

Golubov, S. N., and others, ed., *A. P. Chekhov v vospominaniyakh sovremennikov* (Moscow, 1960).

Gorer, Geoffrey, and Rickman, John, *The People of Great Russia: A Psychological Study* (London, 1949).

Gorky, Maksim, *O russkom krestyanstve* (Berlin, 1922).

Harrison, Jane Ellen, *Russia and the Russian Verb: A Contribution to the Psychology of the Russian People* (Cambridge, England, 1915).

Herberstein, Sigismund von, *Notes upon Russia,* tr. and ed. R. H. Major, vol. i (London, 1851).

Herling, Gustav, *A World Apart,* tr. by Joseph Marek (London, 1951).

Herzen, A. I., *Polnoye sobraniye sochineniy i pisem,* 22 vols., ed. M. K. Lemke (Petrograd-Leningrad, 1919–25).

———, *Byloye i dumy,* 2 vols. (Minsk, 1957).

Hingley, Ronald, *Chekhov: A Biographical and Critical Study* (London, 1950).
——, *Under Soviet Skins: An Untourist's Report* (London, 1961).
——, *The Undiscovered Dostoyevsky* (London, 1962).
——, *The Tsars: Russian Autocrats, 1533–1917* (London, 1968).
——, *The Russian Secret Police: Muscovite, Imperial Russian and Soviet Political Security Operations, 1565–1970* (London, 1970).
——, *A Concise History of Russia* (London, 1972).
——, *Joseph Stalin: Man and Legend* (London, 1974).
——, *A New Life of Anton Chekhov* (London, 1976).
Hitler, Adolf, *Hitler's Table Talk, 1941–1944,* tr. by Norman Cameron and R. H. Stevens (London, 1953).
Ivan IV [the Terrible], Tsar, *Poslaniya Ivana Groznogo,* ed. V. P. Adrianova-Peretts (Moscow and Leningrad, 1951).
Jarintzov, N., *The Russians and Their Language* (Oxford, 1916).
Josselson, Harry H., *The Russian Word Count and Frequency Analysis of Grammatical Categories of Standard Literary Russian* (Detroit, 1953).
Karamzin, N. M., *Istoriya gosudarstva rossiyskago,* 12 vols. (St. Petersburg, 1852–53).
Katkov, George, *Russia 1917: The February Revolution* (London, 1967).
Keenan, Edward L., *The Kurbskii-Groznyi Apocrypha: The Seventeenth-Century Genesis of the 'Correspondence' Attributed to Prince A. M. Kurbskii and Tsar Ivan IV* (Cambridge, Mass., 1971).
Kennan, George, *Siberia and the Exile System,* 2 vols. (London, 1891).
Kennan, George F., *The Marquis de Custine and His Russia in 1839* (London, 1972).
Khokhlov, Nikolai, *In the Name of Conscience,* tr. by Emily Kingsbury (London, 1960).
Khrushchev, Nikita S., *Khrushchev Remembers,* tr. and ed. Strobe Talbott (London, 1971).
——, *Khrushchev Remembers: The Last Testament,* tr. and ed. Strobe Talbott (Boston, 1974).
Kiparsky, Valentin, *English and American Characters in Russian Fiction* (Berlin, 1964).
Kirk, G. S., ed., *The Language and Background of Homer* (Cambridge, England, 1964).
Klyuchevsky, V. O., *Sochineniya,* 8 vols. (Moscow, 1956–59).
Knipper, O. L., *Perepiska A. P. Chekhova i O. L. Knipper,* 2 vols., ed. A. B. Derman (Moscow, 1934, 1936).
Kohn, Hans, ed., *The Mind of Modern Russia: Historical and Political Thought of Russia's Great Age* (New Brunswick, 1955).
Leacock, Stephen, *Over the Footlights and Other Fancies* (London, 1923).

# INDEX TO REFERENCE NOTES

Lermontov, M. Yu., *Sobraniye sochineniy*, 4 vols. (Moscow, 1957–58).

Leskov, N. S., *Sobraniye sochineniy*, 11 vols. (Moscow, 1956–58).

*Literaturnoye nasledstvo: Chekhov*, ed. V. V. Vinogradov and others (Moscow, 1960).

Longworth, Philip, *The Cossacks* (London, 1971).

Mackenzie Wallace, D., *Russia*, 2 vols. (London, 1877).

Mandelstam, Nadezhda, *Hope Against Hope* (New York, 1970).

Mead, Margaret, *Soviet Attitudes Towards Authority* (London, 1955).

Mehnert, Klaus, *The Anatomy of Soviet Man*, tr. by Maurice Rosenbaum (London, 1961).

Miliukov, Paul, *Outlines of Russian Culture, Part I: Religion and the Church*, ed. Michael Karpovich, tr. by Valentine Ughet and Eleanor Davis (Philadelphia, 1942).

Miller, Jack, *Life in Russia Today* (London, 1969).

Miller, Wright, *Russians as People* (London, 1960).

Mirsky, D. S., *A History of Russian Literature*, ed. Francis J. Whitfield (London, 1949).

Nabokov, Vladimir, *Speak Memory: An Autobiography Revised* (New York, 1966).

———, *Lolita: roman*, tr. into Russian by the author (New York, 1968).

Nechkina, M. V., *Dvizheniye dekabristov*, 2 vols. (Moscow, 1955).

Nikitenko, A. V., *Dnevnik*, 3 vols. (Moscow, 1955–56).

Nove, Alec, *Was Stalin Really Necessary? Some Problems of Soviet Political Economy* (London, 1964).

Olearius, Adam, *Podrobnoye opisaniye puteshestviya golshtinskogo posolstva v Moskoviyu i Persiyu v 1633, 1636 i 1639 godakh*, tr. by Pavel Barsov (Moscow, 1870).

Orlov, Alexander, *The Secret History of Stalin's Crimes* (London, 1954).

*Oxford Chekhov, The*, Chekhov's complete plays, and his fiction from 1888 onward; tr. and ed. Ronald Hingley, to be completed in nine or more vols. (London, 1964–    ), eight of which (1–3 and 5–9) have now (1977) been published.

Paléologue, Maurice, *An Ambassador's Memoirs, 1914–1917*, tr. by Frederick A. Holt (London, 1973).

Pares, Bernard, *Russia* (New York, 1943).

Pasternak, Boris, *Doktor Zhivago* (Milan, 1957).

Pipes, Richard, *Struve: Liberal on the Left* (Cambridge, Mass., 1970).

———, *Russia under the Old Regime* (London, 1974; and New York, 1975).

Pitcher, Harvey J., *Understanding the Russians* (London, 1964).

———, *The Chekhov Play: a New Interpretation* (London, 1973).

Pushkin, A. S., *Polnoye sobraniye sochineniy*, 10 vols. (Moscow, 1956–58).

Raeff, Marc, *Michael Speransky: Statesman of Imperial Russia, 1772–1839* (The Hague, 1957).

—— (ed.), *Russian Intellectual History: An Anthology* (New York, 1966).

Redlikh, Roman, *Stalinshchina kak dukhovny fenomen* (Frankfurt-am-Main, 1971).

Rigby, T. H., Review of *Khrushchev Remembers* (1974), *Slavic Review* (Urbana, Illinois), vol. 34, no. 3, Sept. 1975.

Rush, Myron, *The Rise of Khrushchev* (Washington, D.C., 1958).

Sakharov, Andrei D., *Sakharov Speaks,* ed. and with a foreword by Harrison E. Salisbury (London, 1974).

Schlesinger, M. L., *Land und Leute in Russland,* 2nd ed. (Berlin, 1909).

Seton-Watson, Hugh, *The Russian Empire, 1801–1917* (Oxford, 1967).

Shaw, George Bernard, *Shaw on Stalin: A Russia Today Pamphlet* (London, 1941).

Simmons, Ernest J., ed., *Continuity and Change in Russian and Soviet Thought* (Cambridge, Mass., 1955).

Solovyov, S. M., *Istoriya Rossii s drevneyshikh vremyon,* 15 vols. (Moscow, 1959–66).

Solzhenitsyn, Alexander, *Lenin in Zürich: Chapters,* tr. by H. T. Willetts (London, 1976).

Stalin, I. V., *Sochineniya,* vols. 1–13 (Moscow, 1946–51); vols. 14–16 (Stanford, 1967).

Starr, S. Frederick, *Decentralization and Self-Government in Russia, 1830–1870* (Princeton, 1972).

Steklov, Yu. M., *N. G. Chernyshevsky* (Moscow and Leningrad, 1928).

Strong, John W., ed., *The Soviet Union under Brezhnev and Kosygin* (New York, 1971).

Szamuely, Tibor, *The Russian Tradition* (London, 1974).

Tolstoy, L. N., *Sobraniye sochineniy,* 20 vols. (Moscow, 1960–65).

Tourguéneff, N., *La Russie et les Russes,* 3 vols. (Paris, 1847).

Tupper, Harmon, *To the Great Ocean: Siberia and the Trans-Siberian Railway* (London, 1965).

Turgenev, I. S., *Sobraniye sochineniy,* 12 vols. (Moscow, 1954–58).

Tyutchev, F. I., *Stikhotvoreniya* (Berlin, 1921).

Vakar, Nicholas, *The Taproot of Soviet Society* (New York, 1961).

*Vekhi: sbornik statey o russkoy intelligentsii,* 2nd ed. (Moscow, 1909).

Venturi, Franco, *Roots of Revolution: A History of the Populist and Socialist Movements in Nineteenth-Century Russia,* tr. by Francis Haskell (London, 1960).

Vernadsky, George, *A History of Russia* (New Haven, 1944).

——, *The Mongols and Russia* (New Haven, 1953).

Waliszewski, K., *Autour d'un trône: Catherine II de Russie* (Paris, 1913).

Walshe, M. O'C., *A Concise Russian Course* (London, 1949).

Westwood, J. N., *A History of Russian Railways* (London, 1964).

Wilson, Francesca, *Muscovy: Russia through Foreign Eyes, 1553–1900* (London, 1970).

Wittram, Reinhard, *Russia and Europe,* tr. by Patrick and Hanneluise Doran (London, 1973).

Woolf, Virginia, *The Common Reader,* 1st series (London, 1938).

# INDEX

# INDEX

# INDEX

# INDEX

# INDEX

# INDEX

# INDEX